MAN'S DOMINION.

In this feminist critique of the politics of religion, Sheila Jeffreys argues that the renewed rise of religion is harmful to women's human rights. The book seeks to rekindle the criticism of religion as the founding ideology of patriarchy.

Focusing on the three monotheistic religions; Judaism, Christianity and Islam, this book examines common anti-women attitudes such as 'male-headship', impurity of women, the need to control women's bodies, and their modern manifestations in multicultural Western states. It points to the incorporation of religious law into legal systems, faith schools and campaigns led by Christian and Islamic organisations against women's rights at the UN, and explains how religious rights threaten to subvert women's rights. Including highly topical chapters on the burqa and the covering of women, and polygamy, this text questions the ideology of multiculturalism, which shields religion from criticism by demanding respect for culture and faith, while ignoring the harm that women suffer from religion.

Man's Dominion is an incisive and polemic text that will be of interest to students of gender studies, religion and politics.

Sheila Jeffreys is a Professor in the School of Social and Political Sciences at the University of Melbourne. She is the author of *The Industrial Vagina* (2009) and *Beauty and Misogyny* (2005).

MAN'S DOMINION

Religion and the eclipse
of women's rights in
world politics

Sheila Jeffreys

Routledge
Taylor & Francis Group

LONDON AND NEW YORK

First published 2012
by Routledge
2 Park Square, Milton Park, Abingdon, Oxon, OX14 4RN

Simultaneously published in the USA and Canada
by Routledge
711 Third Avenue, New York, NY 10017

Routledge is an imprint of the Taylor & Francis Group, an informa
business

British Library Cataloguing in Publication Data
A catalogue record for this book is available from the British Library

Library of Congress Cataloging-in-Publication Data
Jeffreys, Sheila.
  Man's dominion: religion and the eclipse of women's rights in
  world politics / Sheila Jeffreys.
     p. cm.
  Includes bibliographical references and index.
  1. Sex discrimination against women. 2. Patriarchy. 3. Religion
  and politics. 4. Religion – Social aspects. 5. Human rights.
  I. Title.
  HQ1154.J44 2011
  201'.7208209051 – dc22   2011014008

ISBN: 978-0-415-59673-2 (hardback)
ISBN: 978-0-415-59674-9 (paperback)
ISBN: 978-0-203-80239-7 (ebook)

Typeset in Bembo
by Florence Production Ltd, Stoodleigh, Devon

MIX
Paper from
responsible sources
FSC
www.fsc.org   FSC® C004839

Printed and bound in Great Britain by
TJ International Ltd, Padstow, Cornwall

This book is dedicated to Ann Rowett, whose love and clear understanding of the issues, as always, have supported me so well in the writing of it.

CONTENTS

ACKNOWLEDGEMENTS

I would like to thank the friends who have read and commented so helpfully on draft chapters of this book. They are Ann Rowett, Kathy Chambers, Vicky Swinbank, Lorene Gottschalk and Jennifer Oriel. Their insights resulted in some big changes. I am grateful to all the members of my feminist network here in Australia, particularly my present and past postgraduate students who continue to give me inspiration, and make me thrilled that a new generation of feminists is now changing the world. I thank, too, my feminist sisters who are represented on a radical feminist discussion list, F-agenda, which nourishes an intellectual and activist community in which my ideas can flourish.

ABBREVIATIONS

ACLU	American Civil Liberties Union
AWID	Association for Women's Rights in Development
CEDAW	Convention on the Elimination of all forms of Discrimination Against Women
CPM	Christian Patriarchy Movement
ECOSOC	United Nations Economic and Social Council
ECWR	Egyptian Centre for Women's Rights
EWL	European Women's Lobby
FLDS	Fundamentalist Church of Jesus Christ of the Latter Day Saints
HT	Hizb ut-Tahrir
ICCPR	International Covenant on Civil and Political Rights
IHEU	International Humanist and Ethical Union
MCB	Muslim Council of Britain
MDG	Millennium Development Goal
MECO	Muslim Education Centre of Oxford
NGO	Non-governmental organisation
OIC	Organisation of the Islamic Conference
UDHR	Universal Declaration of Human Rights
UN	United Nations
UNCHR	United Nations Commission on Human Rights
UNDP	United Nations Development Programme
UNFPA	United Nations Population Fund
WAF	Women Against Fundamentalism
WCF	World Congress of Families
WLUML	Women Living Under Muslim Laws

INTRODUCTION

Man's Dominion argues that the domestic and international rise of religion is harmful to women's human rights. I was propelled to write the book by my concern that it was becoming more and more difficult for feminists to criticise religion and point out how much it harms women, at exactly the same time as the increasing political influence of religion was causing serious harms. In the 1970s when I became a feminist in London, atheism was, for most of us, simply an underlying understanding upon which feminist ideas were built. As Dena Attar from the UK states, 'In the early 70s it was possible to believe that religion was in retreat, that feminism could make the great challenge without meeting much of a response' (Attar, 2010, first published 1992, p. 71). Writing in 1992, she says it was no longer possible to hold onto that idea: 'The extent and viciousness of the backlash becomes clearer all the time' (Attar, 2010, p. 72). Attar's concerns are all much more relevant 20 years later. There has been a strong activist feminist response to 'fundamentalism' in countries all over the world, but critical writing and action on religion that is not identified as 'fundamentalist' has been conspicuous by its absence. I argue that the distinction between 'fundamentalism' and 'religion' is problematic, because it can make the latter seem benign, and criticism of it seem churlish, in the face of a pressing emergency. This book is about the three monotheistic religions in general and not just fundamentalism.

Very useful books showing up the misogyny of Christianity were written by feminists who were recovering from their immersion in religious ideology in the 1970s and 1980s, particularly Mary Daly's very significant, *Beyond God the Father* (Daly, 1985b) I paid little attention to these books at the time because I considered, like other progressive intellectuals, that religion would die out. When I read Daly's work today it seems very brave, because the idea that religion must be challenged, rather than 'respected', has come to be seen as rather offensive in multicultural societies and in communities dominated by the 'politics of difference'. I have written this book in order to recover lost ground, to assert once more that which generations of feminist activists and theorists have thought too obvious to mention: that all religions were invented in historical situations where women were radically subordinate to men, and reflect their odious origins in their ideas and practices. I aim to open up the space for debate once more so that feminists may criticise religion without feeling under pressure to show 'respect'.

I am keenly aware that a right-wing movement is developing in Europe at the time of writing this book, which targets Muslims. This makes the task of writing a critique of religion much more controversial. Extreme right-wing, anti-immigrant movements are emerging in Germany, France, the Netherlands and Sweden. In Sweden, a far-right party, the Swedish Democrats, entered parliament for the first time in September 2010, winning 20 of the 349 seats; and a gunman who targeted people with immigrant backgrounds and was believed to have killed one and attempted to murder seven others, was arrested in Sweden in November (Telegraph, 2010). In Norway the gunman Anders Breivik massacred young people at a youth camp in July 2011 in order to register his protest at the 'Islamisation' of Europe (Hedghammer, 2011). In the UK, the English Defence League is conducting a campaign against the 'Islamification' of British cities (Townsend, 2010). Right-wing organisations rail against sharia law, for instance, which is a topic that this book discusses. The fact that racist groups exploit some of the issues that are of great concern to feminist critics of religion must not be allowed to prevent the development of the critique. But it does explain why there is some reluctance, particularly on the Left, to have any truck with the feminist concerns that form the subject matter of this book. Activists surveyed for a 2010 Association for Women's Rights in Development (AWID) report on fundamentalism and women's rights, said that 'any criticism of fundamentalism within a particular community (whether by insiders or outsiders) can feed into racist stereotyping of the community by right-wing groups' (Balchin, 2010, p. 108). Nira Yuval-Davis commented in the report, 'Because people are afraid to be racist then they accept this multi-faithism which fundamentalists then utilize'

(Balchin, 2010, p. 108). It is important, nonetheless, to create a space in which the feminist critique can be developed despite the fact that, in the current charged atmosphere, accusations of racism are, and will continue to be, levelled at critics of religion.

Definition of religion

The definition of religion I use in this book is that offered by Anthony Giddens, 'A set of beliefs adhered to by the members of a community, involving symbols regarded with a sense of awe or wonder, together with ritual practices in which members of the community engage' (Giddens, 1997, p. 584). Giddens rightly points out that 'Religions are clearly influenced by culture, and the sort of religions taken up by societies are likely to relate to the prevailing context which makes some more attractive than others' (Giddens, 1997, p. 584). This book starts from the understanding that religion is socially constructed and produced by culture. Revelations come from nowhere more mysterious than the interests of the dominant groups within particular cultures at particular times. This explains the ubiquity of anti-woman ideologies in cultures of thoroughgoing male domination. This book will be mainly concerned with the three monotheistic religions of Judaism, Islam and Christianity, which are very similar in their attitudes towards women. They all developed in the same cultural crucible in the Middle East (Lerner, 1987). The prevailing culture around them was deeply patriarchal. As these religions expanded into different cultural contexts they were influenced by these new cultures, so that the costume rules for Muslim women are affected by the culture in which they live, for instance, rather than simply by the religion. The three religions all derive from deeply patriarchal roots and incorporate similar norms about women, such as women's innate subordination and the need for obedience to their husbands; the notion of 'honour' and 'shame'; and the idea that women's bodies represent sin and evil. Ideas about women's sexuality and the need to control it are similar in these religions but are modified according to the particular cultural contexts in which they are practised.

I will only consider the three monotheistic religions here, although feminist theorists and activists against religious fundamentalism argue that there are versions of fundamentalism in all the main religions in the world, not just the three from the Middle East, but in Hinduism, Buddhism and Sikhism too. They write about the way in which a newly political Hinduism in India is mobilised by organisations such as Shiv Sena (Nussbaum, 2007), and the political party the BJP, in ways that mandate a narrow and subordinate role for women, and argue that this needs to be included in the fundamentalism that feminists oppose. There are arguments that in Sri Lanka, Buddhism is being directly politicised in ways that suit the non-Tamil Sinhalese majority (Khuankaew, 2008). The forms of women's subordination found in these religions, and the threat posed to women's interests as these religions develop newly politicised versions, are outside the scope of this book.

There is a greater coverage of Islam than the other monotheistic religions here. I am aware that this may be seen as 'Islamophobic' because, as indeed I argue here, all religions are dangerous to women's rights, so why should Islam be singled out. Judaism and Christianity are included in most of the chapters of this book, their founding texts are examined, their fundamentalist versions are scrutinised for their agenda on women, their access to government funding, particularly for faith schools, is problematised, and their involvement in campaigning against women's rights is described. But there is more coverage of Islam, and two chapters – on the covering of women and on Islamic feminism – are restricted to consideration of Islam. The reasons for this do not include any idea that Islam is essentially more problematic for women than the other two religions that were its progenitors. Where there is more attention to Islam in this book it is because the topics being discussed, such as incorporation of religious law into Western legal systems, or the campaign to cover up women and girls, are being promoted particularly strongly in the present by some Islamic organisations.

The Atheist 'movement'

At the present time there is a growing atheist movement worldwide, which is responding to the rise of religion, but this is not a movement that takes much notice of women's interests. It is inspired by the work of men such as Richard Dawkins (2006), Sam Harris (2005) and Christopher Hitchens (2008), who take a rationalist perspective towards religion. These men argue that god does not exist, and use rationalist argument and scientific ideas to prove that no idea of god is needed to explain the world. But feminists have been quite suspicious of both the rationality that male thinkers make claim to, and the scientific objectivity which pretends to truths that are often socially constructed, e.g. that women are naturally different in their mindsets and avocations from men (Harding, 1986). Dawkins' scientific triumphalism fails to appeal – and most of the time seems to be stating the obvious – to feminists whose concerns about religion are not whether god exists, but the fact that religions promote misogyny, and truncate women's opportunities, in countries throughout the world. The way in which Dawkins writes, asserting a superior rationality against the foolishness of those who are easily deceived, could be seen as representing a *hypervirility*. Masculine rationality distinguishes his writing from the behaviour of women, since it is women who have most often been associated with the subjective and emotional spheres, and are likely to be over-represented in churchgoing in Christian religions in the West. Though I hope that this book will contribute a feminist perspective for those involved in the atheist movement who are prepared to include the issue of women's equality in their ruminations, it is not directed to the 'new' atheists so much as to all those concerned with women's rights, who have felt that they should curb their fury so as not to offend and be disrespectful to religion. Disrespect is crucial. Disrespect for the cultures, values and institutions of male domination is the very foundation and *sine qua non* of feminism. Since religion is crucial to the construction of cultural norms in every culture, disrespect for it should be the natural amniotic fluid of feminist thought and activism.

The misogyny of religion

The feminist critique of the way that religions think about and treat women has been profound. Feminist criticism of religion as harmful to women was powerfully expressed in the 1970s, usually in relation to Christianity (Daly, 1985b). Feminist activists and theorists have pointed out the many ways in which Christian religious organisations, as well as those of other faiths, are harmful to women's human rights. From the 1980s onwards these criticisms were extended to Judaism and Islam and feminists have argued that religion is foundational to the ideology of women's inferiority in all patriarchal systems (El Saadawi, 2007). Religion gives authority to traditional, patriarchal beliefs about the essentially subordinate nature of women and their naturally separate roles, such as the need for women to be confined to the private world of the home and family, that women should be obedient to their husbands, that women's sexuality should be modest and under the control of their menfolk, and that women should not use contraception or abortion to limit their childbearing. The practice of such ancient beliefs interferes profoundly with women's abilities to exercise their human rights. Feminist human rights theorist, Courtney Howland, for instance, points out that two elements common to the precepts of organised religions in relation to women – the requirement of women's obedience to their husbands and the modesty rule – chill women's political expression (Howland, 1999). These precepts place an absolute limit on the ability of women in some religious communities to express their opinions, exit their houses, exercise voting rights and engage in any activities where men are present. In this book I shall examine the womanhating attitudes common to the monotheistic religions, and the ways in which they have become the basis of men's rule in religious communities in Western multicultural states, forming the basis of a campaign against women's rights as human rights through the United Nations.

The rise of religion

This book is written in response to the rise of religion. Considering the misogyny that lies at the root of the monotheistic religions, it is impossible for feminists to be sanguine about this phenomenon. This rise has taken Western intellectuals by surprise. The important sociologist of religion, Peter Berger, explains that, like most sociologists until the 1980s, he assumed that modernisation and secularisation would go hand in hand, but now admits, 'The world today is massively religious, and is anything but the secularized world that had been predicted' (Berger, 1999, p. 8). Many other scholars support the idea that religion is on the rise and seek to explain it (Eagleton, 2009). But these commentators give little attention to the implications of this rise for women.

A 2010 issue of the journal *Third World Quarterly*, dedicated to, as the introduction describes it, the effect of 'The Unhappy Marriage of Religion and Politics' on women's equality, covers a variety of ways in which there is a 'rising political prominence of religious actors and movements' (Razavi and Jenichen, 2010, p. 833). The editors explain that in a wide variety of states, political parties and elites have been making alliances with religious leaders in order to garner their votes and shore up their rule. Israel and India are given as examples of this, but the same process has been taking place in countries like the UK and Australia too, in what I call the 'gentlemen's agreement', in which particular groups of patriarchs are handed control over women and children, or even able to get their religious prejudices respected in civil law on issues of crucial importance to women, such as abortion and sexuality. In ethnic nationalist movements, religion has been harnessed to bolster the legitimacy of political leaders – even in Serbia by Milosevic, who was an atheist. Religion has been used to bolster authoritarian regimes, as in Iran and Pakistan, where Islamisation projects have imposed 'an anti-democratic, discriminatory and misogynistic template on society' (Razavi and Jenichen, 2010, p. 841). Democratisation has created the paradox that religious political parties have been able to secure power in states such as Turkey, which has led to the spread of conservative attitudes towards women in both political and civil society. In all of these examples it is a woman's right to control her own body and sexuality, and her right to equality in the 'private' sphere of the family that has been sacrificed as alliances and compromises have been made between patriarchs. In this book I am unable to do justice to developments in individual states such as Pakistan, Turkey, Poland and Nigeria, all of which have been subjected to detailed analysis in relation to the rise of religion and the sacrifice of women's equality elsewhere (Arat, 2010; Pereira and Ibrahim, 2010; Shaheed, 2010). Rather, I have chosen to concentrate on the implications for women of the rise of religion in multicultural societies in the West, through the fertile ground offered by multiculturalist ideas, for instance, and the process of desecularisation.

Multicultural ideology provides support for the development of private religious fiefdoms in which women and girls are subordinated beyond the reach of the state, because it calls for the 'respect' of culture and religion. Respect for religion fosters desecularisation, the process in which states enlist religions in policy formation and delivery, despite the harm to women, girls, lesbians and gay men that are likely to be fostered thereby. Desecularisation is evident in the UK and in Australia, where heads of state such as Tony Blair, John Howard and Kevin Rudd have proclaimed their religious faith and its importance to their policymaking, in ways unthinkable little more than a decade ago (Warhurst, 2006). They have been concerned to propitiate what they perceive as increasingly influential religious minorities in nations in which the religious observance of the citizenry continues to decline. The vaunting of religion has facilitated the implementation of neo-liberal policies of privatisation of state services, and the involvement of 'faith communities' in taking over state responsibilities, inspired by social capital and communitarian ideas. In this process, important areas of state provision, such as education and welfare services, have been outsourced to religious organisations. This has taken place at considerable speed in the UK and Australia from the late mid-1990s onwards.

Religion, women's human rights and equality

This book uses a human rights framework, where this is appropriate, to examine the harm that women suffer from religion. This is a necessary correction, because religious patriarchs are increasingly using rights talk to defend their subordination of women and girls. They justify the harms through the 'right to religion'. Fundamentalist Christian, Mormon and Muslim organisations are using human rights language, such as the need to defend the 'natural family', in United Nations fora in order to turn back the gains made by the movement for women's rights as human rights. Article 18 of the International Covenant on Civil and Political Rights (ICCPR) contains a right to 'Freedom to manifest one's religion or beliefs' but this is tempered by 'such limitations as are . . . necessary to protect . . . the fundamental rights and freedoms of others' (United Nations, 1966). The 'right to religion' therefore may not trample women's 'rights and freedoms'. The language of human rights is important to the international conversation over women's freedom. I assume in this book the usefulness of women's rights as human rights arguments. I will not rehearse all the discussion in feminist and human rights theory as to the effectiveness or appropriateness of using rights talk (Jeffreys, 1997). Women's human rights activists in countries throughout the world are using rights language to raise issues and to delineate harms, and it is this practice that I shall employ in this book.

The understanding of women's equality that I use is one of transformative equality. The 1979 'Women's Convention', the Convention on the Elimination of all forms of Discrimination Against Women (CEDAW), is based upon the notion of equality between men and women. This equality approach has been criticised as assuming a male norm, since it is men that women should be 'equal' to (Fudge, 1989). Men's freedoms, however, are created prior to, and out of, women's subordination, and need to be curtailed if women are to be 'equal' (Pateman, 1988). Men have privileges that enable them to understand 'work' as a paid workday outside the home, because they are generally serviced by the unpaid, and unrecognised work of women (Jeffreys, 2012, forthcoming). Men's 'sexual rights' assume women's compliance with being objects for use, with no concern for women's sexual personhood (Oriel, 2005). Women cannot be 'equal' in these respects (MacKinnon, 1989). Transformative equality does not reduce women to seeking the right to be 'equal' to men, but requires a transformation of the relations between men and women. In this understanding men will lose the privileges that they have gained at the expense of women. I argue in this book that the rise of 'fundamentalism' should be understood as a backlash by patriarchs against this potential loss of privileges, and a campaign to maintain them. The public/private split common to political and legal theory and practice, in which rights are understood as belonging to the public realm, and exclude women's private exploitation and relations of slavery, must cease to exist in transformative equality (Howland, 1999; Cook, 2006). The public and the private realms are understood as indissoluble. I will argue in this book that the rhetoric of religious patriarchs seeks to maintain the 'private' as removed from state interference so that they may subordinate their wives and children according to their own lights. For women to participate in the public realm, the state must be prepared to intervene and alleviate the harms they suffer in the private fiefdoms that are created in fundamentalist versions of religion. Despite the shortcomings of CEDAW, it, and other rights instruments, have an educational and persuasive power that is important to feminist struggle.

A gentlemen's agreement

One of the themes of *Man's Dominion* is the policy of appeasement that has become the dominant response by political actors in the West, particularly those on the Left, to religious political activism. I shall argue that the tolerance of the harms that religions inflict upon women and girls in Western multicultural states is based upon a 'gentlemen's agreement'. This term was the title of a 1947 film about anti-Semitism in the US in which Gregory Peck plays a reporter who goes undercover to reveal 'genteel' anti-Semitism in country clubs and hiring practices, and anti-Jewish quotas. These practices were covert. In the gentlemen's agreement covered in this book they are not. The subordination of women is very clear in matters such as hiring practices, entry to buildings, segregated events, in many religious organisations all over the world, including all

Western multicultural societies. Nonetheless, I argue, patriarchal governments in the West make compacts with them, providing funding through faith schools and access to policymaking through consultations. The gentlemen's agreement is particularly clear in relation to groupings of men that see themselves as 'progressive', Labour parties and Left organisations that seek the votes of ethnic minorities through compacts with their patriarchal leaderships, or bond with religious organisations to organise protests and marches, against Islamophobia, for instance. Carole Pateman, in her mistressful book *The Sexual Contract* (1988), explained how the supposed 'social contract' that underlies government in Western states constitutes a bonding of male governments with their male citizens over and through the bodies of subordinated women. The way that male Left organisations and patriarchal governments work with religions without requiring them to demonstrate their commitments to women's rights, such as allowing women equal employment rights, should be seen as a gentleman's agreement between patriarchs. The religious leaders receive a nod and a wink to the subordination of 'their' women in exchange for their cooperation over certain issues that the ruling patriarchs consider important to their policy agenda. I shall provide many examples in this book of the way in which this agreement is implemented. In this introduction, two examples, in relation to fundamentalist Islam, should suffice to illustrate this problem.

The gentlemen's agreement is clear in the way in which campaigns by Islamic fundamentalist men are aided by the patriarchal compact that exists between Left-wing liberal males and the ultra-conservative Islamist leadership. The Left-wing men, and some women too, may be motivated by cultural relativism, or white guilt, but their endorsement and support for fundamentalist Islam represents a most harmful betrayal of Muslim women. It is a dangerous alliance. This compact was powerfully demonstrated in 2010 in relation to Amnesty International, an institution with a reputation as a fearless advocate for human rights, and even, in the last decade when it has taken up violence against women as an issue, for women's rights as human rights. Gita Sahgal, who was one of the founding members of the brave campaigning group Women Against Fundamentalism in 1989, and researched about and campaigned against fundamentalism for 20 years, has an impressive reputation for courage and integrity on behalf of women. She was director of Amnesty's gender section in London in 2010, when she was forced out over Amnesty's work with a man strongly associated with the Taliban in Afghanistan, an organisation whose agenda towards women is perhaps the most brutal in the world. Sahgal was deeply concerned about the way in which Amnesty gave support to a group called CagePrisoners, run by ex-Guantanamo Bay prisoner Moazzam Begg. Begg set up the organisation to campaign for prisoners in Guantanamo Bay, and others imprisoned without trial on suspicion of terrorist activities inspired by fundamentalist Islam. Sahgal argued that Amnesty's support for Begg was in contradiction to the organisation's commitment to women's human rights, because of Begg's links with the Taliban. Amnesty has promoted Begg as a human rights defender, though Begg has been refused a passport by the British government because of the evidence of his links to the Taliban while he lived in Kabul, and his time in Al Qaeda training camps. Sahgal calls him 'Britain's most famous supporter of the Taliban' and quotes his 2006 autobiography, *Enemy Combatant*, in which he explains his decision to move to Taliban-ruled Afghanistan with his family, to 'live in an Islamic state – one that was free from the corruption and despotism of the rest of the Muslim world' (Sussman, 2010). Begg also states that in 2001 he believed 'the Taliban were better than anything Afghanistan has had in the past 25 years' and he is one of the current advocates of dialogue with the Taliban (WLUML (Women Living Under Muslim Laws), 2010a). Sahgal was strongly supported by feminist organisations that challenge fundamentalism such as AWID and WLUML. These feminist activists believe, like Sahgal, that the Taliban, whose ideology is based upon womanhating, and whose politics in practice in Afghanistan involved brutal suppression of women, including public stoning, caning and execution, cannot be rehabilitated. Taliban supporters, they consider, have no place in human rights organisations because the suppression of women's rights and the championing of women's rights, do not make reasonable bedfellows.

Another example of this kind of gentlemen's agreement is the treatment, by those who consider themselves liberal and progressive, of Tariq Ramadan. Ramadan is seen by many as the moderate face of Islam in Europe and receives many requests for interviews and for his counsel. In recent years his status as the acceptable face of Islam has been seriously questioned (Fourest, 2008; Ireland, 2008; Berman, 2010). In 2004, Caroline Fourest, a French feminist and co-founder of the feminist website 'Pro-Choix', wrote a book examining his writings because of her alarm at his fundamentalist agenda and the implications for women. Fourest, who speaks Arabic, examined the writings and speeches of

Ramadan that non-Muslim audiences do not usually have access to in *Brother Tariq: the Doublespeak of Tariq Ramadan* (2004), which was published in English in 2008. She demonstrates that Ramadan's views are Islamic fundamentalist and not moderate at all. Doug Ireland says in the *New Humanist* that Ramadan is, 'particularly virulent about the role of women', and suggests that they should be forbidden to engage in sports in which their bodies are seen by men, and ensure that they do not, 'use their looks to attract indecent attention' (Ireland, 2008). Ramadan is against equal opportunities, saying, 'Allowing women to work does not mean opening up all types of work to them . . . We are not going to go to the lengths you sometimes see in Western society and say that, in order to prove they are liberated, women must become masons or truck drivers . . . We're not going to be so stupid as to say: prove you're liberated, drive a truck, whore' (Ireland, 2008). Such harmful social attitudes to women should elicit outrage from men committed to women's equality, and it is worrying that this is not always the case.

Ramadan is the grandson of Hassan Al-Banna, founder of the Muslim Brotherhood – the archetypal, fundamentalist, Islamic organisation – in Egypt in 1928. Ramadan says he does not disagree with any of the writings of his grandfather and runs the Geneva Islamic Centre, which is the headquarters of the Muslim Brotherhood in Europe. He exposed his fundamentalist impulses in a television interview in which he was asked what he thought about the punishment of stoning women for adultery (Berman, 2010). He replied that he thought there should be a moratorium on the practice while a conference was convened to discuss what should be done, to which both Western intellectuals and fundamentalist clerics should be invited. Paul Berman, in his book on the complicity of Western intellectuals with fundamentalist Islam through their support of men like Ramadan, compares the treatment of Ramadan by liberal intellectuals Timothy Garton Ash and Ian Buruma, with their treatment of Ayaan Hirsi Ali. These men laud Ramadan as the great hope for a progressive Westernisation of Islam, perhaps because his criticism of capitalism appeals to their Leftish sensibilities, while denouncing Ayaan Hirsi Ali, the Somalian intellectual who was chased out of asylum in the Netherlands by a fatwa threatening her with death for her criticism of Islam. The contrasting way in which Ali (who denounces fundamentalism) and Ramadan (who represents it in his person) have been treated, demonstrates the profundity of the problem of this masculine complicity with womanhating. Ali's work, along with that of other important feminist critics of Islam, such as Fadela Amara, Irshad Manji and Maryan Namazie, will be considered in this book. I argue that feminists need to provide a supportive platform for such criticism rather than accusations of racism, Islamophobia and Westoxication such as are presently being hurled at these women by cultural relativist and post-colonialist academics. As Dena Attar states, 'the left everywhere seems to have lost its ability to provide a critical analysis of religion, or to offer an alternative' (Attar, 2010, p. 72). This book seeks to reinvigorate this critical analysis.

Fundamentalism?

This is not a book about 'fundamentalism', though it includes considera-tion of what is generally called fundamentalism. It is a book about religion in general. There has been a tendency in recent decades to concentrate feminist concern on the rise of fundamentalisms. I consider that this con-centration has obscured the everyday harms of more 'moderate' religious organisations, or even the embrace of 'moderates' on the grounds that they constitute the lesser of the available evils. Fundamentalisms are forms of the major malestream religions of patriarchal cultures, not some odd and eccentric growth. Patriarchal religions, during the times in which fundamentalisms are less active, serve as reservoirs, within which their more strident versions remain dormant but ready to grow again. Thus I find it necessary in this book to address religion rather than 'funda-mentalism'. Nonetheless I require a term to signal that I am discussing the more extreme versions of the patriarchal religions, when that is neces-sary, and I will use the term 'fundamentalist' since this is in common usage in feminist activism against the worst forms of religious subordin-ation of women.

There is some opposition to the term 'fundamentalism' from the Left based on the idea that the term represents hostile and colonising impulses (Pieterse, 1994). Some feminist scholars have argued that the term is unsuitable for different reasons. Ayesha Imam argues that the term 'fundamentalism' is inappropriate to describe any variety of Islam because it was coined to describe a form of Christianity (Imam, 1997). She also considers that a term is needed that makes a greater distinction between believing in the fundamentals of the holy book, which many Muslims would think unexceptional, and a form of Islam that has a clear and harmful political agenda. For this political form of Islam she prefers the term the Muslim Religious Right. Nikki Keddie eschews 'fundamentalism' and prefers the term 'New Religious Politics' or NPR (Keddie, 1998, p. 697). I use the term 'fundamentalism' in this book, not because it perfectly describes the phenomena I address, but because it has a commonly understood meaning among feminist activists and academics.

The need to oppose 'fundamentalism' created a problem for feminist theory and activism. Once the problem with religion was understood to consist of particular extreme forms thereof, rather than religion itself, the feminist critique of religion was profoundly undermined. Fundamentalism represents the distillation of misogynist religious ideology. Confronting only fundamentalism can divert feminist attention from the fact that all forms of patriarchal religion constitute a problem. Energies are focused upon the clear emergency, and the feminists who continue to criticise religion, and not just fundamentalist religion, can come to be seen as a problem. Thus Jennifer Butler, in her book *Born Again*, on fundamentalist Christianity in world politics, argues that 'secularist' feminists have helped to create the problem of fundamentalism (Butler, 2006). They are seen as too extreme, she says, and have caused an extreme reaction. Feminists fighting the main enemy of fundamentalism call for alliances with milder versions of religion to create a united front. For them, continuing to criticise religion can seem tactically unwise if not dangerous. In fact, the advent of religious fundamentalisms does not indicate that some varieties of religion are positive and should be encouraged. It might indicate the very opposite, that the seeds of fundamentalisms lie in all religions and can grow when the conditions are right. I shall argue in this volume that religions that have evolved into forms that are harmless towards women are not numerous. The problem with religion extends far beyond the forms that would normally be seen as fitting the definition of fundamentalism. Presbyterian and Catholic churches that exclude women from ministry, seek the right to reject or sack employees on the basis of religious beliefs or sinful behaviour such as homosexuality, that restrict abortion rights, or emphasise the importance of keeping the family together in cases of men's violence to women or children, may not be understood as 'fundamentalist' but constitute serious dangers to women's equality. Concentrating on 'fundamentalism' may divert attention away from the threats these quite malestream religious formations present. I intend that *Man's Dominion* will complement the copious feminist literature on fundamentalisms, by broadening the analysis to include a swathe of the forms that the three monotheistic religions take, not just those that are most extreme in their prescriptions for women.

Structure of the book

The first chapter of this book looks at the way in which feminists of the 1970s and 1980s criticised religion as a central plank in the subordination of women. All the major feminist theorists of this time saw religion as crucial to the way women are relegated to second-class status, and they drew on the ancient, sacred texts to demonstrate the brutal misogyny therein. I shall look at the attitudes to women in these ancient texts here to remind a new generation of feminists who may not be familiar with these ideas just how harmful they are to women's status. In Chapter 2 I will look at how these ideas are employed today in versions of religion that fit into the usual definitions of fundamentalism, and some that do not. In Chapter 3 the focus is the rise of an international movement of the religious right that seeks to counter the successes of the movement for women's rights to be recognised as human rights. I shall delineate the ways in which the 'right to religion', which is promoted by this coalition, contradicts women's human rights.

In Chapters 4 and 5 I examine the way in which the rise of religion, in forms harmful to women's human rights, has been facilitated in Western multicultural societies, through the ideology of multiculturalism, which mandates that religion should be respected, and desecularisation, in which governments support religions and enable them to increase their influence over women and girls. In Chapters 6 and 7 I look at two harmful cultural practices against women – the covering up of women and polygamy – which have become matters of concern to policymakers in Western states recently. In Chapter 8 I seek to make space for feminist criticism of religion by analysing the way in which the brave feminists who criticise Islam are denounced on the Left and within the feminist academy. I hope that this book will contribute to the creation of a lively debate on why the feminist critique of religion has become so circumscribed, and how it can be widened and strengthened once more.

1

THE DEVIL'S GATEWAY

Religion and the subordination of women

This chapter will introduce the main ways in which feminist theorists have criticised religion. The rejection of all religions, as womanhating ideologies that provided a foundation and justification for the subordination of women, was a central issue for 1970s feminism, as it had been for other influential twentieth-century feminists such as Simone de Beauvoir (Beauvoir, 1972, first published 1949). All of the important feminist texts of the second wave, such as Kate Millett's *Sexual Politics* (1972), Eva Figes' *Patriarchal Attitudes* (1970), Andrea Dworkin's *Right-Wing Women* (1982, first published 1978), recognised the importance of religion as an anti-woman force and the importance of opposing it. This was so much a given at that time, that the idea that it would ever become difficult for feminists to criticise religion would have been unconscionable. These feminist theorists did not spend much time in their work on detailed analysis of the harms of religion, but took it for granted that religious ideas were the foundation stones of the way that patriarchal culture regards women, and that womanhating religious nostrums underlay the sciences and literatures that men created. As Merlin Stone expressed it in her book on the suppression of Goddess religion by the patriarchal monotheists, 'to many of us today religion appears to be an archaic relic of the past' (Stone, 1977, p. 4). Mary Daly, the American radical feminist philosopher, did take on the task of unpacking religion in detail, and her very influential and groundbreaking work will be considered here as a good representation of the central points of the feminist critique (Daly, 1985a; 1985b). Other feminist theorists engaged in historical research to show how patriarchal religions took over from a more woman-friendly alternative (Sjoo, 1987; Gimbutas,1991). This chapter will draw together from the different feminist critiques the main tenets of the three main monotheistic religions in relation to women and show their considerable similarities.

Feminist critique of Christian religion

Feminist critique of religion has a long history. It was understood by those who wrote key feminist texts as the foundation of the subordination of women. Simone de Beauvoir argued in *The Second Sex* in the 1940s that religion is necessary to the subordination of women as a social group because it provides women with a 'supreme compensation' (Beauvoir, 1972, first published 1949). Following the Marxist understanding that religion serves to resign the masses to their subordination and prevent revolt, she says, 'When a sex or a class is condemned to immanence, it is necessary to offer it the mirage of some form of transcendence' (Beauvoir, 1972, p. 632). Religion causes woman to take, 'an attitude of respect and faith towards the masculine universe'. Religion founds men's authority over women and makes resistance difficult, because fear of divine punishment keeps women in their place.

> Man enjoys the great advantage of having a god endorse the code he writes: and since man exercises a sovereign authority over women it is especially fortunate that this authority has been vested in him by the Supreme Being. For the Jews, Mohamedans and Christians among others, man is master by divine right; the fear of God will therefore repress any impulse towards revolt in the downtrodden female.
>
> (Beauvoir, 1972, p. 632)

Religion, she argues, offers woman a refuge from the abuse she suffers at men's hands precisely in the system of belief they have created to keep her down. She finds in 'God' a refuge from the very law of men, delegated from 'God', which subordinates her. Woman is then able to take comfort from the fact that men's faults are sinful but unchangeable, 'Masculine logic is confuted by holy mysteries; men's pride become a sin, their agitation for this and that is more than absurd, it is blameworthy: why remodel this world which God Himself created? The passivity enforced upon woman is sanctified' (Beauvoir, 1972, p. 633). Beauvoir's insights help to explain why women may support religion. It can help them, for instance, to hold back the violence they might otherwise suffer, 'As a human person she has little influence, but once she acts in the name of divine inspiration, her wishes become sacred' (Beauvoir, 1972, p. 634).

Kate Millett argued similarly in *Sexual Politics* (1972), the book that provided a rallying text for second-wave feminism, that religion was the justification that men used for their rule over women, and ensured that male power was beyond criticism.

> Religion is also universal in human society and slavery was once nearly so; advocates of each were fond of arguing in terms of fatality, or irrevocable human "instinct" – even "biological origins". When a system of power is thoroughly in command, it has scarcely need to speak itself aloud; when its workings are exposed and questioned, it becomes not only subject to discussion, but even to change.
>
> (Millett, 1972, p. 58)

The rejection of religion was the solid ground from which these writers embarked on their work. They saw no need to justify such rejection or criticise religion at length.

Mary Daly: shrewd prudes laughing out loud

It was different for Mary Daly, the American feminist philosopher who has made the most significant contribution to the critique of Christianity in second-wave feminism. She started out as a committed Christian, and ended up rejecting religion altogether. Her first two books chart that course. Daly has a considerable profile as a radical feminist philosopher on many issues but her work started with her response to religion. She was brought up Catholic and gained two doctorates in divinity schools. Her first book, *The Church and the Second Sex*, was published in 1968 and written in the wave of excitement that engulfed Catholic women intellectuals after the momentous events of Vatican II, when it appeared that the Catholic Church was opening up to new ideas and abandoning medieval practices, such as that nuns must wear habits. Daly still considered herself a Christian at this time. She was fired, because of the book, from her teaching job at Boston College in 1969, but reinstated and given tenure following protests from her students.

In her first book, Daly delivers a thorough critique of the evolution of Christianity in an age when women were totally subordinate to men and 'a man could sell his daughter as well as his slave', and the messages about women that still appertained from that time. She rejects the maleness of god, which she calls, 'the absurd idea that God is male' (Daly, 1985a, p. 180). She details how the Christian divines throughout history have been antifeminist, antisexuality, and have seen woman's flesh as a temptation, through criticism of the work of Tertullian, Aquinas, Jerome and Pope Leo. But she does not reject Christianity or religion in general. The book contains a section on how Jesus was positive towards women, and explains Paul's prescription that women should not go out unveiled as his not wanting to offend surrounding cultural mores, rather than as misogyny. Interestingly, she makes an argument that would prove central to those feminists who would, in the twenty-first century, seek to both criticise but also protect Islam. She says that Christianity's central message is good, and can be disinterred from the cultural components that have distorted it historically, 'Those who have benefited from the insights of a later age have the task of distinguishing elements which are sociological in origin from the life-fostering, personalist elements which pertain essentially to the Christian message' (Daly, 1985a, p. 84). She abandoned the idea that the essence of Christianity is positive within a few years.

The book was extremely controversial at the time and had a considerable impact on the thinking of feminists and women within the church, but by the early 1970s Daly had moved on and rejected Christianity entirely. The extent of her journey is revealed in the self-mocking preface to the 1985 edition of her first book. The preface is written about the author in the third person, and questions how this author could possibly have believed what she wrote. By the time the preface was written she had developed the delightful and influential wordplay of her later works, which poke fun at patriarchal and religious language. Mary Daly signals a 'tremendous event' in the offing, 'This event is the Self-Realizing of women who have broken free from the stranglehold of patriarchal religion, with its deadly symbols, its ill logic, its gynocidal laws and other poisonous paraphernalia'. She speaks of religion as emanating from 'phallocracy's great prophets' (Daly, 1985a, p. xii) and of the need for 'exorcision of the poisonous patriarchal god and his attendant pathologies', which 'has required and continues to require Courage – the Courage to Leave and, more than this, the

Courage to Live beyond the godfathers' gruesome grasp' (Daly, 1985a, p. xii). Of women who cleave to religion she writes:

> Women under patriarchal religious control become grateful to the paternal predators for their priestly ministrations, believing their dogmas, little suspecting that what these fathers, sons, and holy ghosts bestow upon their faithful followers, who are victims of mass hypnosis, is a bag of illusions.
>
> (Daly, 1985a, p. xiv)

She talks of 'sadospiritual churchmen' and calls the church an 'inherently womanhating, gynocidal institution' in which there is no point in women seeking to be equal (Daly, 1985a, p. xiv). Religious women are described as, 'hooked by churchly love-hysteria' and 'victims of necrophilic love that loves to see women possessed, marching zombie-like in the ranks of the living dead' (Daly, 1985a, p. xv). In an exemplary and powerful passage she calls upon women to show their disgust for religion.

> I suggest that it is Time to let Disgust out of its closet, to celebrate its public Emergence – not disgust for bamboozled women but Disgust for the sacred set-up, the subliminal pornographic seduction, the hidden hard-ons of the holy fathers who induce such grotesque Self-abasement. It is Time to proclaim that the Disgust of a Wholly Disgusted Woman is Holy. This is Her Holinesss, refusing to kneel before his nothingness, calling to other women to rise from their knees, laugh at his lies, acknowledge their own Powers – the Powers of Holy Crones who throw off the chains of hypocrisy, who refuse to allow our strength to be turned against us.
>
> (Daly, 1985, p. xx)

The 'hidden hard-ons' of the holy fathers have been revealed in recent decades as the enormity of sexual abuse within the Catholic Church has become clear (BBC, 2010a). Daly was prescient in this respect. The abuse is not limited to the Catholic Church; similar cases of child sexual abuse of boys and girls, by Qur'anic teachers and others, have occurred in mosques in the UK (Mackay, 2007). Daly did not consider that women should seek formal equality within the church through campaigns for the ordination of women. This would be a mistake because, 'One of the most devastating things the catholic church could do, I think, would be to ordain women, thereby masking its deep-rooted misogyny and further promoting fallacious faith, false hope, and dead love' (Daly, 1985a, p. xx).

The invention of patriarchal religion

Daly's work shows both the approach of accommodation to patriarchal religion and subsequently its rejection. Another important approach for early second-wave feminists was to seek to discredit the monotheistic religions by examining their origins. Feminist theorists pointed to the work of anthropologists and historians to argue that the establishment of monotheistic religions in the ancient Near East constituted a defeat by patriarchs of a matriarchal system (Stone, 1977). The notion that a historical matriarchy existed was supported by evidence suggesting a religion based upon female gods, particularly fertility goddesses, and matrilineal kinship systems in which men followed women into their families, and kinship was established through the female line. Other feminist scholars have disagreed with this account and thrown doubt on the historical existence of matriarchy, pointing out, for instance, that worship of fertility goddesses does not necessarily indicate that real, live women had positions of power and influence, and that matrilineal systems could mean that women were under the control of their brothers and uncles rather their husband and his kin (Bamberger, 1974). Nonetheless there is much evidence that there was considerable conflict as the proponents of the new, vigorously patriarchal religion, sought to suppress believers in the old, more female-focused one. There is evidence, too, that patriarchal monotheism was both established by conquest and instituted a much more severe form of male domination, as women were taken into the control of their husbands, who could imprison them in conditions of purdah and remove them from public life (Lerner, 1987; Plaskow, 1990).

Merlin Stone's *The Paradise Papers* (1977), is a classic example of this literature. Her book opens with the question, 'How did it actually happen? How did men initially gain the control that now allows them to regulate the world in matters as vastly diverse as deciding which wars will be fought when – to what time dinner should be served?' (Stone, 1977, p. 1). She describes the religions that existed before the patriarchal takeover when, in prehistoric and early historic periods:

> . . . religions existed in which people revered their supreme creator
> as female. The Great Goddess – the divine Ancestress – had been
> worshipped from the beginnings of the Neolithic periods of 7000
> BC until the closing of the last Goddess temples, about AD 500.
> Maybe Goddess worship goes back to 25,000 BC . . .
>
> (Stone, 1977, p. 2)

The advent of the Abrahamic religion she puts at between 1800 and
1500 BC, encapsulated in the 'Eve myth' after which the 'female
religion' 'was the victim of centuries of continual persecution and
suppression by the advocates of the newer religions which held male
deities as supreme' (Stone, 1977, p. 3). Stone argues that 'Northern
invaders known as Indo-Europeans' brought the new monotheistic
religion with them to the Near East, and this entailed, 'the worship of
a young warrior god and/or a supreme father god' (Stone, 1977, p. 37).
The female goddesses and their followers were then subjected to attacks
that targeted any 'female creator ideas'. The new religious scholars
undermined the female creator by calling her a 'fertility goddess' and
calling her religion a 'cult' to diminish it (Stone, 1977, p. 4). The Goddess
and her worship were, Stone explains, 'represented as improperly
sensual'. Stone says she does not advocate a return to the old Goddess
religion but argues that women need to understand this history in order
to acquire self-respect:

> It is only as many of the tenets of the Judaic-Christian theologies
> are seen in the light of their political origins, and the subsequent
> absorption of those tenets into secular life understood, that as
> women we will be able to view ourselves as mature, self-
> determining human beings.
>
> (Stone, 1977, p. 15)

Influential Jewish feminist theologian Judith Plaskow details the
conflict between the new patriarchs and the old religion, in which many
gods – including female ones – were worshipped (Plaskow, 1990). She
explains that a subtext in Genesis is the 'establishment of patrilineal
descent and patriarchal control' (Plaskow, 1990, p. 4). She points out
that as late as the ninth to eighth century BC there was evidence for
polytheism in Israel, with references in texts to Yahweh and his Ashera
and many female images. In polytheism, she says, many positions of

influence were open to women, whereas the new religion barred women from leadership and consolidated a new all male priesthood of Yahweh (Plaskow, 1990, p. 43). These new interpretations of religious history were inspiring to second-wave feminists because they indicated that patriarchal monotheism had a starting point, and therefore possibly an end point too. It is not the only religious system that has existed, and may be particularly suited to the severe forms of male control of women that currently exist in most parts of the world. Understanding that there was a 'before' can help to put the male-dominated religions of the present into perspective, and reduce their earthly power.

Womanhating in religious texts

These feminist commentators have been involved in a deliberate political project to expose the patriarchal takeover so as to create confidence in women that they could rebel and seek change. Another aspect of this project was to document how the subordination of women was accomplished in the early texts of those religions, and to map the ground on which women's subjection was justified. In the early part of second-wave feminism the major works of feminist theory incorporated excoriation of the prescriptions of the monotheistic religions for women's role. Julia O'Faolain and Lauro Martines undertook the task of documenting the womanhating pronouncements and practices of the Hellenistic period onwards in their book *Not in God's Image* (1973). The statements of Christian divines, Judaist prophets and the Qur'an, are so uniformly hostile towards women, and in such very similar ways, that it is hard to understand why there should be an increasing respect for religion by political actors in the present, when women's equality has supposedly made advances. I will examine here the similarities between the three monotheistic religions on a series of issues fundamental to women's equality: the idea of women's natural subordination to men; the idea of the feminine evil; the segregation and covering of women and women's inherent disgustingness. Nawal El Sadaawi, the Egytian feminist whose work offers a swingeing critique of the way that Islam is used to justify the oppression of women and girls, argues that the monotheistic religions are similar in their traducing of women:

> Any serious study of comparative religion will show clearly that in the very essence of Islam, as such, the status of women is no

worse than it is in Judaism or in Christianity. In fact the oppression of women is much more glaring in the ideology of Christianity and Judaism. The veil was a product of Judaism long before Islam came into being. It was drawn from the Old Testament where women were adjured to cover their heads when praying to Jehovah, whereas men could remain bareheaded because they had been created in the image of God. Thus arose the belief that women are incomplete, a body without a head, a body completed only by the husband, who alone possesses a head.

(El Sadaawi, 2007, first published 1982, p. 5)

In the following section I shall use a number of feminist sources to illustrate the basic themes of the womanhating revealed in the texts of the monotheistic religions, and show their similarities.

The myth of feminine evil

There was a strong consciousness among feminist theorists of the second wave that harmful attitudes towards women in cultures that are rooted in Judao-Christian-Islamic tradition stem from the creation myths themselves, in which woman is blamed for the birth of evil. As Kate Millett pointed out, in this tradition the world in which god had created man, but woman was as yet unrealised, was a golden age, a paradise of all good things (Millett, 1972). Woman changed all that. She brought sexual intercourse into the world and got Adam thrown out of paradise into a world in which he had to work and bear all the usual problems of human existence. As Millett explains, there are two leading myths of Western culture, 'the classical tale of Pandora's box and the Biblical story of the Fall', and they tell the same story (Millett, 1972, p. 51). The myth of feminine evil consists in the idea that woman was not god's chosen creature, but born of Man as a secondary consideration. She then misbehaved and showed her general unworthiness, in particular by tempting Man, who was born in god's image (and should, therefore, have known better), to forgo paradise and enter into the sin of sexual union. This idea was represented in Greek mythology by the myth of Pandora's box. Hesiod, eight centuries before Christ, described how the smith Hephaestus modelled a woman from clay, who then became enlivened as a woman. As he explains:

Up to this time the races of men had lived on earth free from harm, from toilsome labour and from the painful diseases which bring death to humankind. But the woman's hands raised the lid of the great jar, scattered the evils within it, and laid up the harsh troubles of men.

(O'Faolain and Martines, 1973, p. 24)

Millett identifies the Pandora myth as bearing traces of an older Mediterranean fertility goddess, because, in Hesiod's version, 'she wears a wreath of flowers and a sculptured diadem in which are carved all the creatures of land and sea' (Millett, 1972, p. 51). In this version, Pandora introduced sexuality to the world so that the golden age when 'the races of men had been living on earth free from all evils, free from laborious work, and free from all wearing sickness' came to an end. Pandora was, in his work, the origin of 'the damnable race of women – a plague which men must live with'. Hesiod describes Pandora as a perilous temptation with 'the mind of a bitch and a thievish nature', full of 'the cruelty of desire and longings that wear out the body', 'lies and cunning words and a deceitful soul', a snare sent by Zeus to be 'the ruin of men'. This idea, that woman tempts man with a dangerous sexuality, is common to all the religions of the Middle East. The result of the myth of feminine evil is that:

> Patriarchal religion and ethics tend to lump the female and sex together as if the whole burden of the onus and stigma it attaches to sex were the fault of the female alone. Thereby sex, which is known to be unclean, sinful, and debilitating, pertains to the female, and the male identity is preserved as a human, rather than a sexual one

(Millett, 1972, p. 51)

Millett argues that this idea of the female as 'the cause of human suffering, knowledge and sin' was still, in the 1960s, the foundation of sexual attitudes and 'represents the most crucial argument of the patriarchal tradition in the West' (Millett, 1972, p. 52).

The Pandora's box story was written into the Old Testament as the story of Eve, who was created out of Adam's rib and led to the expulsion of man from paradise because she tempted Adam with the forbidden fruit of the apple, and he did eat. This was, as with Pandora, a metaphor

for sexual relations. The Eve story was taken up by Christian divines
with enthusiasm. Thus for the second-century Eastern Church ideologist,
Tertullian, all women represented Eve and must pay for her seduction
of man:

> And do you not know that you are Eve? God's sentence hangs
> still over all your sex and His punishment weighs down upon you.
> You are the devil's gateway. It was you who coaxed your way
> around him whom the devil had not the force to attack. With
> what ease you shattered that image of God: man! Because of the
> death you merited, the Son of God had to die. And yet you think
> of nothing but covering your tunics with ornaments.
>
> (O'Faolain and Martines, 1973, p. 145)

Eve, and thus woman, is charged in this version with causing the death
of Christ, who had to die and be reborn to redeem humankind of the
sin that Eve unleashed. It is small wonder that womankind was doomed
to suffer in this ideology, since woman was seen as responsible for the
death of god's son.

Male headship and control of the family

An idea of equal importance is that of the necessity of women's
subordination to their husbands and through them to god. The idea that
women should be subordinate, and obey the headship of their husbands,
is particularly clear in the New Testament. Julia O'Faolain and Lauro
Martines point out that, though Paul in Galations said that there were
no distinctions under god of male or female, nonetheless women were
subordinate to men. Thus in Corinthians Paul thunders that 'The head
of the woman is the man' (O'Faolain and Martines, 1973, p. 140).
Women had to cover their heads in the churches to show that they
were under men's headship, but men's heads should be uncovered, 'For
the man is not of the woman; but the woman of the man. Neither was
the man created for the woman; but the woman for man' (O'Faolain
and Martines, 1973, p. 141). Women must, also, be silent in the
churches, 'for it is not permitted unto them to speak' and 'they are commanded to be under obedience' but if they had questions they could ask
their husbands later: 'And if they will learn anything, let them ask their
husbands at home: for it is a shame for a women to speak in the church'

(O'Faolain and Martines, 1973, p. 141). The message about women's subordination to their husbands is repeated forcefully in Ephesians: 'Wives, submit yourselves unto your own husbands, as unto the Lord. For the husband is the head of the wife' (O'Faolain and Martines, 1973, p. 141). The Qur'an, too, contains similar recommendations for how husbands should exercise their headship over women, such as, 'Virtuous women are obedient and careful during their husband's absence . . . But scold those who you fear may be rebellious; leave them alone in their beds and beat them' (O'Faolain and Martines, 1973, p. 126). This advice has formed the basis of the defence of violence against women in fundamentalist Islam and has been the target of revision and revulsion from Muslim feminists. Husbands possessed their wives' bodies entirely and are advised, 'Your wives are your field: go in, therefore, to your field as you will' (O'Faolain and Martines, 1973, p. 126). The idea of male headship, so important to all three religions, is a keystone of the burgeoning fundamentalist varieties of Christianity and Islam.

Seclusion and the veil: segregation in public space

The remedy prescribed for women's allegedly dire seductiveness was that they should cover their beauty so that men would not be tempted. All three monotheistic religions have covering rules. Women must be covered to show obedience to god and to men, and particularly to show their modesty and not tempt men into sin. The covering of women as a subordinated group, and their imprisonment through seclusion, existed in the cultures in which the monotheistic religions developed and was directly transferred. In classical Greece, slaves or labouring women who needed to work outside did not suffer seclusion, but women of rich families did (O'Faolain and Martines, 1973). Classical Greece was much more severe than Rome in this respect. In Rome women might go to dinner parties whereas in Greece this was not allowed. Thus a Roman commentator reported about Greece: 'for there a wife may not be present at dinner, unless it is a family party, and spends her time in a remote part of the house called "the gynaeceum" which is never entered by a man unless he is a close relative' (O'Faolain and Martines, 1973, p. 24). Men in classical Greece did not stay at home, of course, but spent their time in the marketplace. In the ancient Middle East, veiling was introduced as a practice by the lawmaker Hammurabi of Babylon, who required that women who were the property of individual men in marriage should be veiled in the streets to show their respectability, while those who were held in common by men – prostituted women – should remain bareheaded to show their lowly status (Lerner, 1987).

This veiling tradition was incorporated into Christianity. Tertullian, from the second century, trumpets accordingly, 'And so a veil must be drawn over a beauty so dangerous as to have brought scandal into heaven itself' (O'Faolain and Martines, 1973, p. 144). Clement of Alexandria, from the same period, argues similarly, 'By no manner of means are women to be allowed to uncover and exhibit any part of their person, lest both fall – the men by being excited to look, they by drawing on themselves the eyes of men' (O'Faolain and Martines, 1973, p. 145). The fourth-century theologian Augustine explains the necessity for veiling. He said that the problem for women was the 'sex of their body', which prevented them from being in the image of 'God' and this meant that they are, 'bidden to be veiled' (O'Faolain and Martines, 1973, p. 142).

Judith Plaskow argues that the laws of modesty, about women's adornments, movements or general public behaviour, were introduced to the Jewish tradition in the post-biblical literature, and did not exist in the bible (Plaskow, 1990, p. 176). It is rabbinic sources, she explains, rather than the Old Testament itself, that required women to be covered. According to these later sources a husband could charge his wife with misconduct if she bared her hip, leg, shoulder, arm or chest in public, and display of hair was considered an act of immodesty. It was, moreover, 'considered improper for a non-family member to greet a woman, even through her husband' (Plaskow, 1990, p. 176). There were strict laws of chaperonage, which firmly forbade private meetings between a man and woman. These measures were all aimed at protecting men from the temptations that women embodied (Plaskow, 1990, p. 177).

The seclusion and covering rules are part of the range of measures that these patriarchal religions invoked to control women's sexuality. Rules about the importance of virginity, chastity and honour are common to the three religions. These rules included dire punishments for women who were seen to have escaped the control of their male heads. All three religions emphasise the importance of virginity on the wedding night. Judith Plaskow describes the dictates of Jewish law from Deuteronomy as follows:

> If a man married a woman and then accused her of not being
> a virgin, her father had to bring the "evidence of her virginity"

(that is, the bloody sheets) before the elders of the town. If the charges were true, the wife was stoned to death on her father's doorstep.

(Plaskow, 1990, p. 172)

Women's bodies were the possessions of their fathers and husbands to do with as they willed. Thus, as Plaskow explains, women were 'given' and 'taken' in marriage. The practice of Levirate marriage, which required that a childless widow must marry her deceased husband's brother, is an example of this (Plaskow, 1990, p. 173). The importance of being able to ascertain a girl's virginity was such that some strange practices grew up around it. The thirteenth-century Christian scholar Michael Scot argued that virginity could be proved by careful examination of a woman's urine. The colour of the urine was the clue, thus, 'Virgin's urine is quite unclouded, bright, thin, and almost lemon colour when healthy. The urine of the woman who has lost her virginity is very muddy and never bright or clear, save exceptionally when she is more than three months' pregnant' (O'Faolain and Martines, 1973, p. 155). While women were dangerous and tempting, they were simultaneously seen as disgusting.

Women seen as disgusting

Another important theme in Judaist and Christian theology and practice is the impurity of women. The Old Testament lays down rules through which men may escape the contagion of women's polluting secretions. During menstruation women must avoid touching men or allowing men to touch them. Thus Leviticus states:

When a woman has a discharge of blood, her impurity shall last for seven days; anyone who touches her shall be unclean till evening. Everything on which she lies or sits during her impurity shall be unclean. Anyone who touches her bed shall wash his clothes, bathe in water and remain unclean till evening . . . If he is on the bed or seat where she is sitting, by touching it he shall become unclean till evening. If a man goes so far as to have intercourse with her and any of her discharge gets on to him, then he shall be unclean for seven days, and every bed on which he lies down shall be unclean.

(O'Faolain and Martines, 1973, p. 106)

Women's impurity extends to the period after the birth of a child, but the birth of a boy creates fewer cleanliness problems than the birth of an inferior girl child. After the birth of a boy the woman is impure for 33 days, and after birth of a girl, for 66 days (O'Faolain, 1973, p. 106).

Judith Plaskow, argues that womanhating became more overt in the rabbinic and medieval periods when 'terms like *bet hatorfa* (place of rot) were used to designate the uterus and prophetic passages filled with sexual disgust became the basis for legal exegesis' (Plaskow, 1990, p. 177). It was in this era that the period of a woman's menstrual impurity was increased from seven days to the period of menstruation plus seven days, she says. It was in this time that such nostrums were invented as that 'The glance of a menstruous woman poisons the air . . . She is like a viper who kills with her glance. How much more harm will she bring to a man who sleeps with her' (Plaskow, 1990, p. 177). In this period too, the separation of the sexes in the synagogue was enforced because it was understood to protect the 'sanctity of worship' from the 'intrusion of sexuality' (Plaskow, 1990, p. 190). The Qur'an shows a big problem with menstruating women too, stating, 'they are a pollution. Separate yourselves therefore from women and approach them not, until they are cleansed. But when they are cleansed, go in unto them as God hath ordained for you' (O'Faolain, 1973, p. 126). The Judaist tradition of women's impurity is continued in the Christian tradition of the 'churching' of women after childbirth, which is first mentioned in a letter of St Augustine. In the Book of Common Prayer (1559) it is stated that a woman after childbirth 'shall come into the church, and there shall kneel down some convenient place nigh unto the choir door: and the priest standing by her shall say these words, or such like, as the case shall require' (Book of Common Prayer, 1559, ii, 22). The priest intones some words over her, after which the woman is considered purified, must make offerings and is allowed to receive Holy Communion.

Womanhating and religious orthodoxy

The monotheistic religions are steeped in ideas and practices that support male power in communities and families. But some varieties have, historically and in the present, relaxed the misogynist prescriptions to various degrees. In a warning to feminist scholars not to 'essentialise' Islam, for instance, Ayesha M. Imam says that the great variety of ways in which Islam has treated women, historically and geographically, need to be borne in mind (Imam, 1997). She points out, as do other feminist scholars of political Islam (Ahmed, 1992), that in previous historical periods, in various Islamic societies, women have been respected religious scholars, far from the situation currently in most variants of Islam where men are shielded from the pollution of women with the use of barriers or exclude women from mosques. In relation to Christianity there are very clear differences between the ways in which the Christian Patriarchy Movement in the US or the Vatican regard women's role, and that of more progressive groupings such as the Uniting Church in Australia. Similarly, Judaism spans a spectrum from Reform Judaism, which is prepared to accept women and even lesbian rabbis, and ultra-orthodox Judaism, which restricts the ways in which women may look at men before they are married to them.

Those feminists who seek to hold on to religion, rather than rejecting it entirely, strive to excise the most hostile edicts and infuse Judaism and Christianity with new and more woman-friendly beliefs and practices. They seek, also, to become priests, rabbis and religious leaders, with some success. Judith Plaskow has sought to create a specifically 'feminist Judaism', which, she declares, will clearly require a revolution, not just a tinkering with the texts (Plaskow, 1990). Rosemary Radford Ruether has attempted the same feat with Christianity (1993). These feminist thinkers seek to rescue god from masculinity and create a quite different form of their religion. Women have calmed down the misogynist vitriol of these religions in some of their variants, and have even gone so far as to become bishops in the US Episcopalian church, which ordained an openly lesbian bishop in 2010 (BBC, 2010b). But those forms of religion that have most influence in the world and include the greatest numbers of worshippers have not undergone such changes. On the contrary, many have returned to the ancient womanhating texts and taken their message to subordinate women literally; they have become 'fundamentalist'. The next chapter looks at how the womanhating ideas of the original texts are being employed in the present, both by versions of religion that fit the usual definitions of fundamentalism, and some, like the Vatican's version of Catholicism, which do not.

2

FUNDAMENTALISM

The divine right of patriarchs

In this chapter I shall show how the anti-woman ideas from ancient sacred texts are being deployed today in versions of the monotheistic religions that would fit the usual definitions of fundamentalism, such as online Islamic fatwa sites, as well as in some that would not, such as an Anglican group in the UK. The subordination of women is the bedrock of all religions, though the fundamentalist versions show this most clearly. It is surprising, therefore, that though other forces have been involved in the construction of fundamentalism in the twentieth century, there has been insufficient attention in explanations to the ways in which it constitutes a reaction to the 'genderquake' (Wolf, 1994), that is, the significant changes that have been made in the relations of power between men and women as a result of economic change and feminism. Fundamentalism provides an avenue through which men may restore the status quo of male domination against the progress of the movement for women's human rights and the increased participation of women in men's bastions of power, politics, business and the public realm over the past five decades. I shall examine here the ways in which men are seeking their compensations by looking at the precepts and practices of more extreme versions of Judaism, Christianity and Islam that fit into the usual definitions of 'fundamentalism'. Most feminist and human rights theorising and activism around religion and women's human rights have targeted 'fundamentalist' religion, and sought to distinguish this from 'moderate' versions. I shall cast doubt on the clarity and usefulness of this distinction here.

By the 1980s, a new fundamentalism, which aimed at the thoroughgoing segregation and control of women, was developing in all of the monotheistic religions. Feminists in the US had to contend with an increasingly powerful Christian right, which was influencing government as well as developing some very extreme forms of the subordination of women (Joyce, 2009). Fundamentalist Judaism developed apace in the 1990s too, both in Israel (Dworkin, 1982) and in ultra-orthodox communities in the West (Yuval-Davis, 1999; Fader, 2009). After the Iranian revolution of 1979 it became increasingly obvious that Islamic fundamentalism constituted a grave destruction of women's human rights (Moghissi, 1999), and during the 1980s, practices of Islamic fundamentalism were exposed by feminist critics in multicultural Western democracies. The focus of this chapter is the way in which womanhating fundamentalism is developing within Western multicultural democracies.

Fundamentalism is based on the subordination of women

The subordination of women is the *sine qua non* of religious fundamentalism, though the criteria identified for the definition of the phenomenon do not always include it. Feminist commentators have been very clear about the centrality of women's subordination to fundamentalism. The influential UK feminist organisation Women Against Fundamentalism (WAF) was formed in reaction to the 1989 fatwa that was issued against the writer Salman Rushdie. The fact that a religious decree could threaten the lives of citizens in the West broadened the awareness of the threat that religious fundamentalism posed to human rights. WAF had two basic understandings: that fundamentalism was based on the subordination of women and that versions of fundamentalism existed in all religions, not just Islam. WAF states in its first newsletter in 1990:

> Fundamentalism appears in many different forms in religions throughout the world, but at the heart of all fundamentalist agendas is the control of women's minds and bodies. All religious fundamentalists support the patriarchal family as a central agent of such control. They view women as embodying the morals and traditional values of the family and the whole community.
>
> (Women Against Fundamentalism, 1990, p. 2)

It is important to note that these criteria apply to many Christian denominations that are not usually considered fundamentalist, such as those which oppose abortion or alternative forms of the family that are not patriarchal.

The new forms of fundamentalism that developed in the 1980s featured, alongside the subordination of women, belief in the inerrancy of ancient texts and a clear political agenda. Two feminist critics and scholars of fundamentalism, Gita Sahgal and Nira Yuval-Davis, express the political agenda of fundamentalisms thus, 'Fundamentalist movements, all over the world, are basically political movements which have a religious imperative and seek in various ways, in widely differing circumstances, to harness modern state and media powers to the service of their gospel' (Sahgal and Yuval-Davies, 1992, p. 4). Fundamentalisms do not simply rely on ancient texts, they invent traditions of their own and can be wildly creative in the ways they seek to constrain women, such as ultra-Orthodox Jews in Israel making women travel in the back of the bus, or Islamic fundamentalists imposing the burqa on women in places where this was never part of the religious or cultural tradition. They are also modern, in that they do not return to fundamentals to the extent of eschewing the internal combustion engine or even the Internet. Indeed these movements are adept at harnessing modern technologies to the promotion of their spiritual and temporal control. Women are to be maintained in ancient seclusion and subordination, but the minutiae of the religious prescriptions for their behaviour are circulated by male authorities on websites.

In some cases the political agenda is to influence the politics of the state, as with Christian fundamentalism in the US. In others, it is to take control of the state or ensure that religious law is adopted as the basis of state law, as in Iran or Sudan. The Christian Patriarchy Movement (CPM) in the US represents the criteria for recognising fundamentalism by having a political agenda, though this is an unusual one. The CPM is specifically anti-state and seeks to withdraw from the control of the state into homeschooling, home businesses and separation rather than takeover (Joyce, 2009). Not only do they wish to limit state interference in their prerogatives, but some in the movement – the 'dominionists' – want to re-establish the colony of America as a 'land of freedom', returning to biblical government and using Old Testament law and punishments (Joyce, 2009, p. 24). Other fundamentalist cults too want to limit interference by the state in the construction of their patriarchal fiefdoms, such as the Exclusive Brethren in Australia (Bachelard, 2008). The Brethren have an exemption on religious grounds from Australia's compulsory voting system, in recognition of their disdain for the affairs of the political world, but they are not consistent. They engage in funding conservative political advertising campaigns, against the Greens party, for instance.

With the exception of the work of feminist scholars, the causes offered for the rise of fundamentalisms rarely include the feminist revolution that is taking place in women's social position in societies around the world. Rather, malestream scholars focus their explanations on Islamic fundamentalism being a reaction to Western imperialism in the Middle East. They explain that when Muslim countries were entrusted to the Western powers as mandates after World War I, they were held back in their development. When these countries gained independence, their new governments were unable, because of Western impositions and restrictions, to narrow the severe inequality in their societies. This provided a space in which Islamic fundamentalist organisations with political ambitions, such as the Muslim Brotherhood in Egypt, could step in with welfare programmes, which created loyal adherents and spread their ideology. This form of explanation, of Islamic fundamentalism as a justifiably anti-Western and anti-colonialist movement, has enabled the Left in the West to be more sympathetic to it than might otherwise have been expected, and might explain why there appears at times to be a gentleman's agreement between Left theorists and activists, and fundamentalism (Halliday, 1995). Foucault, for instance, argued that the establishment of theocracy in Iran was a positive revolutionary development (Foucault quoted in Miller, 2000, p. 313). This sort of analysis from Left-leaning commentators, when it ignores the subordination of women, could suggest that women are beneath notice.

There is another reason why male Left-leaning thinkers may be surprisingly positive towards the violent nature of some fundamentalist forms of Islam. Robin Morgan, in her remarkable book *The Demon Lover*, about the 'sexuality of terrorism', examines the way in which masculine culture has made the terrorist into a hero: 'The terrorist has been the subliminal idol of the androcentric cultural heritage from prebiblical times to the present' (Morgan, 1989, p. 24). She is particularly critical of the way in which the male Left romanticised the terrorism of counter-cultural groups in the US in the 1970s. She quotes, as an example of this tendency towards romanticism on the intellectual Left, Jean Paul Sartre's preface to Frantz Fanon's book about the decolonisation struggle in Algeria, *The Wretched of the Earth*: 'Make no mistake about it; by this mad fury, by this bitterness and spleen, by [the colonized's] ever-present desire to kill [the European], by the permanent tensing of powerful muscles which are afraid to relax, they have become men' (Morgan, 1989, p. 163). A male Left, excited by violence and masculine aggression, is not in a good position to understand what these practices mean for the status of women.

The role of men's power and women's subordination is rarely mentioned in the origin of fundamentalisms, despite the great changes and challenges the women's revolution has created. There are several ways in which a gendered power dynamic is clearly involved in the development of these religious forms. In some cases the prime cause of this development is precisely the changes that feminists have wrought. In societies throughout the world, men's traditional prerogatives are being challenged by the development of women's educational and workplace opportunities. It is hard to overestimate the importance of what has been called a 'genderquake' (Wolf, 1994). In the West, before the 1970s, evidence of changing gender roles was obscured by the 'family wage', which Jennifer Johnson identifies as part of the concordat between the systems of capitalism and male supremacy (Johnson, 2010). Even where women had been permitted to be part of the paid workforce, this was allowed only on the basis that men would be paid the larger 'family' wage, and their supremacy was uncontested. From the 1970s onwards this ploy to keep women in their place was overtaken by events: the capitalist need for the labour of women and feminism. As women have moved out into the public sphere and into 'men's' jobs in ways previously unimagined, men have sought compensations for their eroding status through the sex industry (Jeffreys, 2009), particularly pornography (Dines, 2010; Johnson, 2010), and through other ways of upholding masculinity, such as religious fundamentalism. One example of this response to the challenge of the genderquake is the CPM in the US, the practices of which will be detailed later in this chapter. The CPM clearly developed as a response to the changes that 'Christian feminists' had created in the ideas and practices of some branches of Protestantism in the US. These included allowing women to become religious leaders or speak in church, practices they identified as 'Christian feminism' (Joyce, 2009). It should be pointed out that followers of this movement proudly call themselves Christian patriarchs. Kathryn Joyce, in her study of the CPM, considers that its ideology is aimed at attracting men back to the church by offering them 'power over women and children as "earthly representatives of the divine" and manly Jesus' (Joyce, 2009, p. 38). Joyce argues that the rallying point for disparate parties within the movement is 'enmity to feminism' (Joyce, 2009, p. 11).

In the case of Islamic states in the developing world, the entry of women into the public sphere, through work and education, has been posited as an important cause of fundamentalism (Rozario, 2006; AWID, 2009). In multicultural states, young Muslim men who are experiencing a loss of their masculine status as a result of unemployment, are using Islamic fundamentalism as a way to shore up their masculinity (Amara, 2006). In the 2010 AWID report 'Towards a Future Without Fundamentalisms', one third of the respondents, human rights and feminist activists, stressed the importance of a backlash against progress in women's rights and sexual rights, as a factor behind the rise of fundamentalisms (Balchin, 2010, p. 19). The backlash, they said, is against women's increased autonomy, which has brought profound economic, political and social changes, and it has been particularly severe where states have attempted to advance women's rights in family law.

In the next section of this chapter I examine the ways in which forms of fundamentalist religion have developed in multicultural states. Some forms of fundamentalism are better known than others. While the brutal suppression of women that takes place in the Islamic State of Iran is well documented in media reports and in academic work, examples of the suppression of women's human rights within Western democracies through the creation of fundamentalist, patriarchal fiefdoms, which are 'respected' by governments, are less well known. Iran's treatment of women can be publicised because this country is not an ally of the West. Fundamentalist oppression of women in Israel and the US are less documented, perhaps because they are Western allies. I will focus on these latter examples in this chapter. Judaist and Christian fundamentalism need to be addressed to make it clear that religious fundamentalism, as feminist critics have pointed out, is by no means specifically a problem of Islam. In the rest of this chapter, I will examine three ways in which fundamentalist religion is enabled to flourish in democratic states in the West. The first is the direct support or funding of fundamentalist organisations, the second is the incorporation of religious law into the legal system, and the third is government respect for the private/public distinction and for the right to religion, which enables the privatisation of practices of severe subordination of girls and women.

Supporting fundamentalism

In the last decade governments in multicultural states such as the UK and Australia have increasingly directed funding to religious organisations to deliver services, such as education, health and youth programmes. These dispensations, combined with tax relief and other favourable conditions, enable religions to become as large as major corporations (Ferguson, 2006). The problematic implications will be further discussed later in this book in the chapter on desecularisation. Some of this funding goes to fundamentalist organisations, through the funding of Islamic state schools, for instance. But there is another way in which the UK government has directly subsidised Islamic fundamentalism, which is through their attempts to support 'moderate' versions of the religion in order to inoculate the Muslim community against the production of terrorists. The Prevent strategy, adopted in 2007, is aimed at 'preventing violent extremism' (Communities and Local Government Committee, 2010). 'Moderate' religion in this understanding is that which does not directly advocate bombing of other citizens, but it may be entirely immoderate in every other way. The agenda for women in these 'moderate' versions may be indistinguishable from 'fundamentalism'. The criteria for identifying versions of religion that are 'moderate' are inadequate since the distinction between 'moderate' and fundamentalist religion can be moot. There appears to be no workable definition of 'moderation' to guide governments that seek to invest in organisations in order to inoculate the body politic against extremism. 'Moderate' religion, I suggest, should promote the equality of women, of minorities and of religions. It should outlaw discrimination against women, lesbians and gay men in places of worship and in ministry. It should abandon any idea that 'God' is male, and explicitly reject any anti-woman sentiments in holy books. It should not seek to gain political control in a polity and it should support democracy and the separation of church and state. According to these quite limited criteria, most religious organisations of all faiths would likely fall short.

The UK government, as part of its campaign to support 'moderate' religion, provided the funds to set up the think tank, Quilliam. This organisation can reasonably claim to be 'moderate' because it explicitly opposes 'Islamism', which is the political version of Islam that seeks to set up a Caliphate and the adoption of sharia law. However, it was founded by three men who were Muslim fundamentalists in their youth and Quilliam has been attacked by Muslim critics as a 'quisling' organisation, founded on government money and working to spy on Muslims (al-Tikriti *et al.*, 2008). It writes reports that indict the propaganda from Islamic organisations and mosques in the UK for the radicalisation of Muslim youth. They point out the dangers involved in the British government supporting, or working with, organisations that purport to be 'moderate', but in fact promote very harmful ideas about women, non-believers and homosexuals, and use inflammatory language about what should be done to them. A Quilliam report demonstrates that one reason for mosques in the UK becoming centres for the radicalisation of young men is that they employ Imams who are not raised in British culture. The report found that 97 per cent of Imams were born abroad and 92 per cent trained abroad (Dyke, 2009). The British government runs a visa scheme for religious ministers and since 2004 applicants have had to prove they can speak English, but only at a low level. The mosques do not service the needs of women, with 46 per cent having no prayer facilities for women, and those that do have such facilities being likely to sequestrate women in a gallery or behind a screen so that they have no access to the Imam. As a female Ph.D. student quoted in the Quilliam report puts it, 'Imams may have imported chauvinistic attitudes and present them as Islamic' (Dyke, 2009, p. 21). Quilliam's credentials for 'moderation' look sound, but the UK government also funds the Muslim Council of Britain, whose agenda for women, as expressed in their guidelines for Muslim students in state schools that will be discussed later in this volume, is clearly fundamentalist (Muslim Council of Britain, 2007).

A UK Channel 4 *Dispatches* programme illustrates the difficulties of differentiating between moderation and fundamentalism in relation to Islam (Channel 4, 2007). The narrator explains that their investigation has, 'uncovered a fundamentalist message spreading from the Saudi Arabian religious establishment through mosques run by major UK organisations which claim to be dedicated to moderation and to dialogue with other faiths'. The mosques that are featured have been represented by government figures as 'moderate' but are clearly anything but, in their attitudes to women and minorities and to democracy. One of the far from moderate mosques investigated in the *Dispatches* report is the 'high-profile' Green Lane Mosque in Birmingham, which calls itself a 'centre for inter-faith communications welcoming people of all religions', but promotes hatred of non–believers, women and homosexuals through preaching and videos. The Channel 4 reporter recorded sermons over several months, particularly by Abu Usama, their main English language preacher. He preaches against Kuffaars, or non-believers, who are 'liars and terrorists', and against 'man-made' laws. As the programme points out, Green Lane's official website (Green Lane Masjid) says the mosque is designed to counter the negative publicity and stereotyping of Islam. This is contradicted both by the preachers they present in the mosque and the videos and online materials they provide.

Abu Usama says that Muslims should not be satisfied with 'living in other than the total Islamic State', which would prescribe extreme punishments such as death by crucifixion for changing religion. Usama's views on women are extremely misogynist: 'Allah has created the woman, even if she gets a PhD, deficient. Her intellect is incomplete. Deficient. She may be suffering from hormones that will make her emotional. It takes two witnesses of a woman to equal one witness of the man'. A video available at the mosque has a Saudi TV Imam saying, 'Men are in charge of women, wherever he goes she should follow him and she shouldn't be allowed to leave the house without his permission'. The Imam says that the hijab should be enforced on young girls, with violence if necessary: 'By the age of ten it becomes an obligation on us to force her to wear the hijab. And if she does not wear hijab, we hit her'. A preacher giving religious rulings at the Green Lane mosque, which were distributed on video, says that marrying off a girl before puberty is permissible because the Prophet married a nine-year-old girl. In relation to homosexuality, Usama quotes what he says are words of a companion of the Prophet: 'Do you practise homosexuality with men? Take that homosexual man and throw him off the mountain'. The mosque has been identified as representing a force for 'moderate' Islam, such that an imam from the mosque, Abdul Hadi, was enlisted by the British government to work on a government task force set up after the 7 July London underground bombings to advise about combating extremism. Britain's first Muslim peer, Lord Nazeer Ahmed, praised Green Lane Mosque as his 'favourite spiritual place in the country' and said he had worshipped there.

Judging from the UK example, the test that governments apply when funding or consulting with 'moderate' religion has been faulty, but this is changing. David Cameron, Prime Minister in the Conservative government elected in 2010, announced that he intends to change the test, saying his government 'will no longer fund or share platforms with organisations that, while non-violent, are certainly in some cases part of the problem' (Wintour, 2011). He stated that women's equality was a value that could not be ignored in the government's interaction with religious organisations (Doward, 2011). When governments cooperate with religious organisations whose agenda for women are filled with malice, they are promoting the subordination of women in direct contradiction to any obligations they may have under rights conventions. CEDAW, for instance, requires states parties to change the attitudes that create harmful cultural practices towards women, rather than facilitate their promulgation. No form of religion should be seen as 'moderate' that preaches such ideas.

The incorporation of religious law into the body politic

Another direct way in which governments in democratic states promote fundamentalism is the incorporation of religious law into their legal systems. Israel is an example of this practice. In Israel, religious law prevails in relation to women in very important respects. As the Jewish feminist theologian Judith Plaskow explains, when Israel was established in 1948, sexual inequality was intensified because Orthodox parties had a role in the formation and governance of the state (Plaskow, 1990, p. 110). These parties guaranteed that, even for the non-Orthodox majority, important areas of women's lives would be shaped by fundamentalist religious law. Though a Women's Equal Rights Law was enacted in 1951, marriage and divorce were exempted. In 1953, the Orthodox establishment was granted complete control of these areas and thus equal rights for women were effectively annulled.

The American radical feminist theorist, Andrea Dworkin, has written of her sense of shock when she visited Israel in the 1990s. As a Jewish girl she was brought up to support Israeli kibbutzim financially and see them as beacons for the Jewish people. However, the situation of women in Israel, she found, was dire.

> In Israel, Jewish women are basically – in reality, in everyday life – governed by Old Testament law . . . The Orthodox rabbis make most of the legal decisions that have a direct impact on the status of women and the quality of women's lives. They have the final say on all issues of 'personal status', which feminists will recognize

as the famous private sphere in which civilly subordinate women are traditionally imprisoned. The Orthodox rabbis decide questions of marriage, adultery, divorce, birth, death, legitimacy; what rape is; and whether abortion, battery, and rape in marriage are legal or illegal.

(Dworkin, 1997, p. 230)

To other Jewish feminists she said in despair, 'Sisters: we have been building a country in which women are dog shit, something you scrape off the bottom of your shoe. We, the "Jewish feminists"'. (Dworkin, 1997, p. 231). She explains that there are separate religious courts in the country for Christian, Muslim, Druze and Jewish citizens. The effect is that 'women from each group are subject to the authority of the most ancient systems of religious misogyny' (Dworkin, 1997, p. 231). Women's status in these courts is completely subordinate: 'women, along with children, the mentally deficient, the insane, and convicted criminals, cannot testify. A woman cannot be a witness or, needless to say, a judge. A woman cannot sign a document' (Dworkin, 1997, p. 231). Dworkin encapsulates Jewish law thus: 'Under Jewish law, the husband is the master; the woman belongs to him, what with being one of his ribs to begin with; her duty is to have children . . . preferably with plenty of physical pain; well, you remember the Old Testament' (Dworkin, 1997, p. 232).

She explains that Old Testament laws on marriage prevail, so that women may not get divorced unless their husbands agree, by signing a piece of paper called a get. As Dworkin describes the situation, a woman 'has to live with an adulterous husband until he throws her out . . . if she commits adultery, he can just get rid of her . . . She has to live with a batterer until he's done with her' (Dworkin, 1997, p. 232). If a woman leaves her husband without formal permission from the religious courts she can be judged a 'rebellious wife', will lose custody of her children and any rights to financial support. There are thousands of 'agunot', literally 'chained women', whose husbands will not grant them divorces, and 'Some are prisoners; some are fugitives; none have basic rights of citizenship or personhood' (Dworkin, 1997, p. 232). Dworkin gives an example of the dire plight of Jewish women in Israel by explaining that 'when a Jewish woman is given a divorce, she has to physically back out of her husband's presence in the court' (Dworkin, 1997, p. 233). Judaist law is not just a problem in Israel, where it is incorporated into the legal system, but in all the countries of the Jewish Diaspora where Beth Din, or religious courts, oversee divorce. The Australian Attorney-General's Family Law Council recognises the harms to women of the Beth Din religious divorce process, in which men can refuse divorce and any children women may have after divorce, even if the wife contracts a civil marriage, are seen as illegitimate and shunned (Family Law Council, 2007). The distinction between fundamentalist and moderate versions of religion are moot in this case, since though the appellation 'fundamentalist' is not usually used in the context of this religious law, there is certainly nothing 'moderate' about the effects on women.

When Dworkin visited Israel in the 1990s, there was already a considerable revival of ultra-Orthodox Judaism taking place, and, as she comments, 'in Jerusalem, Orthodox men throw stones at women who don't have their arms covered' (Dworkin, 1997, p. 237). Since her visit, the influence of ultra-Orthodox Jews in Jerusalem has strengthened with particularly humiliating results for women. The political agenda of Judaist fundamentalism includes greater and greater pressure on local and national governments towards segregation of men and women. There is an increasingly successful campaign in Jerusalem and other cities to segregate buses, sidewalks, and entrances to buildings. The buses that service ultra-Orthodox areas in several cities prohibit women from sitting, or entering, at the front (Benson and Stangroom, 2009, p. 7). As in the American South in the 1950s, when black citizens were required to sit at the back of the bus, and Rosa Parks' refusal to do so was an inspiration to the civil rights movement, a class of persons is being treated as subordinate and forced into humiliating segregation. In 2009, stone throwing was being used to try to get the major bus company in Jerusalem to segregate more lines (Lynfield, 2009). A spokesperson for the pro-segregation activists said that unsegregated bus lines forced Jews to sin because the men and women might be forced into contact with one another, 'there are sudden stops and sharp turns and men fall on the women' (Lynfield, 2009).

Fundamentalist values have surfaced in recent years too, in moves to remove women's faces from public space. In 2008, the major bus line in Jerusalem refused to carry election posters that showed the uncovered faces of women, until forced to do so by the High Court (Zach, 2010). In 2010 there were protests at attempts to segregate the sidewalks, particularly near the Knesset. Ultra–Orthodox segregationists are also demanding separate entrances for men and women in public buildings. As Zach, at the New Israel Blog reports, 'there are increasing numbers of "men only" and "women only" entrances for public buildings such as clinics. Protests have been lodged to the Chalit Health Fund, Israel's largest health-care provider, which has opened gender-segregated clinics in Jerusalem, Beit Shemesh and Bnei Brak' (Zach, 2010). There was trouble at a state school in 2009 when all staff and students were told they must use a side entrance (Margolin, 2009). This order is believed to be the result of pressure from an ultra-Orthodox school opposite the main entrance whose male staff did not wish to have to look at female staff and students as they entered the state school. These practices are in clear breach of women's human rights to access public space and facilities, to freedom of movement, and to take part in electoral processes. The state's inadequate response to the egregious violations of women's right to equality in the public sphere, compounds the violation of women's right to equality in marriage and the family that is enforced through a brutally discriminatory legal system.

Sharia law in multicultural states

The governments of multicultural Western states are under increasing pressure to incorporate elements of sharia law into their legal systems (MacEoin, 2009). As is generally the case with such proposals in relation to religious law, these are the elements that concern the human rights of girls and women. Sharia law is 'fundamentalist', in the sense that it is based on acceptance of the inerrancy of the messages of the ancient texts as interpreted by various male exponents. Many countries apply sharia law to varying degrees, including Algeria, India, Lebanon, Palestine, Sudan, Bahrain, Indonesia, Libya, Philippines, Syria, Iran, Malaysia, Qatar, Tanzania, Brunei, Iraq, Maldives, Saudi Arabia, Tunisia, Egypt, Israel, Morocco, Senegal, United Arab Emirates, Ethiopia, Jordan, Nigeria, Singapore, Yemen, Gambia, Kenya, Oman, Somalia, Ghana, Kuwait and Pakistan. In Canada, the UK, Australia and other multicultural states, governments are being asked to decide whether the demand for sharia law should be accepted as in consonance with the 'right to religion'. Customary and religious law exist in many countries alongside other forms of law, so these demands are based upon precedent. In some countries that the UK colonised, for instance, parallel systems of religious law subsist. In India separate systems exist for Hindus,

Muslims and other religious groupings (Nussbaum, 2007). Customary and religious law is usually applied only to issues that concern personal life, and they are sometimes referred to as 'personal' laws. They are, thus, mostly concerned with the rights and status of women.

In 1996, the campaign for the incorporation of sharia law in the UK received a boost from the new Arbitration Act, which enabled the recognition of agreements reached in arbitration tribunals in civil courts. This provided the opportunity for Muslim Arbitration Tribunals to be set up to claim this advantage. The first tribunal was set up in 2007, and they now number five with plans to expand and to train the leaders of other institutions to follow their practice. The tribunals do not usually cover criminal law and they cannot, for instance, affect the status of marriages that have been registered under UK law, but they can cover other issues such as Islamic divorce settlements, and the decisions are accepted in civil law proceedings in the UK so long as both parties are considered to have fully consented to them. Though campaigners for sharia law usually say that their aspirations are limited to commercial and civil law, some of the issues on which they adjudicate are criminal. Thus the UK Muslim Arbitration Tribunals dealt with 100 cases between the summer of 2007 and September 2008, of which six involved domestic violence, which is a criminal offence. In all six cases judges ordered husbands to take anger management classes and mentoring from community elders but instituted no further punishment or any protection for the wives who had suffered the beatings (Hickley, 2008). A report by the think tank Civitas in 2009 estimated the number of sharia courts and tribunals in the UK, which represent different religious traditions in their interpretation of sharia, at eighty-five (MacEoin, 2009). The Muslim Arbitration Tribunals are the only ones whose decisions are binding in civil law.

There are many reasons why the Muslim Arbitration Tribunals and the sharia courts are not suitable as defenders of women's equality: the proceedings are conducted in secrecy; they are constituted by conservative men; they exclude women, except as petitioners; and they are not susceptible to change. Though Western legal systems still contain many problems for women's equality in their ideas and practice, they can be changed by concerted feminist campaigning. Feminists gained major changes in the nineteenth century over issues such as child custody, the right of women to retain their own earnings and even, in 1928 in the UK, the right to divorce. In the late twentieth century, feminists achieved considerable changes to laws on violence against women. None of this is possible in relation to sharia courts, where the ideology and practice are attributed to ancient texts and interpretations and women have no right to question. Disagreement with Islamic teachings can lead to accusations of apostasy, and the punishment laid down for this is considered by Muslim jurists to be death, 'The majority of them go for killing' (al Qaradawi, quoted in Islamonline, 2003).

An attempt to create a role for sharia law in the state of Ontario, Canada, similar to that which it now occupies in the UK, was defeated by feminist efforts. In Canada, Ontario's 1991 Arbitration Act allowed for decisions by arbitration tribunals to be binding in mainstream law. In 2003 the Islamic Institute of Justice was founded to offer arbitration in family and other disputes and in December 2004 a former Canadian attorney general, Marion Boyd, produced an official report for the Ontario government, which recommended in favour of enabling arbitration according to Islamic law. In response, Muslim women in Ontario made it clear that there could be no equality for women in such a system because women would be under extreme pressure from male relatives and in their community to show that they were good Muslims by submitting themselves to such courts. Indeed the likelihood of this type of force being exerted was made clear in 2003, at the launch of the Islamic Institute of Justice, when Syed Mumtaz, leader of the Canadian Society of Muslims, said that a 'good Muslim' should choose sharia in preference to Canadian secular courts (Lichter, 2010). The new organisation sought to institute sharia tribunals, but the feminist campaign against these courts led Ontario's Premier to bring in legislation banning all faith arbitrations. In September 2005 he announced that the Arbitration Act would be amended to ensure 'one law for all', and the amendment was passed in February 2006. In Ontario, family arbitrations must now be conducted exclusively under Canadian law, and the results of other dispute resolution processes have no legal effect.

The majority of sharia courts, which do not have the legal status of the Muslim Arbitration Tribunals, operate in the UK from the back rooms of mosques, in which male authorities give 'fatwas', or official advice as to the tenets of sharia law to Muslims who appeal to them. These courts are approached mostly by women, and deal overwhelmingly with matters related to personal status, such as marriage and divorce and child custody. The sort of fatwas that they are likely to dispense are available to view on fatwa websites, where groups of imams post responses to questions that are sent in to them. The online fatwa sites offer a very useful glimpse of the constraints that deny women full citizenship in some parts of the Muslim community. My perusal of fatwa websites found that these rulings enforced a requirement of women to sexually service their husbands, women's unequal rights to divorce, and many other discriminatory and harmful attitudes and practices towards women. The London Islamic Sharia Council states that '95% of all letters received by the Council are related to matrimonial problems faced by Muslims in the UK' (Islamic Sharia Council, n.d. a). Most of these are from women wanting to divorce their husbands, because women cannot usually divorce their husbands under sharia law unless the men agree. Advice on divorce on the website explains that, 'Due to financial responsibilities which he has to bear, the right to divorce in Islam is primarily given to the husband' (Islamic Sharia Council, n.d. b). He may divorce his wife 'either verbally or in writing'. He is advised only to divorce her once and only when she 'is not on her menses', for which odd criterion no explanation is given. He must have had 'no sexual contact with her since the time of her last menses', to ensure that she is not pregnant. After the husband has pronounced the divorce, the wife must wait for a given period, called 'iddat', during which she must live with her husband and have no sexual contact. The husband has the right to take her back during this period, but if he does not, she must then leave the matrimonial home. When the husband has pronounced 'three divorces', on three different occasions, he cannot take her back or remarry her.

In marriage, according to the Islamic Sharia Council, a woman has no right to control access to her body. A question about the husband's right to use his wife's body for penetration was entitled, 'Denying husband's marital rights'. Typically the answers include innumerable quotations from sacred texts, many of which seem hardly germane to the issue. One states, 'if a man calls his wife to his bed and she does not come, and he goes to sleep angry with her, the angels will curse her until the morning' (Islamic Sharia Council, n.d. c) This curse applies to 'those who are too slow and reluctant to respond to their husbands' and the website states, 'Allah will curse those procrastinating women who, when their husbands call them to their beds, say "i will, i will [sic]" until he falls asleep'. Women should not 'give silly excuses and try to avoid it'. Another question concerns whether a marriage can be contracted if the bride is not present, and the website answers that this is OK so long as the woman's Wali or guardian is there to stand in for her (Islamic Sharia Council, n.d. d). Negative attitudes towards women are clear in answer to a question about 'why two women are the equivalent of one man in an Islamic court'. The answer references what it calls the 'latest research', which shows that 'Man's mind is uni-focal while the woman's mind is multi-focal' and a 'case of testimony' requires 'more attention and concentration'; also, 'women are kind-hearted human beings who are governed by their emotions' (Islamic Sharia Council, n.d. e). The covering of women is important to the imams who advise on the fatwa sites. A question concerning covering asks, 'Why is it necessary for a woman to cover her whole body whenever she comes out of home' and the answer is that the woman is 'meant to be covered' because 'display of the beauty on the part of woman and free mixing with men leads to scandals like that of Mr Clinton and Monica' (Islamic Sharia Council, n.d. f).

These fatwas have no standing in UK law, and so cannot be enforced, but they are likely to have considerable impact on the way in which Muslim women and girls are able to live their lives. They constitute an informal but powerful authority in Muslim communities, to which women will be under great pressure to conform. They lend support to the authority of the men whose wishes and rules control the women's lives. Fortunately, the majority of Muslims in the UK, particularly older generations, reject the use of sharia law. A 2007 poll by the think tank Policy Exchange found that 75 per cent of those over 55 preferred British law (Mirza *et al.*, 2004, p. 4).

Public equality/private fiefdoms

The fatwas on sharia law websites give a glimpse into the pressures and constraints that women and girls experience in some Muslim communities in multicultural states. They shed light on the rules that patriarchs create to maintain their power in religious fiefdoms. Even where women have public equality in the legal system and religious law is not recognised, they may be subject to severe subordination in the private sphere where patriarchs use quotations from ancient texts to control what women wear, where they may go, how much education they may have, whether they may work and in what ways, how they have sex and reproduce, how they marry and divorce and whether they have access to their children. Such fiefdoms, in which religious rule is applied, exist in all Western states. They may be Mormon, Christian or Judaist, as well as Muslim. Women and girls within these fiefdoms are controlled through fear of hell and damnation, as well as by propaganda, penury and emotional or physical violence. They are brought up in the fear of divine punishment, sketchily educated, without skills, cut off from access to people and ideas unacceptable to the patriarchs. The existence of this form of private subordination that cuts women off from access to the rights male citizens expect, such as freedom of movement, freedom of expression, rights to education and to work, and the right to equality in the family, is generally considered to fall outside the state's jurisdiction or sphere of interest. But the harms to girls and women that take place are egregious and, as I argue throughout this volume, the public/private split must be overcome if women are to enjoy substantive as opposed to formal equality.

The CPM in the US provides a good example of how these private fiefdoms work. CPM patriarchs quote biblical references for man's dominion over women and follow a literalist understanding of the texts. In her fascinating book on the CPM, Kathryn Joyce explains that this movement is part of the Christian right, and promotes a 'submissive lifestyle' for women that is 'increasingly advocated through a number of mainstream conservative churches that urge a return to "complementarian" notions of manhood and womanhood modeled on roles of female submission and male headship' (Joyce, 2009, p. ix). The CPM promotes its ideas through its influence in the homeschooling movement in the US. Homeschooling is important to the CPM because it enables a closed environment for the indoctrination of children, who are not able to acquire any liberatory or critical views. The doyenne of the movement's homeschooling initiative is Mary Pride who publishes the Practical Homeschooling magazine, and she is a resolute enemy of feminism as she demonstrates in her book *The Way Home: Beyond Feminism, Back to Reality* (Pride, 1985). Pride says feminism 'contains ills from communism to witchcraft', that feminism has caused the 'victimization' of women through such things as no-fault divorce laws and casual sex, and its most pernicious product is 'family planning'. To rebut feminism the Christian Patriarchs set up the Council on Biblical Manhood and Womanhood in the 1980s. The council spreads its message through the large and influential group of churches in the Southern Baptist Convention, the Presbyterian Church in America and an evangelical ministry called the Campus Crusade for Christ. The

Council's founding statement said that there was 'widespread uncertainty and confusion in our culture regarding the complementary differences between masculinity and femininity' (Joyce, 2009, p. 14), and its purpose was to heal 'people and relationships injured by an inadequate grasp of God's will concerning manhood and womanhood'.

A good illustration of the CPM's attitude to women is the important founding idea that women should call their husbands Lord. As Joyce explains, Doug Phillips, who is the founder of Vision Forum, and publishes homeschool curricula, is 'one of the most influential proponents of the Patriarchy movement among homeschoolers'. He says, 'Can you call your husband "Lord"? If the answer is no, you shouldn't get married' (Joyce, 2009, p. 3). The materials that the CPM produces are sold through homeschooling conventions, where men have such choices in the 'Biblical Patriarchy collection' as 'Manliness', 'Manly Men Write Manly Letters', and 'Poems for Patriarchs', whereas women have 'Verses of Virtue', 'The Role of Women', and 'What's a Girl to Do?' The women wear homemade skirts and have uncut hair. Various biblical verses are recommended as advice to be followed by women and their male heads. Titus is popular as a source, and recommends training 'young women to love their husbands and children, to be self-controlled and pure, to be busy at home, to be kind, and to be subject to their husbands, so that no one will malign the word of God' (Joyce, 2009, p. 8). Doug Phillips recommends that women should be 'helpmeets'. Women should not struggle after careers, but manage their households. They should seek to win the 'adornment of humility' and, importantly, they should not nag, because of the biblical injunction, 'A constant dripping on a day of steady rain and a contentious woman are alike' (Joyce, 2009, p. 9). Phillips helpfully asks women, 'Are you a dripping faucet?'.

The Quiverfull branch of the CPM mandates that women should try to have upwards of six children. Many have far more, and some women featured in Joyce's book have thirteen or fourteen. Quiverfull is named after the idea that women should have full 'quivers' of children. Women are required to relinquish control over their bodies to god, and may not use contraception or abortion to limit their childbearing. Joyce estimates the number of families that seek to fulfil the Quiverfull mandate as in the low tens of thousands, but considers there are many who don't identify as Quiverfull members yet still follow the philosophy of keeping women pregnant. The CPM imposes strict training and indoctrination on girl children for their role as submissive wives.

Daughters are taught submission to their fathers at father–daughter retreats. Arranged marriage is popular in the CPM and some patriarchs are beginning to demand bride price for the sale of their daughters. For this reason girls are forbidden access to novels and materials that depict romantic love, lest they become corrupted.

Though it may be tempting to see the CPM as extreme in its sexual politics, its ideas have spread widely and are represented even in the Anglican Church in the UK. This shows that the difficulty of distinguishing 'moderate' religion from that which is fundamentalist is a problem for Christianity as well as for Islam. A group within the Anglican Church, which calls itself REFORM, is firmly aligned with the Council on Biblical Manhood and Womanhood, which is a lynchpin of Christian Patriarchy (Brown, 2010). This Anglican group is a leading component of the alliance against the ordination of women or homosexuals as bishops in the church, a stance that has split the Anglican community. REFORM adheres on its website to the men's headship ideas of Christian Patriarchy, and links to documents on the American Council of Biblical Manhood and Womanhood that encapsulate this philosophy as well as ones on the 'inerrancy' of the bible. REFORM includes some women Anglican priests, but considers that women should only fill foot soldier positions in the church and not rise above them. REFORM considers that women should not become 'priests in charge, incumbents, dignitaries and bishops'. The 'headship' of women is 'inappropriate' because of, 'the unique value of women's ministry in the local congregation' and the divine right of patriarchs, called by REFORM, 'the divine order of male headship' (Reform About Reform, accessed 2010).

The Danvers statement, to which REFORM adheres, is a response to 'feminist egalitarianism' in evangelical churches (CBMW, n.d., accessed 2010). It rejects women's equality in no uncertain terms, stressing the importance of 'complementarianism'. Feminism, it says, has created 'widespread uncertainty and confusion in our culture regarding the complementary differences between masculinity and femininity' and the patriarchs of the CBMW are dedicated to sorting out this misunderstanding, which 'unravels' the 'fabric of marriage'. The statement promotes 'the loving, humble leadership of redeemed husbands and the intelligent, willing support of that leadership by redeemed wives'. Women writers on the website expound copiously on how exactly women's submission to their husbands should manifest itself, how hard it is to do, and how many benefits result from it. Barbara Hughes, for instance, explains:

> We know from the very first book of the Bible that "intimacy through subordination" is not only possible, but it is God's plan for us – modeled after the intimacy that exists in the Godhead. So for me, as a Christian woman, submitting to my husband is not an option; it is obediently following God's plan.
>
> (Hughes, 2008, p.122)

Wives have the role of 'helping' their husbands, who have headship in the home. Hughes helpfully reminds doubters that, 'Christian wives must never resent or despise the term "helper" or consider it demeaning. To help is divine! There is no better word to describe the role of a wife than "helper"' (Hughes, 2008, p. 126).

Within the Catholic Church there can be difficulties in making the distinction between moderation and fundamentalism too. The views on correct womanhood that issue from the Vatican are practically identical to those of the CPM, though the Vatican is not so transparent as to name itself Christian Patriarchy Central. Some feminist scholars and activists, particularly those who are Catholics, argue that the ideas and practices of the Vatican should be understood as fundamentalist (Kissling, 1999). Ophelia Benson and Jeremy Stangroom, in their very useful and straightforward dissection of the misogyny of religion, *Does God Hate Women?* (2009), provide a breakdown of late twentieth-century broadsides against feminism from the Vatican. In 1988 Pope John Paul II wrote in the encyclical Mulieris Dignitatem:

> In the name of liberation from male 'domination', women must not appropriate to themselves male characteristics contrary to their own feminine 'originality'. There is a well-founded fear that if they take this path, women will not 'reach fulfilment', but instead will *deform and lose what constitutes their essential richness*
>
> (Benson and Stangroom, 2009, p. 61)

This was clearly in response, as the founding of the Christian Patriarchy movement was, to the encroachment of feminism on the Church's ideological control of women. This encyclical was followed in 1995 by a *Letter to Women* from the Vatican that stated particularly clearly the principle of complementarity, also dear to the CPM. It stated:

The creation of woman is thus marked from the outset by *the principle of help:* a help which is not one-sided but *mutual.* Woman complements man, just as man complements woman: men and women are *complementary* . . . It is only through the duality of the 'masculine' and the 'feminine' that the 'human' finds full realization.

(Benson and Stangroom, 2009, p. 61)

In 2004 the current Pope, when he was Cardinal Ratzinger and had not yet ascended to his popehood, put forth a Letter to the Bishops of the Catholic Church on the Collaboration of Men and Women in the Church and the World, signed by John Paul II. This stated that, 'The ancient Genesis narrative allows us to understand how woman, in her deepest and original being, exists "for the other"' (Benson and Stangroom, 2009, p. 63). The ideas of the CPM, the Vatican and REFORM are strikingly similar, though not all these religious forms may be widely understood as 'fundamentalist'.

Fundamentalist Judaism

Fiefdoms that demonstrate extremely similar forms of subordination and humiliation for women have also been set up by Jewish patriarchs through the creation of ultra-orthodox communities in countries around the world. The Bobover community in Brooklyn, New York, provides another useful example of the way such fiefdoms subordinate women. In Brooklyn, Jewish law for women does not have the imprimatur of the state in the way that it does in Israel. Fundamentalist anti-woman values are imposed within the community. In Boro Park, Brooklyn, 82,000 out of a population of 160,000 are Jewish and three-quarters of those are Orthodox, according to the 2000 Census; these figures are questioned by community leaders who consider that the numbers of Orthodox are very much higher (Fader, 2009). Ayala Fader studied one of the groupings within this Orthodox community, the Bobovers. She explains that ultra-orthodox Jews, the *haredim*, became more fundamentalist in the late twentieth century. She describes how this process took place among Hasidic communities in New York in her fascinating ethnography of the Bobover community of Brooklyn in *Mitzvah Girls* (2009). She explains that they engaged in the inventing of traditions. One example is that where a wig was considered sufficient to cover a woman's hair, she was now to wear a hat as well. The Bobovers, as Fader explains it, engaged in the 'hyperbolization' of gender and Jewish difference. Various methods are employed by Hasidic cults in this 'hyperbolization'. There is gender segregation in the synagogue, and men and women speak different languages. There are Hasidic schools for the boys where they communicate in Yiddish, whereas the girls go to private Hebrew schools. In some Hasidic cults such as the Satmar, girls do not read the bible. Girls are rigorously, and over many years, schooled in 'modesty' so as not to tempt men.

The requirement of Jewish women's modesty lies in the Code of Jewish Law, which notes that married women's hair must be covered, and that a woman must cover 'most of her body that is usually covered' (Fader, 2009, p. 150). For orthodox Jews it is understood that the 'erotic' parts of the body include hair for married women, collarbones, elbows, shoulders, thighs and knees. The pronouncements on the requirements of modesty are made by the rabbi who 'makes decrees regarding communal standards of female modesty and posts them on the streets of Brooklyn, to little girls who remind one another to sit modestly even at home on the sofa' (Fader, 2009, p. 150). Thus the Bobover community commandeers public space to consolidate the patriarchal fiefdom. The role of men in Hasidic communities is to study Torah full time, while women keep house. In the community Fader studied, women were 'obliged to protect men from the potential for arousal so that men can study Torah with pure hearts' (Fader, 2009, p. 150). One of the women in Fader's study told her that she had the responsibility to cross the street or wait if she saw a young Torah scholar approaching, because, as she put it, the streets 'belong to the men', and the sound of women's heels on the pavement could, apparently, be distracting to a Torah scholar. There are strict rules about girls fraternising with boys in the cult, marriages are arranged, and there is no dating (Fader, 2009, p. 179). These rules of separation can be quite extreme. Fader says that for some Hasidim, 'it is the custom to avoid eye contact with the opposite sex' (Fader, 2009, p. 199). Thus at the first meeting of youths intended for an arranged marriage they may have to look at each other in mirrors. Sometimes there is no meeting before marriage.

There are purity classes before marriage for the girls so that they can 'learn how to monitor their bodies during their monthly periods'

(Fader, 2009, p. 200). The prospective wives are taught that they should monitor their bleeding until there is no sign of blood for several days. They must wipe themselves inside and out with a special cloth and inspect it. If the colour on the cloth is ambiguous they must show the cloth to the husband's rabbi so that he can decide if the wife is ready to go to the Mikveh or ritual bath, to prepare herself for penetration by her husband. This is necessary, apparently, because if it were left to women's judgement they might control their husband's access to them by saying that they were still unclean (Fader, 2009, p. 208). Fader is determinedly non-judgmental in her anthropological description of these practices, but I suggest that the term 'ritual humiliation' is the most appropriate to describe them. The Bobover community provides a good example of how girls and women are trained to accept their subordination and the headship of their husbands and fathers. The state plays no direct role in these violations of women's human rights, which take place in the 'private sphere', but can be seen as complicit in its failure to act.

Conclusion

I have sought to show that making distinctions between 'moderate' and 'fundamentalist' versions of religion is fraught with difficulty. The most extreme forms, however, of the monotheistic religions, share the characteristic of offering compensation to men for the privileges they have lost through the 'genderquake' by empowering patriarchs to oppress women and girls in the home and community. As these forms have grown in recent decades in Western democracies, they have benefited from government largesse in the form of funding, and have gained authority, through governments consulting with them on policy. In the case of fundamentalist Islam, the agenda for women's subordination has been aided by the incorporation of elements of sharia law in the legal system in the UK, a move that has aided the respectability of this mechanism for controlling women. Religious fundamentalists of all varieties have benefited from state policies of respecting the private sphere and engaging in studious non-intervention. This has supported the development of closed communities in which thousands of girls and women are separated from the exercise of human rights that other citizens take for granted, such as freedom of movement, the right to choose their marriage partner, or the right to education. As feminist human rights theorists argue, if women and girls are to have human rights then states may have to intervene in these fiefdoms, so that there is not just formal equality for women but substantive equality. These private denials of rights now have an analogue at the international level. Patriarchs of all three monotheistic persuasions began to organise in the 1990s against the progress of the movement for women's human rights through the United Nations. I shall examine international religious organising to maintain the subordination of women in the next chapter.

3

THE RIGHT TO RELIGION TRUMPS WOMEN'S HUMAN RIGHTS

The rise of religion that undermines women's human rights comprises not just a variety of forms within nation states, but also an international campaign to defeat women's rights through the United Nations. The movement for recognition of women's rights as human rights had achieved considerable success. The Convention on the Elimination of All Forms of Discrimination Against Women (United Nations, 1979) was followed by vigorous feminist activism leading up to the 1995 third United Nations (UN) World Conference on Women in Beijing. The Beijing declaration, which was created at this conference, added usefully to the rights outlined in CEDAW (Beijing Declaration, 1995). The years since this advance, however, have been marked by a steady increase in the power of organised international religious networks determined to stymie this progress and turn it back. These religious networks can be seen as constituting a countermovement spurred into development by the success of the transnational movement for women's human rights (Friedman, 2003). The attack on women's rights is orchestrated under the banner of the 'right to religion', and adapts language from fundamental human rights documents such as the 'natural family' to attack homosexuality and support heterosexual marriage. This chapter will examine this backlash, which involves efforts by the US religious right, the Holy See – which is represented as if it were a state at the UN – and the Organisation of the Islamic Conference and its allies, to block women's rights in the area of sexuality and reproduction in particular.

Religion and women's human rights

CEDAW was created as a result of thirty years of work by the United Nations Commission on the Status of Women, which was set up in 1946 to promote women's rights. The Convention was a recognition that women's human rights needed special attention, and that women could not be subsumed into the rights of 'man'. Women are for the most part glaringly absent in the human rights instruments drawn up by the United Nations in the decades before the adoption of CEDAW. In a wave of feminist activism on women's rights as human rights in the 1990s, feminist legal scholars examined both the standard human rights documents, and even CEDAW itself, and found them severely wanting (Cook, 1994; Peters and Wolper, 1995; Askin and Koenig, 2001). These theorists pointed out that the 'first generation' human rights documents used masculine language and only covered issues important to the relationship of bourgeois men with the state, thus they concentrated on matters such as the right not be imprisoned without trial, the right to exercise political rights such as the right to vote, the right to life and the right to privacy (Charlesworth, 1995). Women are included in the rights covered by the Universal Declaration of Human Rights (UDHR) in 1948, and the Convention on Civil and Political Rights (ICCPR) in 1966, to the extent that women's rights in the public sphere are similar to those of men and so need protection in similar ways. However, these rights instantiate the public/private split in legal theory and practice. Women's ability to exercise these political rights is likely to be challenged by what is done to them in the supposedly 'private' world of the home and family. Women who are prevented from leaving the home cannot vote, for instance (Howland, 1999). First generation rights also included the right to religion, but this right has only recently been employed as a weapon against women's human rights.

Feminist legal theorist, Courtney Howland, argues persuasively that acceptance of the right to religion chills women's political rights under the first and fundamental UN Convention, the ICCPR. She explains the importance of this chilling of women's rights by pointing out that civil and political freedoms have 'long been regarded as at the core of democracy and forming the foundation for an individual's liberty within a democracy' (Howland, 1999, p. 93). Thus to the extent that these rights are limited for women by the right to religion, the democratic project is fundamentally undermined for all. She explains that in the 1980s and 1990s the notion of the right to religious freedom, enshrined in the ICCPR, has been taken up by religious groupings and transformed from its original purpose, of protecting the rights of individuals. The right to religion was created to protect individuals in their religious practice in the wake of the holocaust and out of mindfulness of the extent of the harms involved in state persecution of religious minorities. But in recent decades religious communities, organisations and states have touted the 'right to religion' to justify persecution of women. Broad and vague notions of religious freedom are used by theocratic states 'as the justification for the state controlling an ever-enlarging public sphere that may well encompass every aspect of public and private life' (Howland, 1999, p. 95). In states in which an authoritarian theocracy is not in place, there is an increasing sympathy to 'broadening claims of religious freedom' by religious groups, with the result that such groups gain 'large autonomous zones of so-called privacy within which women's rights may be severely limited' (Howland, 1999, p. 95). Howland argues that these 'broadening claims' are 'in effect trumping women's rights by allowing claims of religious freedom to transform parts of the public world into the "private"' (Howland, 1999, p. 95). Howland says that the ICCPR is able to be turned into a weapon against women's equality because the right to religion is a core political right within the document.

She points out that women's ability to participate in democratic politics depends upon the degree of inequality in the home (Howland, 1999, p. 97). If a woman's husband demands obedience she will not have an equal right to participation. Democracy starts in the home and for women it can simply never begin, not just in theocracies, but in multicultural states where the government considers that it should not intrude into the privacy of a man's home. Howland identifies two rules of what she calls fundamentalist religions that reduce or exterminate women's political rights: the obedience rule and the modesty rule. She considers that these rules subsist in Buddhism, Christianity, Hinduism, Islam and Judaism. The obedience rule requires a wife to submit to the authority of her husband and gives him the right to discipline her, 'in other words to batter her' (Howland, 1999, p. 97). The modesty rule requires a woman to be 'modest in matters of behavior and dress' and often, 'segregation of the sexes in education, health, and employment' (Howland, 1999, p. 97). Some states have laws that prescribe women's obedience and modesty, she explains, but these are rarely recognised as affecting not just the 'private' realm but the traditionally 'public' and political realm too. They impinge upon women's rights to 'freedom of belief without coercion . . . the right to hold opinions without interference, and the right to freedom of expression . . . since a woman may not seek, receive, or impart information without her husband's permission' (Howland, 1999, p. 98). Modesty requirements threaten women's rights to 'freedom of peaceful assembly . . . and association' (United Nations, 1966, Article 21), because women may not be allowed by their husbands to take part in meetings. A woman's freedom of expression is inhibited also by the fact that she may not be allowed to associate with others, particularly men, and 'covering' may prevent her ability to 'communicate through facial expression' (Howland, 1999, p. 98). Obedience rules can require a wife 'to vote a certain way, forbid her to run for election, and even to obtain information about political parties'. Even if a wife obtains her husband's permission to run for election, 'the modesty code . . . may make this impossible in practice' (Howland, 1999, p. 98). States that have laws instantiating modesty rules upon women, such as the Sudan or Iran, should be seen to be contravening the political articles of the ICCPR.

Women's political rights in the ICCPR are abrogated particularly clearly by the violence they experience in the 'private' realm of the home. The right to life in particular, as well as political rights of participation in the public realm, are chilled by explicit violence and bullying that underlie the requirements for obedience that are exercised against women by the men they live with, their families and communities. Violence against women is a practice that does not have a counterpart in men's experience; they are not hit and raped in their homes by women, for example. For this reason, feminist legal theorists and activists have had a hard struggle to get men's violence against women understood as a human rights violation. The struggle is hard, also, because traditional understandings of human rights allowed only violations by the state and its agents to be recognised, not those by individual men such as husbands. Violence is not mentioned in CEDAW. Feminist theorists and activists have gradually created the understanding that, though in many cases the state is not directly implicated in violence against women, it is responsible for setting in place laws, policy, policing and effective treatment in the judicial system to allow these abuses to be combatted (Jeffreys, 1997). The result of feminist work to incorporate violence into human rights practice was the 1993 Declaration on the Elimination of Violence Against Women. This Declaration has no legal force, however, and the issue of violence against women still does not appear in a convention.

A good example of the way in which violence against women, as well as other significant rights violations, can be incorporated into state law through religion, exists in the marriage laws in many countries. The marriage law for both Muslims and Christians in Lebanon demonstrates this (KAFA n.d.). The Lebanese human rights organisation, KAFA, provides sample questions and answers for women about their rights in marriage. The Shiite Muslim marriage law permits the husband to imprison his wife in the home. The answer to the question 'Do I have the right to leave the marital home?' is 'The wife cannot leave the marital home without her husband's consent and approval. She will be considered disobedient, and she will be deprived of some of her rights'. Another question asks whether the husband has the right to chase down a wife who has exited the family home and drag her back, the right to 'file for cohabitation'. The answer is, 'Yes, the husband has the right to file for cohabitation'. The wife has no similar right against her husband. A woman who does not return is again to be considered 'disobedient', which covers 'failing to fulfil her sexual obligations, committing repulsive things (unspecified) and leaving the house without his prior permission'. The document comments that use of the police to retrieve the woman is rare. The Christian marriage laws in Lebanon violate women's human rights in similar ways. The wife still has no right to leave the marital home, unless, 'marital life between the spouses becomes intolerable or in case the husband jeopardizes his wife's life or threatens to kill or harm her and his threats were serious'. Otherwise, no, she cannot leave. Imprisonment may not usually be understood as violence against the person, though it may constitute emotional violence, but physical violence is likely to be encountered as men put into action their rights to prevent egress or drag the woman back. Imprisonment is against first generation human rights in the ICCPR, of which Article 9(1) states, 'Everyone has the right to liberty and security of person . . . No one shall be deprived of his liberty except on such grounds and in accordance with such procedures as are established by law' (United Nations, 1966). Such private slavery gives the lie to any of the political rights covered by the ICCPR but, unfortunately, the right to liberty enshrined in the Convention is generally understood to relate to imprisonment by the state rather than by husbands.

Reservations to CEDAW

States have used religious arguments to justify placing reservations to particular articles of the Women's Convention when they sign on to it. The Women's Convention is distinguished by having a much higher rate of reservations than other Conventions, which indicates the level of importance many states place on being able to continue treating women unequally (United Nations, 1979). The commonest form of reservation is that made by Islamic states that they do not consider themselves bound by a particular article in the Convention unless it conforms to the requirements of Islamic law. Some Islamic states have entered reservations against Article 2 of the Convention, which is its most important and substantial clause, dealing with recognition of the equality of men and women and the outlawing of discrimination against women, including the taking of measures to 'modify or abolish' customs and practices that discriminate against women. These states include Algeria, Iraq, Libya, Morocco, Singapore and Syria. The substance of their reservations is that they will only agree with this Article to the extent that it conforms to their national laws, which incorporate sharia, or to Islamic law in general. Islamic states have also entered reservations to Article 16, which deals with equality in marriage, on the grounds that this is not in conformity with Islamic law. States may withdraw their reservations and some have chosen to do so, but there are still reservations to Article 16 from Algeria, Bahrain, Egypt, Iraq, Israel, Maldives, Micronesia, Morocco, Singapore, Thailand and United Arab Emirates. In theory, reservations to Conventions should not be in opposition to their substantial purposes, and many states have objected to the reservations placed by Islamic states on the grounds that these fall into that category. The placing of reservations was for some time the main way in which hostility to the principle of women's rights as human rights was demonstrated by states that used religious arguments. In the 1990s this hostility became much more organised.

The religious backlash against women's human rights

In the 1990s a new development took place in UN fora. Fundamentalist religious organisations representing Protestant and Catholic Christians, Mormons and Muslims, joined together across their differences to create an international 'pro-family' block. This move was stimulated specifically by their recognition that a 'women's rights as human rights' agenda was gaining traction at the UN and having influence internationally. The 'women's rights as human rights' campaign was seen as endangering the confinement of women within the family and marriage, and the control of their reproductive bodies by men. The creation of this religious grouping resulted from the 1994 Cairo International Conference on Population and Development (Friedman, 2003; Steans and Ahmadi, 2005). The religious organisations were alarmed at the likelihood that the increasingly influential movement based on the uniting slogan 'women's rights are human rights' would enshrine women's rights to abortion and contraception, and the right to free expression of sexual orientation, in the conference document. For the 1994 conference, and thereafter for all conferences concerned with women's rights, they sought to gain consultative status as non-governmental organisations (NGOs) with the United Nations Economic and Social Council (ECOSOC), so that they could attend such meetings and seek to stymie or turn back women's rights. This was a quite new development. Previously NGOs affiliated with ECOSOC that attended women's conferences were organisations that supported women's rights rather than those dedicated to direct opposition. In this way, the mechanism by which women's organisations had advanced understandings of women's rights, the ten yearly UN World Conference on Women, was endangered. NGOs recognised by ECOSOC can send as many delegates as they wish to UN fora. Religious groups, replete with funds, could potentially outnumber the delegates that were sent by coalitions of women's groups from poor countries. Their strength of numbers can seriously impede or skew debate.

The conservative alliance consisted of some Catholics and some Muslim delegations led by the Vatican. It was constructed by Pope John Paul II who saw the similarities between the conservative Catholics and conservative Muslims that would serve to unite them. The Pope's concern began in response to the Clinton–Gore presidential campaign, which he saw as presaging more liberal attitudes to abortion and contraception in the US, which were promoted through US funding in poor countries. He not only organised the global Catholic Church, but also sent emissaries to Muslim countries to get support against abortion on demand being accepted as a universal human right, and against rights to freedom of sexual expression. The Pope used moral arguments to forge his alliance, but played to the gallery of Islamic fundamentalism by using arguments against imperialism and Western individualism. In 1995 a Catholic–Islamic commission was set up to foster interfaith dialogue. The main areas of consensus between the conservative Catholics and Muslims was over the 'divinely ordained and biologically determined different yet complementary masculine and feminine roles' (Bayes and Tohidi, 2001, p. 6), as well as attitudes towards the family, women's role as mothers, sexuality as appropriate only to marriage, opposition to abortion, the central role of religion in society, emphasis on religious values, opposition to pornography and degrading images of women in the media and opposition to the individualism of Western culture that would 'give women's individual rights priority over women's communal family and religious duties' (Bayes and Tohidi, 2001, p. 4). Bayes and Tohidi argue that the conservative bloc represents a 'supra-national alliance . . . an attempt to maintain and reinforce a hierarchical sex/ gender regime based on male supremacy and justified by religious beliefs' (Bayes and Tohidi, 2001, p. 6).

The new alliance was active at the 1995 third UN World Conference on Women in Beijing, which produced the Beijing Platform for Action. The conservative campaign targeted reproductive and sexual rights in particular and for this reason the Platform for Action had the terms 'sexual rights' and 'sexual orientation' removed (Steans and Ahmadi, 2005). Jill Steans and Vafa Ahmadi describe Beijing as the event that 'prevented further substantial feminist gains' and as an event where feminists had to furiously defend their language of women's rights, and many governments were unwilling to even restate what they had said five years before. They consider that the UN conference process, which had provided the structure for the transnational women's movement to organise and make advances, was lost after Beijing. The alliance was prominent, too, at the Beijing Plus Five Committee on the Status of Women conference in 2000 at the UN building in New York, when feminist activists sought to make advances on the Platform of Action that had emerged from the Beijing conference of 1995 (Bayes and Tohidi, 2001). There was a major split among delegates caused by a 'new transnational and cross-cultural conservative and religious alliance against equal rights for women' focusing on issues such as sexuality and sexual orientation, and women's control of their bodies including abortion (Bayes and Tohidi, 2001). The Beijing Plus 5 meetings at the Commission on the Status of Women in 2000 demonstrated that earlier feminist practices could not continue: 'NGOs decided not to hold the large-scale strategy session used before, which they knew would be . . . disrupted' (Steans and Ahmadi, 2005, p. 315). At least 300 delegates from the conservative coalition attended in a total attendance of 1,700 NGO representatives. The conservative delegates were largely from the

Religious Right in the US, incorporating Mormon, Conservative Catholic and Conservative Evangelical groupings.

As the coalition organised to attend the 2000 meeting, the implacability towards women's rights became clear in the strength of their rhetoric. Austin Ruse, for instance, the Director of the Catholic Family and Human Rights Institute, called for 'pro-family and pro-life advocates' to attend and fight against, 'the Beijing Platform for Action . . . one of the most radical and dangerous documents you can imagine' (Butler, Jennifer, 2000). Ruse continued, 'You will work alongside Catholics, Evangelicals, Jews, Muslims, Mormons . . . We are the children of Abraham . . . arising to fight for faith and family' (Butler, Jennifer, 2000). Some members of the coalition became a little excited in their rhetoric. Thus Daymond Duck argues rather vehemently against progressive interpretations of human rights:

> The United Nations is trying to establish a long list of universal values to guide nations and individuals. These values . . . will not be Christian values. They will be the values of the politically correct humanists, witches, mystics, goddessworshippers, peaceniks, environmentalists, and a wide assortment of other ungodly activists who deem the blood of Jesus a repulsive thought and bow down before the altars of Satan.
>
> (Buss and Herman, 2003, p. 19)

The same strength of feeling is clear in the campaigning talk of the World Congress of Families (WCF), one of the new umbrella groups established to take up the fight against the women's human rights agenda. It is the child of the Howard Center for the Family, Religion, and Society in the US, and its tactics demonstrate a canny twisting of human rights ideas to defeat feminism through support for the 'natural family'. WCF considers that feminists are the most direct threat to its conservative ideology, as a 2010 article on its website proclaims: 'Today, we focus on one of the greatest mythmakers of all time – Feminism. In the process, we will look at how the falsehoods that have been perpetuated in the name of feminism are harming women, devastating marriage, and destroying the family' (Crouse, 2010). The Congress uses the language of human rights to support its notion that the 'natural family' is the foundation of society, predates the state and should be fought for. It quotes human rights documents that talk about protecting the family and makes such protection the foundation of its contemporary campaign. The term 'natural' family, the Congress explains, 'signifies a natural order to family structures that is common across cultures, historical, and overwhelmingly self-evident' (World Congress of Families, n.d.). This 'natural' order does not include homosexuality. As an example of the hatred of homosexuals by some states at the UN, in 2010 a UN resolution against 'Extrajudicial, summary or arbitrary executions', after being in existence for ten years with lesbians and gays included as an example of the groups covered by the resolution, was changed in committee to remove this category (IGLHRC, 2010). The amendment removing the reference to sexual orientation was sponsored by Benin on behalf of the African Group in the UN General Assembly and was adopted with 79 votes in favour, 70 against, 17 abstentions and 26 absent. It clears the way for the slaying of lesbians and gay men.

The right-wing religious coalition has seized upon the infelicitous use of the word 'natural', in connection with the family in the UDHR, to lend legitimacy to its campaigns to shore up traditional male dominance (Buss and Herman, 2003). The Opening Remarks of the Congress of 1999 give a full rundown of mentions of the family, and statements that the WCF considers family-related in the UDHR, in particular Article 16: 3, which states, 'The family is the natural and fundamental group unit of society and is entitled to protection by society and the State' (Carlson, 1999). The words 'natural' and 'family' are not adjacent in the document but the Christian Right finds their closeness felicitous and joins them together in its propaganda. The WCF's campaigning ideology purports to be central to human rights concerns because it stands upon and seeks to promote the 'natural family'. It demands legal protection of the family by the state on the grounds that the 'natural' family predates the state and must not be interfered with, 'We affirm that the natural family exists prior to the state. Public policies must respect this family autonomy' (World Congress of Families, 2009). It is not clear as to the precise form of the historical family they have in mind, not polygamous certainly, but they support extended families. The Roman familia, which was extended, included slaves and the complete subordination of women and is not necessarily excluded. Indeed, if there were a 'natural' way for humans to organise their emotional, sexual and childbearing lives, then it would not need the help of state governments and religious prescriptions to flourish. The fact that the 'natural' family needs so much help indicates that it is a political construction. Some Muslim organisations are similarly hostile to the project of women's rights as human rights. A text on the Islamic website 'SoundVision.com' demonstrates considerable alarm at the Beijing Platform for Action (UN threat to Islam, n.d.). It quotes an action alert from the Islamic ezine Albalagh about the 2000 Beijing Plus Five conference, which states that 'It is the greatest challenge to the supremacy of Shariah that the Muslim world has ever faced collectively. If we fail to challenge it this time, we may have to pay the price for that lapse over the next decades or centuries' (UN threat to Islam, n.d.). The Beijing Platform for Action is described as, 'a clearly anti-religious, secularism-based vision of women's rights'.

The Holy See

The Vatican is in a position to coordinate the right-wing religious coalition and exercise particularly strong influence at the UN, because of the unique position it occupies there. It participates as a territorial state, under the title the 'Holy See'. The organisation of progressive Catholics, Catholics for Choice, which focuses on opposing the Vatican's prescriptions on contraception and abortion, set up a campaign called See Change to change the status that the Vatican holds at the UN. See Change seeks to get the Secretary-General to 'review the church's current status as a Non-member State Permanent Observer' so that it will participate in the UN in the same way as the world's other religions do, as a non-government organisation. The Holy See sought to gain full membership as a state but this was denied in 2004 in a resolution that gave it further participation rights but not statehood. The Holy See does not fulfil the internationally accepted definition of a state for the purposes of international law, which is 'a) a permanent population; b) a defined territory; c) government; and d) capacity to enter into relations with the other states' (Sippel, n.d.). As Frances Kissling, from Catholics for Choice, points out, the Vatican has '1000 male citizens and an electoral body comprised of men appointed by the Pope' (Kissling, 1999, p. 197). She argues that under the criteria used by the UN to admit the Vatican as a state, 'EuroDisney should similarly be able to seek statehood' (Kissling, 1999, p.197).

Catholics for Choice details the heinous behaviour of the Vatican in the obstruction of women's rights at the UN (Sippel, n.d.). The Holy See used its position at the UN to oppose the inclusion of 'forced pregnancy' in a proposed list of war crimes when the International Criminal Court was established. In 1999 it used its position to condemn the provision of emergency contraception to women who had been raped in the Kosovo conflict, and in 2001 to condemn the use of condoms for HIV/AIDs prevention. The Vatican's opposition to women's control over their own bodies through contraception and abortion does not represent majority catholic opinion. Catholics for Choice argues that the decision revealed in the Papal pronouncement 'Humanae Vitae' (Of Human Life) in 1968 to forbid contraception had the effect of splitting the catholic communion and forcing the majority of practising Catholics in the West into relying on their own consciences and disregarding their Church authorities (Catholics for Choice, 2008). Humanae Vitae states, 'Each and every marital act must of necessity retain its intrinsic relationship to the procreation of human life'. The pronouncement is in direct contradiction to the advice that bodies set up by the Vatican to work on this issue had given. In 1963 a papal commission was set up to work on a new statement on marriage. It overwhelmingly voted to recommend the rescinding of the church's ban on artificial contraception. The Vatican could not accept this and brought in fifteen bishops to make the final report. The bishops too voted nine to three, with three abstentions, to change the teaching on contraception. A concern that weighed on the minds of those who supported the status quo was that those who had been sent to hell for using contraception could not be recalled just because the church had changed its mind (Catholics for Choice, 2008, p. 5).

Humanae Vitae was counterproductive because of the way in which it undermined the authority of the Vatican. According to Catholics for Choice, by 1999 nearly 80 per cent of Catholics believed that a person could be a good catholic without obeying the church hierarchy's teaching on birth control (Catholics for Choice, 2008). Thus the Holy See should perhaps be seen, not only as not being a nation state, but not representing a religion either, since so many Catholics are unfaithful to the messages that it advocates. The Holy See, as Frances Kissling maintains, is fundamentalist whereas the majority of Catholics are no such thing, yet its representatives pretend to carry the mandate of a religion in promoting its opposition to human rights. In 2010 the Pope made statements in an interview that have been seen as representing a change of heart on condom use (AFP, 2010). He said that condom use was permissible by men and women in relationships if one party was

HIV positive. This change represents the end point of a considerable campaign to allow condoms to be used in Africa to reduce the ravages of the HIV epidemic.

The Cairo Declaration

Another important player in the conservative bloc is the Organisation of the Islamic Conference (OIC), which is increasingly active at the UN. The OIC is an international organisation with a permanent delegation to the UN and was founded in 1969. It is composed of fifty-seven member states, from the Middle East, Africa, Central Asia, Caucasus, Balkans, Southeast Asia and South Asia. The OIC is responsible for two initiatives that represent serious threats to women's human rights: the Cairo Declaration on Human Rights in Islam, and the various resolutions 'Combating the Defamation of Religions'. The Cairo Declaration was created in 1990. Attempts to get this accepted by the UN's Human Rights Council have failed up to now and there is increasing opposition to this possibility. The resolutions on defamation, however, have been increasingly successful and have been adopted by the Human Rights Council in succeeding years, and even at the UN General Assembly. While the Declaration is in direct contradiction to the UDHR and CEDAW, and would subject women's rights to the test of compatibility with the particular interpretation of Islamic law that patriarchal jurists favour in particular states, the resolutions would make it impossible for women to question their subordination within religions, particularly Islam.

The Declaration makes grand and universalising claims for Islam in its preamble, 'Reaffirming the civilizing and historical role of Islamic Ummah which God made the best nation that has given mankind a universal and well-balanced civilization' (Cairo Declaration, 1990, Preamble). It uses exclusively masculine language at a time when some awareness of women existed in other fora as a result of second-wave feminism. Thus the Declaration aims to, 'protect man from exploitation and persecution' (Preamble). The opening of Article 1 is starkly different from the UDHR in subjecting humans to a male god and the creation myth, 'All human beings form one family whose members are united by submission to God and descent from Adam' (Cairo Declaration, 1990, Article 1a). The Declaration states straightforwardly that women have a different and inferior role and rights. Women are equal to men in 'human dignity' but not in the family: 'Woman is equal to man in human dignity, and has rights to enjoy as well as duties to perform; she has her own civil entity and financial independence, and the right to retain her name and lineage' (Cairo Declaration, 1990, Article 6a), but 'The husband is responsible for the support and welfare of the family' (Cairo Declaration, 1990, Article 6b). There are separate spheres for men and women, and a woman is to be dependent on her husband. There is a warning against abortion in the Declaration and a recognition of the rights of the foetus, which is a major difference from other human rights documents, 'Both the foetus and the mother must be protected and accorded special care' (Cairo Declaration, 1990, Article 7).

The language is emphatically masculine in sections of particular importance to women's equality, the 'private' sphere of home and family in which most violence and oppression of women is carried out. Most worryingly the document states, 'Everyone shall have the right to live in security for himself, his religion, his dependents, his honour and his property' (Cairo Declaration, 1990, Article 18a). This clause shows up one of the difficulties with the ICCPR (United Nations, 1966), which uses similar language in Article 17 (1), 'No one shall be subjected to arbitrary or unlawful interference with his privacy, family, home or correspondence, nor to unlawful attacks on his honour and reputation'. Men's honour resides in the bodies of the women they control, and the 'security' of this honour is used to justify honour killings of wives, daughters and sisters (Welchman and Hossain, 2005; Wikan, 2008). The ICCPR uses the language of 'privacy' and so does the Cairo Declaration, affirming that 'everyone' shall have the 'right to privacy in the conduct of his private affairs, in his home, among his family, with regard to his property and his relationships' (Cairo Declaration, 1990, Article 18b). But the Declaration makes even more of the idea of 'privacy', stating, 'A private residence is inviolable in all cases' (Cairo Declaration, 1990, Article 18b). In fact it is precisely this inviolability of the home that must be breached if women and children are to be protected in cases of domestic violence and child sexual abuse. These rights serve men's interests in the creation of little fiefdoms in their homes over wives and children, but they do not serve the interests of women. It is ironic that it is in replicating men's rights to privacy in the family, and to their 'honour' that exist in the ICCPR, that the Declaration repeats precisely the idea in that convention, the notion of a public/private split, of which feminist human rights theorists have been most critical. This serves the Islamic fundamentalist agenda well.

The Declaration indicates a severe restriction on freedom of expression, stating, 'Everyone shall have the right to express his opinion freely in such manner as would not be contrary to the principles of the Shari'ah' (Cairo Declaration, 1990, Article 22a). The criticism of the sharia that is so vitally necessary to women seeking to survive in Islamic theocracies is likely to be outlawed by such a prescription. The Declaration ends by submitting all its 'human rights' to Islamic law, 'The Islamic Shari'ah is the only source of reference for the explanation or clarification of any of the articles of this Declaration' (Cairo Declaration, 1990, Article 25). The concerns of feminist human rights scholars as to the male bias of first generation UN instruments are mild in comparison with the problems implicit in the Cairo Declaration, but the Declaration is not garnering much support at the UN, while the Resolution on Defamation is.

Defamation of Religion

The Resolution on the Defamation of Religion, which the OIC has been promoting, states, 'defamation of religions and prophets is inconsistent with the right to freedom of expression'. This Resolution constitutes a problem for human rights in many ways. It does, as the International Humanist and Ethical Union (IHEU) points out, create considerable problems for freedom of expression and for the rights of unbelievers (Cherry and Brown, 2009). It serves also, to chill the political expression of women and feminists who might like to criticise the religious regimes under which they seek ways to survive. The draft resolution was first presented to the UN Commission on Human Rights (UNCHR) in 1999. It was adopted with amendments. In 2002 UNHCR adopted a similar Resolution from the proposal by the OIC entitled, 'Combating Defamation of Religions'. This was adopted in a variety of versions by the UNHCR in subsequent years, and similar resolutions were adopted by the UN General Assembly itself in 2005, 2007 and 2008. In 2010 there was more opposition to the Resolution in the Human Rights Council, which nonetheless passed it by twenty votes to seventeen, with eight abstentions (UN Watch, 2010). The resolution was proposed by Pakistan and based largely upon the Pakistani blasphemy law, which outlaws 'derogatory remarks' against Islam, the Qur'an and the Prophet Mohammed, and under which hundreds of

Pakistanis have been persecuted over the last two decades (Cherry and Brown, 2009, p. 11).

The Resolution is focused on Islam, and is against the creation of 'stereotypes' of Islam, though in parts it purports to be a general Resolution, and Judeophobia and Christianophobia were added in 2010 in an attempt to make it more credible. Resolutions do not have the force of law, but the OIC seeks to create an instrument that does, in order to implement its aims on defamation. However, Resolutions do create precedents that shape the creation of future laws (Cherry and Brown, 2009). The serious implications of this possibility are clear in the 2010 case of the Christian woman Asia Bibi. Bibi was sentenced to death in Pakistan for blasphemy, stemming from her rejection of a call for her to embrace Islam by fellow farm workers (WLUML, 2010b). In January 2011, the Governor of Pakistan's Punjab province, Salmaan Taseer, was assassinated by one of his bodyguards on account of his support for Bibi and calls to repeal the blasphemy law (Hanif, 2011). His death was greeted with celebration by fundamentalists and rose petals were showered upon the head of his assassin outside the courtroom.

The IHEU makes cogent arguments about the 'right to religion', which is used to justify the resolutions. It points out that the Articles as to 'freedom of religion or belief' in the UDHR and the ICCPR apply 'only to individuals' as does the concept of human rights in general, and they not give rights to 'religions or beliefs *per se*'. The right to freedom of religion does not protect the 'content of religious beliefs' from criticism nor 'protect the feelings of believers who may take offense at criticism of their beliefs' (Cherry and Brown, 2009, p. 5). Moreover, it points out, 'The right to discuss and criticize any or all religions or beliefs is a necessary component of the freedom of religion.' Defamation laws, the IHEU explains, cannot apply to religion because they exist to protect the reputations of individual persons who must 'be identified, must have suffered measurable damage, and must prove the "defamatory" statements are false' (Cherry and Brown, 2009, p. 6). Religions, opinions and ideologies do not have personal reputations that they can lose and are not protected by international human rights law.

The promotion of defamation proposals at the UN mirrors the creation of religious vilification legislation and blasphemy laws in an increasing number of states, which is one significant aspect of the rise in the influence and power of religion. In Victoria, Australia, the Racial and Religious Tolerance Act of 2001 says that 'A person must not, on the ground of the religious belief or activity of another person or class of persons, engage in conduct that incites hatred against, serious contempt for, or revulsion or severe ridicule of, that other person or class of persons' (Victoria, 2001, Article 8i). The introduction of a 'class of persons' that should be protected from vilification of their religion takes this legislation into the category of protecting religions rather than individuals. The legislation occasioned one spectacularly contentious trial and has since not been used. An attempt by the Blair government in the UK to create legislation similar to the Victorian example, on 'Racial and Religious Tolerance', failed to pass without severe amendments that omitted a clause that would enable 'exposing a religion to ridicule, insult or abuse' to constitute an offence. Evidence of the vexatious possibilities inherent in the Victorian legislation was tendered in the debate. Blasphemy legislation was passed in Ireland in 2009. In an opinion piece on blasphemy in the *Guardian* in response to the Irish legislation, Ophelia Benson points out that, 'To many people it's "blasphemy" to use the female pronoun for God' (Benson, 2010). This suggests the chilling effect that blasphemy laws are likely to have on women's right to criticise religion.

Harmful cultural practices and religion

In the last decade there has been increasing concern in the community of human rights NGOs and bodies about the harm that the new conservative religious alliance is doing to the progress of women's rights. Concerned human rights actors are seeking to expand the understanding of 'freedom of religion' to include an understanding of how women's freedom can be circumscribed by religion. One example of the organisations engaging in resistance is the European Women's Lobby (EWL), which is an umbrella group of women's organisations in the European Union and has members in all member states and in candidate countries. The EWL has expressed its concerns at the way in which 'ultra-conservative religious lobby groups' are growing in influence at the UN and in Europe and threatening women's rights, and in 2005 wrote a Position Paper in support of Council of Europe Resolution 1464, 'Women and Religion in Europe', which calls on the member states of the Council of Europe to 'fully protect all women living in their country against all violations of their rights based on or attributed to religion' (European Women's Lobby, 2005). Religious arguments are used, they say, to justify 'dress codes that render them invisible' or require shaving of the head, restriction of movement in and out of the home, exclude women from positions of authority in the churches, restrict education or access to working outside the home. Violations of women's rights in relation to choice in marriage, the right not to have children or limit childbearing, the right to divorce or not and gain equal rights on divorce, and in relation to women's freedom to express themselves sexually are all, they say, justified in religious terms. They argue that since women have little chance to influence religious doctrine, the more influence religions are allowed in public life, the more problematic this will be for women's rights.

This growing concern is particularly directed at the way in which religion is being used to justify harmful cultural practices against women and girls. Article 2(f) of CEDAW states that parties to the Convention will, 'take all appropriate measures, including legislation, to modify or abolish existing laws, regulations, customs and practices which constitute discrimination against women'. CEDAW also enjoins states parties to take measures to:

> . . . modify the social and cultural patterns of conduct of men and women, with a view to achieving the elimination of prejudices and customary and all other practices which are based on the idea of the inferiority or the superiority of either of the sexes or on stereotyped roles for men and women
>
> (United Nations, 1979, art.5(a))

Harmful cultural or traditional practices are identified in later UN documents as: being harmful to the health of women and girls; arising from the material power differences between the sexes; being for the benefit of men; creating stereotyped masculinity and femininity that damage the opportunities of women and girls; being justified by tradition (Jeffreys, 2005). The UN Rapporteur on violence against women, Radhika Coomaraswamy, produced a report in 2002 on harmful cultural practices within the family (Coomaraswamy, 2002). She included not just those that would most easily fit within definitions of violence, such as female genital mutilation and honour killings, but included practices such as early marriage, polygamy and covering. She states, as do all UN documents on this issue, that there can be no cultural relativist arguments in relation to such practices, 'Cultural relativism is therefore often an excuse to allow for inhumane and discriminatory practices against women in the community' (Coomaraswamy, 2002, p. 7). She says that states should not invoke 'any custom, tradition or religious consideration to avoid their obligation to eradicate violence against women and the girl child in the family' (Coomaraswamy, 2002, p. 3). She opines that, 'the problems caused by cultural relativism' will in the 'next century' be 'one of the most important issues in the field of international human rights' (Coomaraswamy, 2002, p. 7). In fact it is the right to religion, rather than simply the right to culture, which is being wielded with most authority and effect to justify harmful cultural practices. Religion provides a gravitas to men's demands to subordinate women that culture lacks.

Abdelfattah Amor, the UN Rapporteur on Freedom of Religion, was also concerned at the way in which religion was being used to justify harmful cultural practices. He conducted a study in 2002 specifically on the 'Freedom of Religion or Belief and the Status of Women from the Viewpoint of Religion and Traditions' (Amor, 2002). Amor starts the report with a strong statement about the ways in which women have been defined negatively by religions, and argues that religious traditions are socially constructed. He asserts that 'Cultural and religious specificities must give way if there is prejudice to women's dignity' (Amor, 2002, Article 29). He argues that though CEDAW does not refer to discrimination based on religion, it does refer to prejudices and customary practices that are commonly seen as religious or justified by religious arguments. States 'must have' he argues, 'the will to address negative practices which are based on or imputed to religion' (Amor, 2002, Article 87). He points out that a 'common denominator of all forms of religious extremism or fundamentalism is often violent rejection of gender equality' (Amor, 2002, Article 97) and that this 'institutionalises discrimination against women' (Amor, 2002, Article 98). He provides a thorough account of the harmful cultural practices that are justified by religion including polygamy and forms of prostitution. He criticises the way in which religious and priestly functions are reserved for men and may exclude women from public prayer on the grounds of menstrual 'impurity'. He concludes his report by pointing out that there is no global instrument with direct bearing on freedom of religion and the condition of women, with the implication that there should be. Though such an instrument would be extremely useful to confront the increasing power of religious extremism at the UN, that power itself is likely to make it extremely difficult to achieve.

Conclusion

Conservative religious groups and representatives, from the Pope to the OIC, have campaigned from the 1990s onwards to reverse the advances made by feminists in recognising the harms that women suffer as human rights violations. They have been successful in closing down an important avenue through which this progress has been made: UN conferences on women and on women's issues. The fightback has begun, however. Feminist activists are demanding that the Holy See should lose its status as a state at the UN. They are working through organisations in many regions and at the UN to get the understanding of the term 'freedom of religion' to be expanded to include the right to be free of religion and its restrictions, and the right of women to be free of the ways in which religion is used to contradict women's rights as human rights. In particular the feminist fightback has opposed attempts to justify harmful cultural practices, which, after having been defended as 'cultural', are now being defended by the right to religion. This struggle has its corollary within nation states as feminists seek to defend women within immigrant communities from violation of their human rights, in the name of culture and religion. At this national level in Western democracies it is the ideology of multiculturalism, based upon the idea that culture must be respected, that makes it difficult to criticise and oppose religious oppression of women. The next chapter examines the ways in which multiculturalism has trapped certain groups of women in second-class status, excluding them from access to the human rights that less 'cultural' women may expect.

4

MULTICULTURALISM AND 'RESPECT' FOR RELIGION

This chapter will argue that multicultural theory and practice has made it more difficult to criticise the religious oppression of women. Multiculturalism requires that there should be respect for cultural difference and the right of citizens to practise their 'culture' within the private sphere of marriage and the family without the interference of the state. Unfortunately, as feminist critics point out, 'cultures' are based on understandings of sexual difference that are dangerous to women's safety and equality, mainly through the subordination of women in marriage and the family. In this chapter I will explain the critique of multiculturalism that has been developed by feminist theorists. In recent decades multiculturalism has morphed into multifaithism. Culture and religion are being confused or understood as one and the same, and governments in states such as Australia and the UK are increasingly exercising 'multicultural' policies through religion or 'faiths' with particularly harmful consequences for women. Religion is more problematic than culture because it reifies 'cultural' difference in the name of something ineffable and above politics. Religion is used to justify the subordination of women that provides the foundation for culture and makes this more difficult to challenge. Multiculturalism and multifaithism are both more accurately described, from a perspective that notices the existence of women, as 'multipatriarchy'.

Feminist activists have been trenchant critics of multiculturalism since the 1980s. Women Against Fundamentalism, for instance, states categorically, 'We want to live in a country of many cultures, but reject the politics of what has come to be known as "multiculturalism"' (Katz, 1995, p. 43). Susan Moller Okin's edited collection, *Is Multiculturalism Bad For Women?* (Okin, 1999), kick-started the serious academic criticism of multiculturalism as problematic for women. Her incisive feminist approach was severely criticised by the defenders of multiculturalism as 'colonialist, ethnocentric, imperialist and Orientalist' (Macey, 2009, p. viii). Before the impact of Okin's work, masculinist theorising of multiculturalism in the academy had paid no attention to the way in which a requirement of respect for different cultures might disadvantage women. Women's interests have routinely been entirely omitted from masculinist political science as Okin has pointed out (Okin, 1989). A gender-blind multiculturalism became unquestionable in the 1980s and 1990s, as the correct approach to social disadvantage and to challenging racism. The feminist critique is central to this book because the acceptance of multiculturalism serves to make it more difficult for feminists to challenge religious oppression of women by imbuing any challenges with implications of racism.

The origins of multiculturalism

Multiculturalism developed as a theory and practice in Western societies such as the UK and Australia in response to an intake of immigrants in the post World War II period. Before this time the arrival of groups of immigrants, such as Italians into the UK and Australia, had not been met with a specially developed policy. Such issues as how they might learn English, integrate and preserve their 'culture' or not, were not considered matters of state. The arrival of new and large numbers of immigrants from British colonial territories into the UK, however, created a new situation (Macey, 2009). Multiculturalism was conceived as an advance on 'assimilation' in which immigrants were expected not to stand out, and to integrate seamlessly into British society. Multiculturalism came from the understanding that 'culture' was necessary to self-esteem and happiness and therefore to whether immigrants would make a successful transition to living in their new countries. Marie Macey defines multiculturalism as being 'characterised by the accommodation, rather than assimilation, of minority cultures and religions into liberal democratic societies' (Macey, 2009, p. 28). The language and policy of multiculturalism have taken over from the idea of combating racism. In the 1980s some communities in the UK, including Mirpuri Muslims, took to the promotion of cultural and religious difference rather than joining in with demonstrations and campaigns against racism. 'Culture', became a euphemism for 'race'. Anne Phillips expresses it thus:

> Culture is now widely employed in North America and Europe as the acceptable way of referring to race, such that people describe a society as multicultural when previously they would have said multiracial or talk about there being many cultural minorities when really they mean many people who are black.
>
> (Phillips, 2007, p. 53)

Anti-racist critics and activists argue that multiculturalism can, by occluding racism, make their struggle more difficult (Pitcher, 2009).

Multiculturalism is generally based upon the unproblematic understanding of culture as a good thing, and this understanding of culture has now been extended to religion. The idea of cultural relativism, expressed through the politics of difference and multiculturalism, gives a good deal of authority and *dignitas* to culture, and, increasingly, to religion. Cultural relativism was developed within anthropology as part of a critique of the way in which 19th-century explorers and anthropologists attributed negative valences to cultures which were not their own, seeing them as primitive and morally retrograde. It requires the treatment of cultures as equally worthy of respect, simply different from, rather than inferior to, the culture of the social scientists who examine them (Benedict, 1934). Cultural relativism was not a product of feminist thought, but was adopted by some feminist theorists in the 1980s and 1990s as a politically correct approach to what were called 'differences' between women (Mohanty, 1991).

Criticism of multiculturalism

Multiculturalism has attracted increasing criticism from political theorists in the last decade on grounds quite distinct from feminist concerns. In particular the development of terrorist threats and serious riots in the UK, all involving members of the UK's Muslim community, have raised questions about the ways in which multiculturalism may polarise people around, and essentialise, religious differences. Theorists have criticised multiculturalism for creating limited identities based around culture and religion that can foster the growth of isolated hostile communities, which deliberately hold themselves aloof from the wider societies in which they exist. Multicultural policies that privilege religion, for instance, may encourage citizens to identify as Muslims before all else. They may also be apostates, women, lesbians or gays, intellectuals, musicians, but the state identifies them as Muslims and directs funding towards them on that basis. Indeed, the more exaggerated and fundamentalist their religiosity, the more likely it may be that the state will recognise them as authentic targets of government policy. Thus the state may be seen to be offering prizes for religious extremism. Amartya Sen writes incisively about the dangers of privileging just one aspect of identity, the religious, in India, where this has sparked violent communalism between Hindus and Muslims (Sen, 2006). This has had murderous results in events such as the 2002 Gujarat massacre and mass rape in which up to two thousand died (Nussbaum, 2007). In the UK, the creation of separatist enclaves through multicultural policy has been indicted, among other factors, for fostering the violence of Muslim male youths in northern England who rioted in 2001 (Cantle *et al.*, 2006; Macey, 2009). The status that had been accorded to multicultural ideas was tarnished further by the actions of young Muslim men who created mass murder on underground trains and buses in London in 2005. Respect for culture and religion became less self-evidently a good idea.

Feminist theorists have offered rather different criticisms of multicultural ideas. Susan Moller Okin argues that the cultures that multiculturalism respects, have serious inequalities within them relating to the subordination of women (Okin, 1999). She examines the harmful cultural practices of female genital mutilation and polygamy to challenge the notion that culture is a positive for women, and asks, 'What should be done when the claims of minority cultures or religions clash with the norm of gender equality' (Okin, 1999, p. 9). Seyla Benhabib criticises the acceptance of 'cultural defence' by 'elite' men in criminal trials in which men from cultural minorities murder their wives (Benhabib, 2002). She characterises this as a form of what I call the 'gentlemen's agreement', likening it to 'that "traffic in women" through which the males of the dominant and minority cultures signal to each other their recognition and respect for the customs of the other?' (Benhabib, 2002, p. 89). Other feminist theorists have concentrated on arguing that multiculturalism essentialises culture, and thus protects harmful cultural practices that subordinate women. Nira Yuval Davis has argued that migrant communities seek to preserve their cultures of origin 'in aspic', so that they are unchanging though the culture in the home country changes, as all cultures do, in response to social and economic forces (Yuval Davis, 1997). Young women in southern Italy may be wearing mini skirts while parents in Australia inflict upon their daughters clothing rules of a bygone age, for instance. Uma Narayan, too, has made a swingeing critique of the essentialism of culture (Narayan, 1997). Respect for cultures under multicultural policies prevents the ordinary and inevitable transformation that cultures undergo. When an important part of those cultures involves the subordination of women, respect prevents advances towards more egalitarian values from developing, and the privileges of men in those cultures to exploit and suppress women are protected.

An important question to ask in relation to the importance of respecting culture is: whose culture is at issue, men's or women's. Men and women may attach quite different understandings to their notions of what culture represents. Research among Muslims in Kyrgyzstan on how people understood ethnicity provided results that could equally have come from a question about culture (Handrahan, 2001). Women associated ethnicity with food, clothing and cultural artefacts, while men associated ethnicity with actions, violence and activities of female subjugation such as bride kidnapping (Handrahan, 2001, p. 74). When there are calls to respect culture it is necessary to work out whether it is men's culture or women's culture that is meant.

The development of the idea of 'difference' within some branches of feminist theory in the 1980s became an obstacle to the critical theorising of multiculturalism in the feminist academy (Moghissi, 1999). Difference came to stand in for subordination and oppression of women, economic class, race and sexuality. Difference is a neutral and potentially positive term that precludes serious analysis of the structural nature of these forms of oppression and the differences between them. Indeed, 'difference', if it is constructed in contradiction to a stigmatised other can be very dangerous and not at all worthy of respect. It is quite surprising, therefore, that in the 1980s a 'politics of difference' came to predominate in certain areas of feminist discussion, over the concept of women's oppression. The 'politics of difference' were a good fit with multiculturalism and made it more difficult for feminists to criticise these ideas.

Feminism and the politics of difference

'Difference' theory is based in cultural relativism. The feminist theorists who took up this approach set out to emphasise the importance of 'differences' between women, and the fact that there were not necessarily any universal characteristics of oppression that women had in common that were greater than their differences from one another, by virtue of race, culture or class. Such theorists are generally those who started out as socialist feminists and later adopted post-modern, or post-colonial feminist ideas. While socialist and postmodern feminists emphasised the differences between women (Young, 1990; Mohanty, 1991), radical feminists, who took as their standpoint the fact that women share a common oppression, emphasised the similarities (Bell and Klein, 1996). This divergent understanding of what constitutes feminism led to bitter disagreements between these feminist thinkers of different persuasions in the 1990s. The 'difference' approach led to a much greater respect for multiculturalism, and its foundation in cultural relativism, than radical feminists were able to adopt.

The feminist theorist Iris Marion Young is particularly associated with the 'difference' approach. In her 1990 book entitled *Justice and the Politics of Difference* she was writing about women's rights in the workplace, the language rights of non-English speakers and American Indian rights, not multiculturalism as such, but the concept that she developed of the importance of creating 'difference' represents a central idea of multi-cultural theory. She states that groups that are socially excluded or stigmatised are aided by the creation of difference, 'The assertion of a positive sense of group difference by these groups is emancipatory because it reclaims the definition of the group by the group, as a creation and construction, rather than a given essence' (Young, 1990, p. 172). Though Young's intention was that 'difference' should be used in an 'emancipatory' way, the idea of difference, once combined with cultural relativist understandings, came to be used to challenge the feminist understanding that women experience a universal oppression. This latter usage is clear in the work of the post-structuralist theorist Judith Butler, who clearly adopted a cultural relativist approach in a book subtitled 'contemporary dialogues on the left' (Butler *et al.*, 2000). She is against the idea that women share a universal oppression: 'A recent resurgence of Anglo-feminism in the academy has sought to restate the importance of making universal claims about the conditions and rights of women (Okin, Nussbaum) without regard to the prevailing norms in local cultures, and without taking up the task of cultural translation' (Butler, Judith, 2000, p. 35). She accuses universalists of being not just culturally insensitive, but allied directly with US colonialism, 'feminism works in full complicity with US colonial aims in imposing its norms of civility through an effacement and a decimation of local Second and

Third world cultures' (Butler, Judith, 2000, p. 35). This is the sort of silencing accusation that makes it very hard for any serious feminist criticism of culture to take place.

Critics of 'difference' feminism have pointed out that questioning what women have in common stems from a determination to downgrade the importance of women's oppression (Bell and Klein, 1996). There is, after all, little serious work directed at showing that the racially oppressed or the poor, have very little in common. The idea that differences between women should be taken more seriously than that which they have in common, means that race and class take precedence over 'sexism'. The term 'sexism' in common usage does not have the weightiness that is attached to the term 'racism'. Radical feminist theorists have explained this disparity in seriousness as the result of the fact that the oppression of women concerns a socially unimportant category: women. Women, as Catharine MacKinnon expresses so clearly, lack full human status (MacKinnon, 2006). Denise Thompson expresses a similar insight, explaining that, 'The categories of "race" and "class" also contain men, and any category which includes men tends to be dominated by the interests of men' (Thompson, 2001, p. 92). As a result, racism and class exploitation, 'are more readily perceivable than the oppression of women, because they involve the dehumanization of men' (Thompson, 2001, p. 92). Women's oppression cannot be seen to be as important as race, class and religion because all these latter categories include men, and men are important.

The US historian Joan Hoff is incisive in her criticism of the 'difference' approach. She sees it as aiming to make feminism unthreatening and creating conflict between groups, 'By replacing historical reality (meaning socially constructed gender, race, and class differences) with a thousand points of power, difference, and identities, post-structural historians of gender do not threaten mainstream society as some of them claim' (Hoff, 1996, p. 404). Rather, she says 'established power in the US' welcomes 'diversity arguments', because these can serve as a form of social control and keep individuals and groups 'at odds with one another' (Hoff, 1996, p. 404). The radical feminist theorist Catharine MacKinnon sums up the problem with the difference approach with her usual acerbic brevity, 'Nice neutral word, difference, and it has all that French credibility . . . It doesn't improve one's ability to analyze hierarchy' (MacKinnon, 2006, p. 52). MacKinnon puts the feminist critique of difference theory and multiculturalism in blunt terms,

'Multiculturalism is a politically normative version of the anthropological notion of cultural relativism premised on the view "that all cultures are equally valid" . . . Defenses of local differences, as they are called, are often simply a defense of male power in its local guise' (MacKinnon, 2006, p. 52). The 'local differences' that multicultural theory defends are most 'local' when they exist in the private sphere.

Multicultural politics tend to exempt the so-called private sphere from scrutiny and shore up the public/private split in which only the public sphere is seen as political. Feminist political and legal theorists have pointed out that there is nothing private about the home and family for women. These are the areas in which women's subordinate status is particularly clear and in which women experience most risk to their lives and well-being, and they are very political (MacKinnon, 1989). Okin points out that 'advocates of group rights pay no or little attention to the private sphere', which is the 'context in which persons' senses of themselves and their capacities are first formed and in which culture is first transmitted – the realm of domestic or family life' (Okin, 1999, p. 9). The work of the theorist of multiculturalism, John Rex, shows this problem in multicultural theory with particular clarity (Rex, 1997). He explains that in the 'ideal' form of multiculturalism 'One might envisage a society which is unitary in the public domain but which encourages diversity in what are thought of as private or communal matters' (Rex, 1997, p. 208). Multiculturalism, he says, 'involves on the one hand the acceptance of a single culture and a single set of individual rights governing the public domain and a variety of folk cultures in the private domestic and communal domains' (Rex, 1997, p. 210). The term 'folk cultures' here may, perhaps, be understood as a euphemism for the subordination of women. He goes on to say that 'matters relating to the family, to morality and religion belong in the private sphere' (Rex, 1997, p. 212). This approach is gender blind in the extreme, failing to recognise the extremely severe forms of oppression of women that occur specifically within this private sphere, such as unpaid labour, domestic violence and marital rape, unwanted childbearing and forms of marriage that might be better described as servitude (Jeffreys, 2009).

The 'difference' approach is unsuited to the internal power dynamics of the private sphere, which is the area to which many women are exclusively confined: the home and family. When attention is paid to the issue of domestic violence, for instance, the differences between women who are in some kind of relationship to men can seem considerably less significant than the similarities. Women are systematic-ally assaulted physically and sexually by the men they live with (Romito, 2008). Women's ability to escape the violence and the justifications with which it is defended, such as being identified as a response to an offence against 'honour', do depend upon the women's cultural and religious context, and the extent to which states support the particular patriarchal value systems, but the violence is ubiquitous. Men are not victims at the hands of women, because the power dynamics of households do not favour women. Domestic violence is suffered by women at the hands of male partners in all parts of the world, including the white middle classes of the rich world. This demonstrates that women are united in a status category that is subordinate to that of men, whatever the other 'differences' between them. Moreover the fact that women's lives are threatened, and oftentimes ended, by this violence makes this factor that unites women a very significant one.

In the 1990s the 'difference' approach was challenged by feminist human rights theorists who pointed out the harm to the concept of universal women's rights that was wrought by the idea that cultural difference should be respected, through respect for customary law in countries such as India, for instance (Hossain, 1994). The powerful body of feminist human rights theory that emerged in the 1990s was founded upon countering cultural relativism and establishing the necessity to universalise women's rights as human rights (Cook, 1994; Peters and Wolper, 1995; Nussbaum, 2000). The developing concept of 'harmful cultural practices' by the UN Rapporteur on violence against women (Winter *et al.*, 2002), undermined respect for cultural difference by demonstrating how arguments as to culture were used to defend harmful practices such as female genital mutilation, violence against women, son preference and child marriage (Jeffreys, 2005). Susan Moller Okin (1999) and other influential feminist theorists pointed out that while feminists in Western universities dithered and became radically uncertain as to whether it was reasonable to question culture and harmful cultural practices through fears of being colonialist, a strong feminist movement on the ground in Asia and Africa was developing, which had no such qualms (Jaggar, 1998). Western academic feminism, though it had roots in a feminist movement, was fast becoming something impotent and irrelevant.

The difference approach laid the groundwork for the difficulty that the majority of academic feminists had in the 1990s in criticising culture and the oppression of women that is carried out in its name. Nonetheless, as the 1990s progressed and the problem of the cultural oppression of women became clearer, particularly in feminist human rights work, and the feminist opposition to religious extremism developed, the dominance of the difference approach was undermined. Significant theorists of difference published new works showing some anxiety about the way in which the difference approach was proving unsuitable for the analysis of the new problems facing women. Iris Young published *Inclusion and Democracy* in 1999, which is less positive about the difference approach featured in *Justice and the Politics of Difference* (1990). Chandra Mohanty wrote Under 'Western Eyes Revisited' (2003), which took a step back, because of the 'shift to the right', including the rise of fundamentalisms, from her opposition to the idea that women from different cultures have a shared oppression (1991). 'Western' and 'Third World' feminists, she said, now needed to work together. But the damage was already done. The difference approach had made it very difficult for feminist theorists to question culture or religion without implications of racism being directed at them. Anne Phillips introduces her important book *Multiculturalism without Culture* (2007), as being inspired by her misgivings about the extent to which feminist thought had been paralysed by cultural relativism. Feminism was, she said, 'becoming prone to paralysis by cultural difference, with anxieties about cultural imperialism engendering a kind of relativism that made it difficult to represent *any* belief or practice as oppressive to women or at odds with gender equality' (Phillips, 2007, p. 1).

Culture is founded in sex difference

Susan Moller Okin has been criticised for failing to respect culture and suggesting that cultures might need to be discontinued in the interests of women's equality (Okin, 1999). This idea was highly controversial because of a failure on the part of theorists to accept her argument that 'cultures' are not neutral, but are founded at their root in the subordination of women. Women reproduce cultures physically by producing the humans who practise the culture, and practically through education and ritual and the training of children, but the cultures they transmit are controlled and regulated by patriarchs. The control and exchange of women between men to create the alliances and kin structures of male-dominated societies, for instance, is not an optional extra of a culture equally created by men and women, but a practice constructed by men to maintain their dominance and enable the creation of cultures constructed in their own image and out of their interests (Rubin, 1975). Women have not been sufficiently powerful members of cultures to create their foundational ideas and practices, and the same is true of religions. The cultures and religions deemed worthy of respect in multicultural theory originate in periods of history when women were chattels. They include the dominant cultures of Western multicultural societies, which are generally exempted from scrutiny although they also owe their origins to historical periods, such as classical Greece, where women were similarly subordinate, and manifest similar biases. In the West, the subordination of women is justified as 'sexual difference', the idea that women are both physically and mentally different from men and naturally destined for separate roles. The contemporary religious version of this idea, as we have seen, is 'complementarity'.

Cultures are created and nurtured to a large extent in the private sphere, and the notion that culture should be respected sanctifies and protects this sphere from criticism. Feminist political theorists have understood the false distinction created by traditional male political science between the private and the public spheres as fundamental to the subordination of women (Pateman, 1988; MacKinnon, 1989). In this traditional understanding, politics takes place in the public sphere – the world outside the home – of marketplaces, parliaments and mosques. As Okin explains this, 'To a large extent, contemporary theories of justice, like those of the past, are about men with wives at home' (Okin, 1989, p. 13). Women have either been forbidden from taking part in this public world, made to wear clothing that extinguishes their personhood, faced with insurmountable difficulties that prevent participation, such as childcare and housework, required to be obedient to their husbands or simply treated with such disdain and disapproval in the face of men's bonding behaviour that they are effectively excluded. Women's special sphere has been understood as the home, in which they create the peace and happiness of male citizens by keeping the toilet clean and the children quiet (Delphy and Leonard, 1992). The home itself has not been understood as a political domain. Feminist political theorists have sought to change this understanding. They have pointed out that women's subordination and exclusion from the public sphere starts in the home. It is women's double shift of unpaid as well as paid work that prevents their full citizenship (Lister, 1997). Moreover the power dynamics of the home, in which men are in control and may mete out severe violence, mean that it is the most directly and clearly political sphere for women. The exclusion of the home from 'politics' is a fundamental flaw of multicultural theory.

Women's subordination in the 'private sphere' founds cultures. Susan Moller Okin's work on the relationship between patriarchal family structures and the possibility of creating just societies is very useful for understanding this (Okin, 1989). Okin does not write about 'culture' but simply about an undifferentiated 'family' in Western society. She considers that the possibility of equality in the society as a whole is constructed out of what takes place in the family, which is both fundamentally unjust because of the dependency of women upon men, and also acts as a 'school of justice', in which children learn how power relations work (Okin, 1989, p. 17). For children, she says, 'The family is a crucial determinant of our opportunities in life, of what we "become"' (Okin, 1989, p. 16). The family is important, she explains, because it is, 'the linchpin of the gender structure' and it 'must be just if we are to have a just society, since it is within the family that we first come to have that sense of ourselves and our relations with others that is at the root of moral development' (Okin, 1989, p. 14). She points out that religion 'inculcates' the hierarchy that founds the family 'on allegedly natural male dominance and female dependence and subordination' and enhances this with the 'mystical and sacred symbol of a male god' (Okin, 1989, p. 66).

Okin explains that there are many factors within families that make girls and women vulnerable, and one of them is the 'anticipation of marriage'. The anticipation of a situation in which women will leave work, or work part time, and be dependent on a higher-earning male partner affects how they view education and employment. This is highly significant in relation to the removal from school of girls from Muslim families in the UK, for instance, at sixteen so that they can be prepared for arranged marriages (Sanghera, 2009). In such a situation the anticipation of marriage can close down women's options of financial independence for their lifetimes. Multicultural policies start from the perspective that there are areas of private life that should not be the concern of politics. Once the oppression of women and children is deprivatised, policies of multiculturalism and multifaithism cannot look just or reasonable. They clearly fix women's oppression and make any amelioration of women's private slavery much more difficult. Religion privatises, that is its most dangerous function. It removes the vulnerable from the protections of the democratic state and privatises their oppression.

The traditional family is founded in an understanding of sexual difference as natural, which implies that women simply do unpaid parenting and housework as a part of their divinely or genetically ordained fate. But the idea of sexual difference founds culture in other ways too. It is embodied in the different ways that women are required to dress and bedeck themselves, and is surprisingly hard for social theorists to recognise as problematic, despite the extremity of the 'difference' involved. Women in Western culture are required to wear clothes that are tight and reveal large areas of their bodies; to wear shoes that make walking all but impossible; to wear make-up to cover their faces when out in public and to primp and undergo the knife to shape their bodies and body hair to the demands of 'femininity' (Jeffreys, 2005). Men, on the other hand, may still, for the most part, wear loose, comfortable clothing, flat shoes and escape make-up and the knife. Men and masculinity are the norm against which women's 'difference' is created. This extraordinary exercise in the construction of visible sexual difference, with all its associated physical and mental harms (American Psychological Association, 2007), is invisible to most social commentators, who see it as somehow natural and inevitable. Even some feminists see this hugely energetic creation of a status category as an expression of choice and agency, which men mysteriously decline to embrace (Lehrman, 1997; Walter, 1999).

The roles of women in Western culture are not as circumscribed as those that are enforced in other cultures that have experienced less social and economic change in the status of women. Two centuries of feminist activism, plus capitalist development that has required women to enter the paid workforce, has led to an amelioration of women's condition in the West. In mid-nineteenth-century Britain men owned their wives' persons, in that they were permitted to recapture a fleeing wife and imprison her. They owned her property, she had no separate status in law, they could use her body at will, they owned her children and she was not permitted to divorce (Hollis, 1979). But despite significant legal changes in all these particulars, which have important symbolic value in relation to women's status, women's traditional roles within male dominant culture have changed only in circumscribed ways. Women have entered the paid workforce, do well in tertiary education and they have equal rights in divorce and child custody but they still act as 'wives' doing the vast majority of unpaid domestic labour and childcare (McMahon, 1999), they still cannot easily refuse to be sexually used by male partners (Jeffreys, 1993), and they must service male sexual demands in relation to their appearance by adopting sexualised femininity in body, clothing and gait (Jeffreys, 2005). The subordination of women is deeply cultural in Western culture and is centred in the home and the body. Ideas of what constitutes the family, sex, beauty and work are constructed out of women's subordination and regulate women's lives. Western culture is gendered to the eyeballs and it is hard to think of many aspects that would survive the removal of women's subordination.

Considering that sexual difference is so fundamental in the shaping of what is understood as Western culture (see Guillaumin, 1996), there is no reason to expect that it would be less significant in the shaping of other cultures that have not been leavened by centuries of law and attitude change, and feminist campaigns. Cultures are so riddled through and constructed out of women's subordination that they may not be susceptible to minor tinkering. Against this understanding, of the necessity of cultures to be radically transformed if not abolished, it is not hard to see that a political ideology and practice based upon the idea that all cultures need to be equally respected cements women's subordination and rules any chance of alleviating it out of order.

Muslim women speak

In the last few years there have been government funded projects in the UK to find out what Muslim women consider to be matters of concern and importance, in order to facilitate policy development. They demonstrate the degree to which Muslim women suffer in some communities from cultural or religious oppression. There is a difficulty with the idea of consulting 'Muslim' women, which is the principle that religion can and should be the organising principle of the lives of the women in question. It excludes women who are apostates and have given up Islam or do not consider themselves Muslims. These women may take part on the grounds that they are 'culturally' Muslim and therefore de facto included, but they are not invited to contribute and their views may be of particular importance. The exclusion of apostates means that the views of critics of Islam are likely also to be excluded. Atheist feminists from a Muslim background may be those with the must useful suggestions to change Muslim culture but their views will not be heard. It is assumed that Islam will be the way in which 'Muslim' women identify.

Despite this limitation, two UK consultations in 2006 found that 'Muslim' women were very concerned about issues of violence, forced marriage and honour abuse committed against them by men in the community (Mahoney and Taj, 2006; Muslim Women's Network, 2006). They were also angry about discrimination at mosques – including mosques that did not admit women at all – and at the fact that quite inappropriate male community leaders were considered suitable to speak on their behalf. A Welsh inquiry into the views of six hundred 'Muslim' women found that the women considered 'that their culture was a stronger influencing force on their social behaviour than their faith' (Mahoney and Taj, 2006, p. 6). As one woman commented, 'I can deal with Allah . . . when I die – but I have to face my neighbours tomorrow' (Mahoney and Taj, 2006, p. 6). It was 'culture' that imposed on them codes of conduct related to honour, for instance. The report comments that forced marriage and 'Honour related abuse' were important issues for these Muslim women, 'We have heard many anecdotes relating to the disappearance of vulnerable women as young as eleven and as old as sixty-five', and these were 'sidelined' by service providers because they did not want to look 'into the inner workings of the family and the community' (Mahoney and Taj, 2006, p. 7). Women were not expected to 'play a visible role in discussions' within the community, and mixed groups of men and women were 'not viewed in a positive light by the community', and 'women taking a stand' were 'considered harridans' (Mahoney and Taj, 2006, p. 11). The report states that honour-related abuse is taking place in Wales and describes it as being born from 'ancient tribal customs' (Mahoney and Taj, 2006, p. 11). The sort of honour-based infractions by women that might draw violent retribution from men include, 'not serving a meal quickly enough to *allegations* of women entering into illicit sexual relationships' (Mahoney and Taj, 2006, p. 13). These infractions are similar to the sorts of reasons that spark everyday men's violence to partners in non-Muslim communities (Dobash and Dobash, 1980). The report refers to a 'tide of honour based violence in Wales' (Mahoney and Taj, 2006, p. 13). It calls for the removal of the 'current stigma that favours "political correctness" instead of the pursuance of justice in the name of human rights' (Mahoney and Taj, 2006, p. 13).

There is a problem in seeing the kind of abuse Muslim women suffer as exclusive to, or necessarily connected with, a particular religion and culture. The difference between the violence that Muslim women experience, and that of non-Muslim women, is that it can be justified by the perpetrators as ordained by religion. As a woman quoted in the Muslim Women's Network consultation in the UK explains, 'Men in all societies may control women, however they don't use religion as a justification, the way it is wrongly used by Muslim men within the community' (Muslim Women's Network, 2006, p. 13). It is useful to note that the *Muslim Women Talk* (Mahoney and Taj, 2006) report argues that forced marriage should be criminalised. Despite a considerable momentum of support in the early 2000s for criminalising this practice, the UK government chose not to take this step on the grounds of precisely the sort of cultural relativism that is criticised in these consultations (Macey, 2009).

Women under multiculturalism as a development problem

In communities within multicultural states where there is entrenched poverty and disadvantage, the empowerment of women through a gender and development approach may be more appropriate than respect for 'culture' or 'religion'. Marie Macey's work (2009) offers a good example from the UK of the ways in which failure to recognise how women's subordination constructs culture and religion leads to misguided policy. She explains that multiculturalism in Britain was aimed at rectifying the profound inequality of some groups such as Muslim communities originating in Pakistan and Bangladesh. In 2010, the median incomes per week of Indian and white adults in Britain were very similar at £417 and £412 respectively, while the median income of Pakistani and Bangladeshi adults, taken together, was only £238, a considerable difference (Hills *et al.*, 2010). Lack of respect for the culture of the Muslim groups, manifesting in discrimination, racism and presently 'Islamophobia' has been generally considered the cause of their poverty. Macey argues that this is fallacious. If racism or Islamophobia were responsible then all those who could be identified as belonging to a different ethnicity or religion would be likely to suffer a similar fate. The fact that some Muslim groups, particularly Mirpuris from Pakistan and Bangladesh, suffer an unchanging and severe inequality in relation to other ethnic minority groups that originate in the Indian subcontinent requires, she considers, a different explanation.

Her explanation is that the subordination of women is particularly severe among Mirpuris and causes the severe inequality. Mirpuri men traditionally marry uneducated, young girls who are their cousins and bring them to Britain from Pakistan and Bangladesh. This practice of consanguineous (cousin) marriage fosters ties to homeland communities and repays obligations. If an extended family in Pakistan originally helped the emigration of a family member to the UK, then that relative is obligated to bring in more family members via marriage so that the family can make further economic progress. There are a number of problems associated with the practice that help to trap Mirpuri families in disadvantage. The young wives are likely to be uneducated and unable to speak English. They may be segregated within the Mirpuri community and within their homes. They do not have the skills – and are unlikely to be allowed – to work outside the home as women in other communities do and thus advance the economic status of the family. Their lack of education does not provide a good model for their children and may cause their sons and daughters to lack educational ambitions. The wives' inability to communicate in English, plus their confinement to the home to protect their 'modesty', may create more isolation and lack of integration for the family.

Khola Hasan identifies a number of 'human rights concerns' that result from cousin marriage. These include forced marriage and lack of integration (Hasan, 2009). The rates of cousin marriage, she points out, are rising in the UK though falling in countries of origin. The marriages occur among the two-thirds of those British Pakistani citizens whose families originate in the Mirpur region. Migration takes place through the acquisition of spouses from the homeland. Families in Mirpur expect to get the right of first refusal in offers of marriage for each other's children and 'rejection causes offence' (Hasan, 2009, p. 276). Hasan reports that an estimated three out of four marriages of Mirpuris are between first cousins. The effects are considerably increased rates of disability among the offspring of such marriages, with 'British Pakistanis' being thirteen times more likely to have children with genetic disorders than the general population. British Pakistanis account for 3 per cent of births nationally but 30 per cent of all British children with genetic disorders (Hasan, 2009, p. 281). This high rate of disability leads to heavily increased workloads for mothers and to greater poverty. It also exacerbates the problem of forced and arranged marriage for wives brought into the UK. Often they do not know that the husbands they have never met have disabilities and that they will be required to care for them and accept reduced expectations of what marriage might entail. The economic prospects of the Mirpuri community, and any community that keeps women subordinated, less educated, unable to work outside the home and unable to control their childbearing because of the prohibition of contraception, are severely reduced. It might, therefore, be appropriate to apply to government policy towards such communities, a gender and development approach, rather than a multicultural one.

Economic empowerment of women is critical

A gender and development approach recognises that the 'empowerment' of women, meaning the collective empowerment of women in a way that challenges the status quo, is a necessary foundation for the relief of poverty. Naila Kabeer explains that 'empowerment' must 'challenge power relations' (Kabeer, 2005). Radical feminist critics have pointed out that the term 'empowerment' can be victim blaming (Kitzinger and Perkins, 1993). Empowerment does not give women 'power', in the sense in which men have power over them. When women are encouraged to 'empower' themselves while leaving gendered power structures in place, the idea of empowerment could lead to blaming the women for their lack of progress. Despite this serious difficulty with the concept, the term 'empowerment' is in common usage in human rights work by NGOs and UN agencies and I will use it within these limitations here.

The gender and development literature and development agencies at the UN such as the United Nations Population Fund (UNFPA) and the United Nations Development Programme (UNDP) stress that the 'empowerment' of women, while important in its own right for women's human rights, is also fundamental to the elimination of poverty in communities. The UN's Millennium Development Goal (MDG) 3, for instance, is to 'Promote gender equality and empower women' (UNFPA, n.d.). It states that women's empowerment is an 'engine of development'. A key aspect of this empowerment is the ability of women to 'decide freely the number and timing of children'. Women's equality is the basis of enabling women to 'unleash their productivity'. UNFPA states that, 'Gender equality' exists 'when both sexes are able to share equally in the distribution of power and influence; have equal opportunities for financial independence through work or through setting up businesses; enjoy equal access to education and the opportunity to develop personal ambitions'. This is a situation markedly absent for many women in multicultural societies who are trapped by ideas and practices of women's subordination within the private sphere that are justified by culture or religion. UNFPA calls for the 'empowerment of women', which will enable them to identify and redress 'power imbalances' and give them the 'autonomy to manage their own lives'. MDG 3 and the UNFPA understanding of gender and development are anachronistic when seen in relation to the determined maintenance or adoption of traditional male domination in some communities across Western multiculturalist states. The MDGs and the UNFPA statement are not intended to apply to developed nations like the UK, but their message is fully relevant to the existence of segregated communities within Britain in which disadvantage and poverty are continually recycled. It may be that there is one rule for poor countries in which Western aid agencies operate, but quite another for poor and disadvantaged communities within those Western countries themselves in which cultures are to be respected rather than transformed. The understandings implicit in the MDGs should, perhaps, be made the foundation of multicultural policies in rich nations, in the same way as they found UN approaches to reducing poverty and disadvantage in poor ones.

Agency under multiculturalism

The degree to which feminist theorists are prepared to be critical of multiculturalism, depends to a large extent upon their attitude to the issue of 'women's agency'. The concept of 'agency' is rooted in the ideas of liberalism and the free will of the individual. Marxist philosophers have criticised the notion of agency for ignoring the material constraints of class relations and ideology, and as a foundational concept of capitalist ideology (Wilson, 2007). Feminist theorists have criticised the language of liberalism, that is the use of terms such as agency, choice and empowerment, to address women's experience of harmful cultural practices such as beauty norms (Gill, 2007), and prostitution (Jeffreys, 2009). This liberal language fails to capture the structural constraints within which women live their lives, which can include severe violence as well as economic dependence, and the psychological violence of surviving in families that require their subordination. Approaches to multiculturalism which stress the individual woman or girl's ability to exercise choice or agency in the face of family, cultural and religious constraints, fail to understand the forcefulness with which women's subordination can be implemented in the private realm. Anne Phillips' critique of multiculturalism, is far-reaching, but falls short of the outright rejection that scholars such as Susan Moller Okin favours (Phillips, 2007). Phillips argues that, 'multiculturalism can be made compatible with the pursuit of gender equality and women's rights so long as it dispenses with an essentialist understanding of culture' (Phillips, 2007, p. 9). The difference between her approach and that of more swingeing critiques is that she considers that women are not controlled by 'culture', and can exercise agency to escape its thrall. She says that 'a defensible multi-culturalism has to put human agency at its core' (Phillips, 2007, p. 179). She recognises that women experience severe pressures from 'culture' to behave in certain ways but remains convinced that very few women really have little choice but to follow the dictates of their culture.

> Personally, I do not believe there are many such individuals. There are plenty of people around who put up with aspects of their lives they dislike because of other aspects they value . . . I do not think there are many people so ground down by their circumstances that they have entirely internalised its norms.
>
> (Phillips, 2007, p. 179)

Women who are unable to act against the constraints of their circum-stances she describes as 'those who are so brainwashed by their oppression that they cannot even perceive that something is awry' (Phillips, 2007, p. 179). This formulation shows a lack of understanding of the effects of psychological and physical violence, and of the seriousness of the threat of being expelled from family and community.

Right to exit

Phillips' approach places too much emphasis on 'culture' as the adversary that women face. She shows insufficient consideration for the straight-forward violence and force and severe parental pressure that underlie 'culture'. Phillips, like Sawitri Saharso, and indeed the masculinist theorist of multiculturalism, Chandran Kukathas (2003), emphasises the importance of the 'right to exit'. Susan Moller Okin explains that the 'right to exit' is fundamental to liberal multicultural theory, and it 'trumps any group rights' (Okin, 2002). Okin, however, is severely critical of the work of most theorists of multiculturalism for failing to recognise that women's inequality, particularly within the family, makes the 'right to exit' extraordinarily hard to realise for women and girls: 'women are far less likely than men to be able to exercise the right of exit' (Okin, 2002, p. 206). In order to realise a right to exit a person must have access to education and skills training, to work, to equal family relationships, particularly marriage, to the wider society and its support systems. But most importantly, a person must be able to not just conceptualise but to 'want' to exit, despite the severe losses they will suffer. In all these respects, women and girls in particularly patriarchal minority cultures are very unequal in comparison with men. The 'right to exit' means that individuals, such as women seeking to escape an arranged marriage, must be able to leave oppressive communities and express their choice and agency. This right, Phillips considers, can be facilitated through schools, which should give pupils information about such practices as female genital mutilation and forced marriage so that they can take evasive action.

Sawitri Saharso is particularly cavalier in her belief that a putative right to exit is available to women (Saharso, 2003). She writes about hymen reconstruction surgery in the Netherlands, which is undertaken by women who need to be able to appear virginal on marriage, to avoid repudiation and possible violence or murder for offending against honour. Saharso says that feminists should support the availability of such surgery on the public health service as a matter of justice for such women. She offers, in support of this idea, the argument that the girls and young women involved have the 'right to exit', and thus hymen repair surgery is a choice for them. They could choose not to undergo the procedure and instead exit their community. There are, she says, some refuges for Muslim girls in the Netherlands and this provides the necessary means of escape. If they decide upon reconstructive surgery they are making a choice between two reasonable possibilities: surgery or escape. Saharso's argument shows a brutal lack of understanding of the pressures upon young women that make the 'right to exit' quite inadequate. The biggest obstacle, as Okin understands very well, is likely to be the fact that they do not want to exit, 'women, are not only less able to exit but have many reasons not to *want* to exit their culture of origin; the very idea of doing so may be unthinkable' (Okin, 2002; 2007). Exit is likely to require the entire loss of family and community. It may condemn women to a lifetime of having to conceal their identities and be on the run, lest vengeful family members are able to find them. It will require exit into a society in which they will have no obvious supports and have to embark on life all over again. They may not have the requisite education and skills to find work or a support structure to make that possible. But also, as Okin explains, having been indoctrinated for a lifetime in a culture and religion, they may value it and not be able to imagine a life separated from it.

For adult women the constraints can be even more severe. If they have been removed from education to prepare for their roles as wives, as is commonly the case in the UK, where the numbers of girls still in education after sixteen is much smaller than boys (Sanghera, 2009), and suffered an arranged marriage at a young age, they will have had much less opportunity to exercise any freedom to choose or to imagine what that might represent. If their religion offers them no access to leaving a marriage or the right to divorce, then they are particularly vulnerable. Okin points out that it would be very wrong to assume, from the failure of girls and women to exercise their supposed 'right to exit', that they therefore positively choose to remain. She explains that girls in some minority cultures are raised to have very low self-esteem and to treat males – particularly fathers and husbands – with studied deference. Together with all the other severe constraints on women's equality and ability to engage in free behaviour in pursuit of their own interests, this lack of self-esteem means they are unlikely to contemplate disobedience. The formal 'right to exit' is not necessarily a 'realistic' right to exit, because it does not take account of 'the depth of acquired cultural attachments, which can render the exit option not merely undesirable but unthinkable' (Okin, 2002, p. 222).

Okin emphasises the importance of arranged marriage and religious schools in constraining women's 'right to exit'. Of 'faith' schools she comments that if parents are allowed to educate their children in religious settings where they are taught, 'that it is the will of an omnipotent and punitive God that women's proper role in life is to be an obedient wife and full-time mother', then the girls will not be aware of any alternatives (Okin, 2002, p. 226). She explains that 'fundamentalist' schools will socialise children 'into the inevitability of sex roles and sex hierarchy and the godlessness of any departure from them' (Okin, 2002, p. 226). Okin stresses that a seventeen-year-old girl has little room for manoeuvre when forced to choose between leaving school early to marry a 'virtual stranger' and losing her ties with her family and her religion. She asks, 'What kind of a choice is one between total submission and total alienation from the person she understands herself to be?' (Okin, 2002, p. 229). The 'liberal state', she concludes, 'should enforce individual rights against' groups that subordinate girls in this way, and 'encourage all groups within its borders to cease such practices' because not to do so 'is to let toleration for diversity run amok' (Okin, 2002, p. 230).

The responsibility of the state to intervene to enable women and girls in religious fiefdoms to exercise human rights is taken further by Clare Chambers. She devotes her incisive critique of liberal multicultural theory *Sex, Culture and Justice: the Limits of Choice* (2008) precisely to an examination of the inadequacy of the notions of choice and the right to exit. She comments, 'By reducing questions of justice to questions of choice, liberals effectively deny the importance of culture to practice, the importance of power in perpetuating practices' (Chambers, 2008, p. 42). She argues that the imposition of cultural norms that negate 'choice' within the family and through bodily practices that create psychological processes, are clear in the fact that feminists who know that high-heeled shoes derive from male domination and are harmful to health, continue to wear them, for instance. Even understanding does not necessarily un-work the way in which norms enter the body and mind. She explains that 'As people respond to the circumstances within which they live, they become accustomed to those particular responses and, over time, repeat them with little or no conscious awareness or choice . . .' (Chambers, 2008, p. 53).

Conclusion

Multiculturalism has provided the rationale, under the aegis of respecting cultural difference, for respecting the rights of patriarchs to control fiefdoms in which they have power over women and children. Acceptance of multicultural ideas has made it more difficult for feminists to criticise not just 'culture', but 'religion'. The lack of active feminist engagement with harms to women from religion in recent decades can perhaps be explained by a sensitivity to accusations of racism that stems from multiculturalist respect for religion. The ostensible object of this respect has moved from culture to religion to a large extent. Multiculturalism is transforming into multifaithism in those states that express commitment to this form of politics. Though in theory, multiculturalism could reasonably be seen to include 'cultures' such as those of Italy, Greece and Poland, and the Caribbean islands, since these are all countries from which the UK has received migrants, it is not these European and Caribbean cultures that are alluded to in debates and policies on multiculturalism. Rather those 'cultures' that are seen to have problematic religions are the focus of these debates. Governments recognise the groups that require to be addressed by 'multiculturalism' by their religions, and seek to enlist these groups through the usually male and patriarchal ruling elites of their mosques and churches. In this way multiculturalism has become multifaithism. Multicultural theory and practice has enabled a growing respect for and reliance on religion in public policy. In the next chapter I shall examine the way in which multifaithism in the UK and Australia has contributed to the development of politics of 'desecularisation' in which governments deliberately enlist religious organisation both to consult on and to deliver services, such as education, employment and youth services with problematic implications for women's equality.

5

DESECULARISATION AND WOMEN'S EQUALITY

Desecularisation has taken place in Australia and in the UK in the last decade as religious organisations have been invited by governments to take a much greater part in public life. This process is an example of the way in which multiculturalism has developed into multifaithism, and is one manifestation of the rise of religion. Religious groupings have received contracts to run welfare services, received money to set up interfaith organisations and have been invited to take part in consultations on policy. Deliberate government policy has directed the setting up of more religious schools or the handing of state schools to religious organisations to run with state funding. The term desecularisation has been developed by scholars of religion and politics to describe the increasing prominence of religion in government policies and in the public sphere in states that had previously adopted some degree of secularisation (Berger, 1999). The respected sociologist of religion, Peter Berger, considers that Europe – the UK in particular – and Australia fulfil the sociological expectations of a progressive secularisation. I will argue here that this thesis holds true in terms of the levels of religiosity among the citizenry. It ignores, however, the phenomenon in the last decade in which a labour government in the UK and a liberal government in Australia both sought as a matter of purposeful policy to re-religionise the population and increase the role of religion in public affairs, despite the lack of enthusiasm on the part of their constituencies. This chapter will focus on the deployment of religion by governments in Australia and the UK, and argue that this is likely to be harmful to women's equality. Feminist political theorist Anne Phillips asserts that there has been a global trend towards what she called the 'de-privatisation' of religion, and its increasing salience on the political stage

(Phillips, 2009, p. 4). Desecularisation is of concern because, as she puts it, 'I shall simply assert – without argument – that a fusion of state and religion is not favourable to gender equality. Religions are not democracies' (Phillips, 2009, p. 9).

Desecularisation has been carried out by the British and Australian governments despite the fact that the citizenry in these countries is becoming progressively less religious. The 2001 census in the UK, for example, showed that 72 per cent of the population claimed Christianity as their religion, 15 per cent stated that they had no religion, and 5 per cent nominated non-Christian religions (Berkeley, 2008, p. 8). However, the expression of a religious affiliation does not connote any serious commitment to religion. An analysis of findings from the 2001 Citizenship Survey in the UK found that only 20 per cent of respondents 'felt their religious beliefs to be an important part of their sense of self-identity' (O'Beirne, 2004, p. vii). Despite this, the governments of the UK and Australia in the last decade have sought to reinfuse religiosity into public life. This development has attracted the considerable concern of democracy theorists and public policy academics. But this concern is generally directed at the ways in which these developments affect democracy and multiculturalism, and the rights of unbelievers, rather than at their potential effects on women. There has been only limited, and quite recent, commentary on the effects for women (Bloch, 2009; Macey, 2009; Winter, 2009). In this chapter I will suggest that the desecularisation taking place in Australia and in the UK threatens women's equality.

Desecularisation in Western states is manifested in the choice by political leaders to demonstrate their religiosity and to deploy religion in political life (Warhurst, 2006). In the last decade there has been a tendency for politicians to adopt the language of religion, and to seek to show what good believers they are, in acts of public worship. This was clear in the era in which George Bush in the US, Tony Blair in the UK and John Howard in Australia, pronounced their Christianity and expressed its importance in their relationships with each other, particularly over the invasion of Iraq in 2003. George Bush, for instance, once told Palestinian leaders, 'God would tell me, "George, go end the tyranny in Iraq" and I did' (McSmith, 2006). This public religiosity on the part of politicians was a surprising development of the 1990s. Though US politicians had a habit of seeking to appeal to their considerable Christian constituencies, British and Australian politicians had largely unbelieving constituencies, or at least ones that cared little about religion. John Howard in Australia formed closer and closer ties with religious extremists in his own party and in the country as a whole (Maddox, 2005). Tony Blair has publicly expressed his belief that faith should motivate the behaviour of nation states in international politics and since leaving office he has converted to Catholicism, set up a Faith Foundation, and taken on a role as a Religious Studies Professor at Yale. In 2009, President Obama invited Tony Blair to lead the US National Prayer Breakfast. Blair talked about the global importance of religion, saying that faith should be restored 'to its rightful place, as the guide to our world and its future' (Doyle, 2009). These politicians did not restrict their ambitions for religion to the international sphere. In the domestic sphere they created a greater role for religion through government consultation and funding of religious organisations to an unprecedented level, and in previously unimagined ways.

Feminists should be interested in the implications of desecularisation because the womanhating attitudes and practices of religions are in contradiction to women's equality. Despite attempts by some women believers to alleviate the womanhating culture and ideas of their chosen religions, the majority of religious organisations worldwide practise deliberate and egregious discrimination against women. They do not allow women to preach or administer the sacraments, maintain allegiance to the negative attitudes to women that appear in their sacred texts, or maintain the separation of women in special balconies and behind curtains so that they cannot contaminate the mysteries taking place or the thoughts of male worshippers. A study of the way in which mosques provide for women worshippers in Sydney, Australia, explains that though some mosques in the UK forbid women to attend, few mosques in Australia, 'if any, purport to ban women completely' (Hussain, 2009, p. 55). The study details, however, the ways in which women are discriminated against, such as having to enter by back stairs, worship on balconies and behind screens, having toilet facilities in a basement with two staircases to the prescribed area and no seating or very little to allow for women with disabilities. In one case, women had to worship in a yard facing the dustbins on a day when male worshippers needed the women's usual space inside.

Another problem with religious organisations from a feminist viewpoint is that they are likely to practise extreme discrimination in their hiring practices. Though some Christian denominations now admit women to the priesthood, most religions do not, on principle and on the grounds of scriptural revelation, allow women into positions of authority. On the other hand, since the beginnings of second-wave feminism in the 1970s, local authorities have made considerable progress in their equal opportunity policies (Farnell *et al.*, 2003). The handing over of public services to organisations that are publicly in opposition to equal opportunity in hiring practices cannot bode well for the sensitivity with which they will handle issues of gender and sexuality. A review of its Equal Opportunity Act by the state government of Victoria, Australia, for instance, provides a useful example of the problems that can arise. The options paper for the review suggested that the exemptions granted to religious bodies to discriminate on many grounds against employees in their partially or wholly state-funded welfare and education services should be reconsidered (Department of Justice, 2008). Some religious groups put in very angry and forceful demands that their right to discriminate be continued, the Catholic Church and the Presbyterian Church in particular. As a result the Attorney General, Rob Hulls, announced that the Churches should be allowed to continue to discriminate on the grounds most important to them, that is against lesbians and gays, and against single women who become pregnant or have *de facto* partners, so long as they gave up their right to discriminate on other grounds such as disability and race (Fyfe, 2009). In the UK similar issues arose during the passage of the Equality Bill (Accord, 2009).

There is a quantity of research that suggests that people who adhere to religions are likely to hold views that are hostile to the interests of women's equality (Norris and Inglehart 2004; Seguino and Lovinsky, 2009). Seguino and Lovinsky looked at the correlations between intensity of religiosity and attitudes and outcomes unfavourable to women's equality. The outcomes they considered were how women fared in labour markets, in political representation and in political decision-making. Using world attitude surveys and other statistical data for a number of countries, they found that 'religiosity is indeed strongly linked to gender inequitable beliefs' (Seguino and Lovinsky, 2009, p. 40). Where religious organisations are involved by governments in consultations on policy and in the delivery of education and other services it is not unreasonable to expect that such discriminatory values and practices will have negative effects on the equality of the girls and women who are the recipients. Research from the UK found that, when there is a clash between the equal opportunity policies of local council funders and religious organisations over educational projects for boys only, or facilities that only boys may use, for instance, this can cause significant difficulties for the professionals involved (Farnell *et al.*, 2003).

An examination of Pentecostalism is useful here because this is the fastest growing variety of Christian faith in the world (Berger, 1999), and harmful attitudes and practices within Pentecostal churches affect very large numbers of girls and women. Pentecostalism is Australia's fastest growing religion and Pentecostal churches have narrow understandings of women's role and of sexuality (Levin, 2007). Between 1996 and 2001, while attendance at Catholic churches fell by 13 per cent, that of Pentecostals rose by 30 per cent. The main Pentecostal church, Hillsong, generated more than $177 million in revenue in 2005. If their government-supported schools are included then the revenue increases to $263 million. There has been a particular closeness between the Pentecostal churches and Australian politicians from both leading parties. As an indication of the closeness of the Howard Liberal Government to the Hillsong church, in 2004 the then treasurer, Peter Costello (son of a Baptist lay preacher), gave an enthusiastic speech at a Hillsong conference, saying, 'We need a return to faith and the values which have made our country strong' (Brissenden, 2004). Prime Minister John Howard opened Hillsong's Baulkham Hills convention centre in October 2002. In 2007, as part of the election campaign of that year, in which the Labour Party's Kevin Rudd, became Prime Minister, both Howard and Rudd appeared at a Hillsong church to speak of their Christian values and garner Christian votes via a live telecast (Carter, 2007). In 2010, Julia Gillard took over from Kevin Rudd as the first woman Prime Minister in Australia and announced that she was 'not a religious person' in answer to the question 'Do you believe in God?', and this has caused speculation as to whether the Australian Christian Lobby will have less influence on her government than it has had on previous ones (Wright, 2010).

The closeness that has appertained until now, however, is problematic for women's and lesbian and gay equality because of the traditional patriarchal ideology that Hillsong propagates. The harmful nature of this ideology has been revealed by ex-member Tanya Levin in her book *People in Glass Houses* (Levin, 2007). Hillsong propounds what Levin calls 'prosperity theology': that is, how to be wealthy. She explains that it is run by men, is hostile to homosexuality and preaches the subordination of women by their husbands. In 2007, Sy Rogers, a speaker at a Hillsong Sense and Sexuality Workshop in Sydney, who identifies as an 'ex-gay' said, 'Happily, homosexuality can be turned around . . . it is not what God planned for human sexuality' (Levin, 2008). An American-style fundamentalist Christian group with links to Hillsong, Mercy Ministries, was reported in 2008 to be performing exorcisms on teenage girls suffering mental health problems or who admitted to having same-sex relationships (Zwartz, 2010). The young women were taken in for six-month programmes and had their Centrelink (welfare) payments paid directly to the organisation. The closeness of politicians and governments to churches that propound and practise these harmful ideas about women and girls, lesbians and gays is worrying, but governments are currently going further than simply seeking to appease churches and garner votes to engage in government through 'faith communities'.

Government through 'faith communities'

The discriminatory ideas and practices of religions should suggest that they are unsuitable partners for governments that purport to be committed to equal opportunities for women, but governments in Australia and the UK – countries in which progress was made in the 1980s towards women's equality – have both allied themselves with these discriminatory organisations in the last decade. In both these states the process of desecularisation owes its ideological origins to an enthusiasm for communitarianism and the ideas of social capital theorists. Robert Putnam, US theorist of social capital explains, 'Faith communities in which people worship together are arguably the single most important repository of social capital in America' (Putnam, 2000, p. 66). Social capital ideas are an offshoot of communitarianism, and this latter ideology has been criticised as expressing a conservative and elitist idealism by political theorists. It ignores all the other variables that might lead to social breakdown, particularly that of class inequality (Daly and Silver, 2008). It has been taken up with particular enthusiasm in countries in the top four in the developed world for inequality, such as the US, the UK and Australia (Wilkinson and Pickett, 2009). This suggests that governments have enlisted 'faith' to deal cheaply with the social distress caused by market failure, including the alienation of unemployed youth from ethnic minorities, without altering their commitment to market-driven, small government policies. Mary Daly and Hilary Silver argue, for instance, that the enthusiastic adoption of social capital ideas stems from the ideology of 'deprioritizing of the role of the state' (Daly and Silver, 2008, p. 552). As they explain, 'social capital can provide a rationale for the state to exit poor communities and leave the problem-solving to civil society or individual action' (Daly and Silver, 2008, p. 553). The idea of 'social capital' implies, 'that redistribution is unnecessary, since the poor simply need to bond together and turn their social resources into economic assets' (Daly and Silver, 2008, p. 554).

Feminist political theorists have pointed out serious problems with the rose-tinted view of 'community' that underpins communitarian and social capital ideas. One major shortcoming is that it can serve to reify male power (Fraser and Lacey, 1993). 'Communities' have typically been male dominant and recuperating an old-fashioned ideal form will have the effect of establishing male authority on a firmer footing. Another difficulty is the fact that when governments decide to 'consult' with communities they select unelected local representatives who are generally male and carry the values of the traditional model. They are quite unlikely to be women, lesbians and gays, or apostates. A study of the barriers to effective consultation with the South Asian 'community' in Bradford, UK, for instance, found that the 'minorities within minorities' did not do well out of outreach programmes based on the identification of representatives of particular communities (Blakey *et al.*, 2006). Gay men felt that they were excluded from such policies, and lesbians experienced much more complex levels of exclusion. Lesbians felt uncomfortable in the support group set up for gay Asians, as this was male dominated. Their issues were very serious, such as how to avoid arranged marriages without suffering severe violence, and they needed separate spaces in which to discuss these. Lesbians and gay men faced discrimination and violence both within and outside the South Asian community because of their homosexuality. Women as a minority within this community are not covered in the report, apparently because the researcher dedicated to this issue left the project. But it does seem likely that women would have had great difficulties having their concerns taken seriously, particularly when some women are not expected by their menfolk to issue forth into public space at all, being required to follow the modesty rule. The problem of the seclusion of women within the home is one that profoundly challenges all policies of consultation and engagement with 'faith communities' in which some male members enforce this harmful cultural practice upon women.

Despite these shortcomings, the talk of 'communities' and the idea that carrying out government policies through 'communities' is a positive way forward, has become dominant in policy speak. It has become particularly prominent in the language of multiculturalism, to refer to 'faith' or 'ethnic' communities. Thus Bikhu Parekh, author of the influential report 'The Future of Multi-Ethnic Britain' writes 'Britain certainly needs to be "One Nation" – but understood as a community of communities, and a community of citizens, not a place of oppressive uniformity based on a single substantive culture' (Parekh, 2000, p. 56). Unfortunately women are not usually seen as constituting a community in their own right, but are the subordinate class in the communities that are recognised. They do not have representation. A version of multiculturalism that is based upon communities presents the problem, well expressed by Amartya Sen in *Identity and Violence* (2006), of forcing people to fit themselves into one identity category and suppress all the other identities to which they might subscribe, such as being women, being homosexual, being Bengali or being poets. Sen recommends the acceptance that people possess a plurality of identities as a way forward. The Runnymede Trust noted that though the government is supposedly aware of the problem of representing these 'communities', it 'continues to identify particular leaders even while other members of a particular "community" object to that leader's capacity to represent them' (Runnymede Trust, 2007, p. 22). Similar problems, such as how to access and include women from communities that apply the modesty rule, bedevil the issue of interfaith dialogue.

Interfaith dialogue?

Another aspect of desecularisation, and the idea that 'faith communities' can provide a solution to social problems, is the setting up of 'interfaith' groups by governments. In both the UK and in Australia there has been a concerted effort by governments in recent years to stimulate 'interfaith dialogue'. Considerable funding as well as pressure from government has been directed to this end. In a 2007 report, Hazel Blears, Secretary of State for Communities and Local Government in the UK, explained the thinking behind the promotion of interfaith dialogue (Communities and Local Government, 2007). The growth in 'active faith', she says, 'has seen faith communities putting into practice their values and teachings to enrich and benefit wider society' (Communities and Local

Government, 2007, p. 5). The promotion of interfaith dialogue was at the behest of the Prime Minister, Tony Blair, who wanted, 'to see stronger inter faith dialogue where people find the common ground that exists between different religions and communities in the UK and the creation of local inter faith councils in every community' (Communities and Local Government, 2007, p. 6). The underlying motive was 'resilience to extremism in all its forms', which seems likely to refer to forms of violence purportedly based upon extreme Islamism (Communities and Local Government, 2007, p. 6). The report shows awareness that interfaith activity presents particular difficulties of exclusion for women, with a section on the 'challenges and barriers' women face. These relate to the fact that those drawn together to 'dialogue' are usually the male leaders of the religions, but there are other problems such as male domination of the discussions and the fact that many women feel uncomfortable with the formality of the discussions and with being in a room with men or dominated by them (Mubarak, p. 2006).

Concerned feminist scholars in Australia have raised several problems of a general nature with 'interfaith dialogue', not just those related to women's equality. The promotion of 'interfaith dialogue' has taken place in Australia as well as in the UK, and has been identified by a feminist critic as a 'rising phenomenon within and between multicultural communities' (Bloch, 2009, p. 181). The Australian government has spent millions of dollars on interfaith activities since 2002. One major problem is that 'interfaith dialogue initiatives' contribute to 'the collapse of multicultural discourse into religious discourse, whereby "culture" and "religion" are conflated' (Bloch, 2009, p. 181). As Bronwyn Winter puts it in the Australian context, there are attempts to 'cultivate religion as the new "ethnic"' (Winter, 2009, p. 207). Barbara Bloch explains that interfaith dialogue is unlikely to be a good way to counter the terrorism that governments have been so concerned about since 2001, because the extremists and right-wingers are quite unlikely to take part in interfaith activities (Bloch, 2009). She argues that the idea, promoted by governments wedded to an interfaith agenda, that people just need to learn about each other's religions in order to become tolerant citizens, is unlikely to protect against the growth of violence. The promotion of interfaith dialogue provides a diversion from addressing racism directly and is indeed quite helpless against it. It also marginalises those who have no religion and are not invited to take part, while bolstering the public role of religion with its ensuing alienation of those hostile or indifferent to this missionising. Bronwyn Winter makes similar points about interfaith dialogue in Australia (Winter, 2009). She explains that 'interfaith dialogue' has been advanced as the new expression of a multicultural society in a way that displaces discussion of racism. Moreover the framing of 'intercultural dialogue' in religious terms, 'is premised on the assumption that everybody is religious, that everybody is religious in the same way, and there are clear links between religion and culture'(Winter, 2009, p. 205).

Once governments start to categorise citizens according to faith for such purposes they find themselves enmeshed in a tangled web. Atheism, too, has to be made into a faith in order to show fairness of representation. A 2004 report from the UK Home Office Faith Communities Unit called 'Working Together', explains that consultation with 'faith communities' will 'in most cases . . . tend to improve the quality of public policies and services for all' (Home Office, 2004, p. 81). This suggests that the British public in general can be well represented by faiths, even though most are likely to have little 'faith' or none at all. But just in case the unbelievers might feel short changed, the report includes a section on 'People with no religious beliefs' and comments that when consulting faith communities, 'Departments should usually give an opportunity to comment to organisations representing those with non-religious beliefs, such as humanists and secularists' (Home Office, 2004, p. 81). Many unbelieving citizens are unlikely to feel represented by a humanist or secularist organisation and may not even know that these exist. Courageous ex-Muslim apostates, such as Maryam Namazie, who are frequently women and feminists, are unlikely to be captured in such consultations (Rix, 2008). Humanists and secularists might object to being turned into a faith group with 'beliefs'. In a progress report on the Working Together document described above, humanists are expressly included in a list of 'religion/belief' associations, who have been 'actively consulted' (Home Office, 2005, p. 30).

Urban regeneration

There are equality concerns, too, about another way in which religion has been enlisted by government in the UK: as a partner in the project of 'urban regeneration'. Concern about urban regeneration is stimulated by worries about the possibility of religious extremism and terrorism arising in neighbourhoods with socio-economic problems. Funded by the government, faith organisations have been enlisted to report on the 'economics' of faith. Thus reports into faith economics in the North West and in Wales list all of the ways in which the resources of churches could be used to bolster regional and urban development. The resources include in particular the labour of volunteers, which is seen as potentially providing the state with a large unpaid labour force. In Wales, for instance, the report states that the Christian voluntary sector delivers services through 42,000 volunteers who form the equivalent of 2,000 full-time paid workers (Gweini, 2008). Over 600 churches operate community centres, and churches oversee 1,600 listed buildings. One moneymaking opportunity that local governments are now funding is the promotion of 'faith tourism', that is the idea that those with 'faith' might want to do tours of church buildings. In fact many people are likely to pop into churches and other religious buildings on their travels with no interest in faith at all, but an appreciation of history and architecture. They may not be amenable to finding themselves suddenly converted into 'faith tourists'. The economic benefit to Wales of these Christian religious resources was said to be £102 million. The upshot of this sudden valuing of the churches in economic terms is that local authorities are now adjured to fund them when handing out funds for development purposes. The churches say that they have been unfairly discriminated against in not getting enough funds from local government. The problem that they and government reports identify is resistance from local government officers to the idea of funding religions and the proposed answer is that these officers should receive education on faiths. This raises the interesting spectacle of determinedly secular public servants being engineered out of their ethical understandings of how to do their jobs in order to enforce a faith agenda (Communities and Local Government, 2007).

A study from 2003 on the issue of *'Faith' in Urban Regeneration?* is unusual in giving considerable attention to the problem of the clash between religious ideologies and practices and funding priorities (Farnell *et al.*, 2003). The study interviewed regeneration professionals and representatives of a variety of religions in four urban centres in the UK: Bradford, Coventry, the London Borough of Newham and Sheffield. The report comments that

> Regeneration professionals are working in a context of ideological liberalism and scarce material resources, yet are confronted by demands from ethno-religious communities for 'special' treatment.

How do they reconcile these with legal requirements in such spheres as equal opportunities and race relations?

(Farnell *et al.*, 2003, p. 32)

The researchers give examples of the dilemmas the funders face. These can include what to do when an Asian project is actively promoting 'forced' marriage; when a Christian project bans gay men and lesbians from voluntary work; when a Muslim 'educational' project is for boys only. A female national community development professional who was interviewed stated, 'the way that faith is operating goes against, and cuts across, a national consensus about, say, the position of women . . . The activity that is faith based is also in our view misogynist' (Farnell *et al.*, 2003, p. 34). The comments of one male Muslim community development worker from Bradford provide a good example of the clashes that can arise between the attitudes of male religious authorities and the rights of women. He remarked that, 'Our women *choose* to live in purdah' (Farnell *et al.*, 2003, p. 34). A male local councillor/mosque president from Newham, London, commented, 'Women are not outgoing, but want to remain within those four walls (home)' (Farnell *et al.*, 2003, p. 34). Regeneration professionals are forced to either put aside their ethical and political commitments to equality or face the complaints of religious organisations of discrimination and racism.

Delivery of services through religious organisations

Other equality concerns exist in relation to an increase in the delivery of services through religious organisations in the UK and Australia, a development that fits in with the privileging of faith and adoption of faith-based social capital ideas. This government funding to religious organisations is considerable and has helped to make them very influential businesses. Governments support the economic growth of religions through preferential taxing arrangements. Churches and their enterprises are generally exempt from the tax that other businesses would have to pay; depend on volunteers; and are able to offer lower tenders to take over government services. This is particularly clear in a report on the business clout of religions in Australia from 2006, after the Howard government engaged in a considerable redistribution of the welfare dollar from state and non-religious agencies to religions. Adele Ferguson explains that if the top ten religious groups in Australia were to form a corporation then it would be one of the 'biggest and fastest-growing in the country' because it accounted for more than $23 billion in 2005, up 8.2 per cent on 2004 and not including donations, employing hundreds of thousands of staff and 'wielding unsurpassed political and social clout' (Ferguson, 2006, p. 42). The growth is possible because of their 'winning a bigger and bigger share of government concessions and grants', because of tax-free status and being able to operate outside the control of regulatory authorities.

The churches in Australia receive more than $10 billion a year in government grants to fund church schools, but also run public hospitals and residential aged-care and disability services. In 1996 they scored a coup with a big injection of money when the government privatised its Job Network services and directed much of this money to the churches. They also got government contracts to run counselling for parents involved in custody disputes, a particularly controversial issue since churches are likely to favour keeping families together and may not favour women's rights in this respect. They even receive $20 million annually to provide abortion counselling services, which are likely to be infused with religious messages, such as the importance of avoiding abortion. One upshot of this transfer is that the poor are those most likely to come into contact with religious organisations and be religionised whether they want it or not. It is the poor, and poor women in particular, who need housing and unemployment services. The churches, such as the Catholic Church and the Salvation Army, are now being handed contracts to run women's services such as refuges from domestic violence and for homeless teenage girls, which were previously run by feminist inspired women's agencies. These church-run facilities are at liberty to change the ideology and focus of the services, employ men, prioritise the homelessness of boys or make the facilities mixed, and could have a negative impact on the women and girls who require safety and support. Hospitals run by the Catholic Church, as Ferguson points out, will not conduct vasectomies, tubal ligation or abortions, although they are routine in other public hospitals (Ferguson, 2006). Many areas do not have alternative providers, so women will simply lose access to control of fertility with grave impacts upon their lives.

When religious organisations are responsible for services that are vital to women, and particularly to poor women, they are likely to be influenced by discriminatory ideas about women and sexuality and discriminate in their employment practices to exclude or dismiss those who are lesbian, live with partners out of wedlock or fail to show a proper respect for the precepts of the Church. These problems are amplified in relation to 'faith schools' funded by the state in which the harmful ideas may be enforced upon children.

Faith Schools

In the UK and Australia government policies of promoting 'faith' have led to considerably increased funding to 'faith schools'. There is very little discussion of the implications of this for girls (Hanman, 2006). The rationale behind this promotion of religious schools is that they will improve educational performance, provide parental choice, and also provide 'values education'. This is despite the fact that the values of the organisations that run them include ideas such as women are not fit to be priests, should not have sex outside marriage, should not be lesbians, should not finish their educations, and in some cases, should be obedient to their husbands. The enlistment of 'faiths' in the delivery of education has gone further in the UK than in Australia. When the Blair government took office some state educational provision consisted of schools run by religious organisations, the Anglican Church and the Roman Catholic Church. The policy of the labour government was to establish new state-supported 'faith' schools, or to encourage existing independent 'faith' schools to enter the state system, and to accommodate a wider variety of 'faiths' in the provision of state education. Presently the 6,900 'faith' schools constitute a third of state schools, mostly at the primary level, and they are run by Christian, Jewish, Muslim, Hindu and Seventh Day Adventist organisations. The Church of England has 4,657, the Catholic Church has 2,053, and there are 36 Jewish, 8 Muslim, 2 Sikh, 1 Hindu and 82 other Christian schools (Berkeley, 2008). The faith schools policy has occasioned considerable opposition in the UK from a variety of directions, including the National Secular Society, the British Humanist Association, and Schools Out, which represents lesbian and gay school students. Some critics have attributed the roots of this policy to a desire to privatise the education system by stealth (Berkeley 2008). Others have argued that faith schools create social division. Amartya Sen singles out the creation of faith schools as one of the problems that stems from the UK government's conceptualisation of multiculturalism as 'an imagined national federation of religious ethnicities' (Sen, 2006, p. 165). This concentration on categorising people according to religion 'miniaturises' people and prevents the recognition that people are a collection of identities, and that identities are not just socially constructed but 'chosen'. Faith schools then, have the effect that 'young children are powerfully placed in the domain of singular affiliations well before they have the ability to reason about different systems of identification that may compete for their attention' (Sen, 2006, p. 13).

The faith school policy became more controversial as a result of the recognition, after serious rioting in northern British cities in 2001 and later the September the 11th massacre in New York, that what was called community 'cohesion' was an important goal in order to prevent such events. The wisdom of creating separate development of those of different 'faiths' was called into question, and the possibility that the schools might be more likely to create division has been the main concern of critics. The report on the way in which faith schools promoted equality and cohesion by the Runnymede Trust, an organisation devoted to opposing racism and creating multicultural harmony in the UK, was entitled, 'Right to Divide?' in reference to this problem (Berkeley, 2008). In 2007 the government imposed on state schools, including faith schools, the duty to promote 'cohesion'. The report concludes that the schools are unlikely to be successful in this area, saying that an impasse exists because faith organisations are 'unwilling or unable to change the nature of their schools significantly, offering to do little more than tinker at the margins of their provision to address issues of national concern – namely community cohesion' (Berkeley, 2008, p. 6). The government's faith schools policy is in contradiction to the views of the British public. An *Observer* newspaper poll in 2001 found that only 11 per cent were in favour of more faith schools. A poll by the market research company ICM in 2005 found that 64 per cent agreed that 'the government should not be funding faith schools of any kind' (Berkeley, 2008, p. 18).

The ways in which faith schools may affect the equality of girls has not been researched, despite the potential for discrimination that clearly exists when organisations that adhere to ideas hostile to women's equality are given such responsibilities. In a report by the journalist Christina Odone, there is some evidence to suggest that Islamic state schools engage in discriminatory practices; in one such school in Leicester, boys and girls are placed in separate wings and it has been organised for them to enter and leave the building at separate times so that they may not encounter one another (Odone, 2008). There is also reason for concern about what may develop in such schools in guidelines from the controversial, but influential, Muslim Council of Britain (MCB), which show a commitment to discrimination. The MCB is an umbrella group representing 500 organisations, which is consulted by, and has received hundreds of thousands of pounds of funding from, the UK government. In 2006 it received £300,000 for purposes including the production of 'teaching materials for Muslim schools and madresas' (Department for International Development, 2006). The guidelines, produced the following year, are entitled, *Meeting the needs of Muslim pupils in state schools* (Muslim Council of Britain, 2007). This publication makes demands on state schools in general and it is not unreasonable to suppose that they are already accommodated to some extent in Islamic state schools. In response to media criticism about implementation of aspects of the guidelines in Stoke on Trent in 2010, the MCB stated how influential they considered the set of guidelines to be, 'many thousands of schools and education authorities have used it' (Muslim Council of Britain, 2010).

The demands of the MCB include many relating to segregation and to modesty. Boys and girls are to be allowed to dress modestly, with both sexes wearing tracksuits for exercise, and girls covering all parts of the body but the face and hands at all times. They should have single-sex swimming lessons and changing facilities at primary and secondary schools. They should not be expected to be naked in front of other members of the same sex, so individual changing and showering rooms should be provided, and they should not have to use the communal changing rooms in the swimming baths because some members of the public, presumably of the same sex as the children, might be naked there. Dance is un-Islamic and children should be allowed to excuse themselves from such classes, the problem being that dance is lascivious and includes sexual movements. Sex education should include Islamic morality on issues such as 'sexual conduct and behaviour, abortion, contraception, sexual orientation, hygiene, forced marriages, drugs, child abuse and relationships between males and females' (Muslim Council of Britain, 2007, p. 48). In particular Islamic morality forbids boyfriends/girlfriends; homosexuality is not acceptable; and sex should only take place in marriage. Explicit pictures depicting 'private organs', or explicit discussion should not be used in teaching (Muslim Council of Britain, 2007, p. 48). Sex education should not take place during the month of Ramadan because sexual thoughts are not allowed at that time. In 2009 the government announced that faith schools may teach sex education according to their faith, including in relation to issues such as contraception, abortion and homosexuality (Bloom, 2009). So prescriptions such as those of the MCB may become more common.

There is more information about the problems that lesbian and gay students experience in faith schools than there is about girls. Anti-homosexual sex education is a particular concern because it is likely to be implicated in the bullying and violence that lesbian and gay students suffer. Christian and Muslim teachings as to homosexuality being a sin, dirty and despicable may correlate with the bashings and murders of lesbians and gay men (Macey and Beckett, 2001). In 2007, a report by the respected lesbian and gay rights organisation, Stonewall, found that homophobic bullying was reported by 65 per cent of students in British schools in general, but more of those attending faith schools (75 per cent) had experienced it (Stonewall, 2007). Lesbian and gay students who attended faith schools were significantly less likely to tell anyone about homophobic bullying than those attending non-faith schools, 23 per cent versus 58 per cent, and only 4 per cent of gay pupils felt able to tell their local religious leaders about bullying (Stonewall, 2007, p. 8). Faith schools, which are run by religious organisations that profess women's subordination and preach that homosexuality is a sin, cannot, in good faith, be expected to promote a human rights agenda, as a non-faith school may be required to do.

In Australia, funding to religious schools, which are not part of the state system, increased considerably under the Howard government as part of what Barbara Bloch describes as an 'increase in the public profile of religions in Australia over the past decade' (Bloch, 2009, p. 182). This is reflected in the growth in attendance at private religious schools, which depend upon generous state funding. This growth has been most evident in the area of the new evangelical Protestant denominations rather than in more traditional religious schools belonging to the Catholic, Anglican and Uniting Church (a Nonconformist alliance), with more than 40 per cent of non-government school students (200,00) attending faith schools outside traditional religions. The increasing attendance at evangelical schools that receive generous state funding is problematic, considering the values that such religions promote. In the state of New South Wales, the Pentecostal church, Hillsong, provides programmes for schools that create rigid gender stereotyping for girls (Bibby, 2008). The programme is called 'Shine' and girls are taught how to put on make-up, do their hair and nails, and walk with books balanced on their heads. It is being run in at least twenty state schools, numerous small community organisations and within the juvenile justice system. Hillsong describes it as a 'practical, life-equipping, values-based course'. Pentecostal churches, and other religious entities such as the Exclusive Brethren, an offshoot of the Plymouth Brethren, are committed to the promotion of ideas and practices hostile to the rights of women, lesbians and gays (Bachelard, 2008). State funding of such organisations is in direct conflict with decades of work by feminists and lesbian and gay activists to improve equal opportunities and human rights through the education system.

Conclusion

This chapter has argued that the policies of desecularisation that have been implemented by governments in the UK and in Australia have negative implications for women's equality. The religious organisations with which governments are consulting and to which they are delivering public services may be in opposition to women's equality in relation to their employment practices and ideologies. Consultation with faith communities is fraught with difficulties because it is unlikely to be women who are consulted, and in some cases they may not be able to exit their homes or enter mixed company. There is some evidence that funding faith communities for the purpose of urban regeneration pits professionals with good intentions towards equality against organisations for which discrimination is an article of faith. Faith schools are the most problematic aspect of desecularisation from the point of view of women's equality, because some of the religious organisations that receive state funding are committed to segregation and modesty rules, to harmful ideas about the importance of virginity, against contraception and abortion and against homosexuality. These forms of desecularisation are in direct collision with the considerable progress towards the equality of women and girls in the public realm that has been made in recent decades. Unfortunately there is little attention to the impact of these policies on girls and women in government documents and research reports, and research is badly needed. As we have seen above in relation to the MCB's guidelines for the segregation of girls, schools in the UK and in other European states are becoming testing grounds presently for fundamentalist Islamic movements. These movements seek to establish influence through their demands for the covering up of girls, or through other rules on issues such as mixed-sex handshakes. In the next chapter I examine the political movement to cover up girls and women.

6

COVERING UP WOMEN

This chapter examines a harmful cultural practice against women that is justified by religion: covering up women. Covering up women fits well into UN understandings of what constitutes a harmful cultural practice. It harms the health of women and girls; is for the benefit of men; derives from the subordination of women; creates stereotypes of the sexes and is justified by tradition – religious tradition in this case (Jeffreys, 2005). Unfortunately, the use of religious justification has made arguments that the practice is harmful, a topic of controversy. In fact the veil is the clearest sign – in both Western multicultural societies and those that have majority Muslim cultures – that a political movement of Islamic fundamentalism, based on women's subordination, is gaining in strength. The increasing adoption of headscarves and more extensive forms of covering, by women whose mothers fought to banish them, or in countries where they have never been worn before, is not about a sudden wave of piety. Piety is possible without covering after all, and most practising Muslim women in the West do not adopt it (Saeed, 2010). The contemporary campaign to get women veiled is the product of a political Islamist movement, which is constantly escalating its confrontations with more moderate Muslims and with non-Muslim governments and institutions, in a battle for influence and power. Feminist criticisms of the practice of covering women's bodies in Christianity, in Judaism and in Islam are straightforward. Such practices mark women as different and inferior; they shore up masculinity and male power; they essentialise men's sexuality as predatory and women's as the source of evil; and they create forms of at least psychological and physical discomfort, and at the worst complete social exclusion (Manji, 2003; Amara, 2006; Lazreg, 2009). These concerns stem from the understanding that covering is a rule created by male domination and aimed at the maintenance of women's oppression. This clarity has been muddied and undermined in recent decades as growing Muslim fundamentalism has promoted the covering of women in the East and the West, and cultural relativist academics and apologists have sought to represent covering as the exercise of women's 'choice' and 'agency' (Lazreg, 2009). I shall argue that apologists for the veil, who choose to see women as being empowered by covering and exercising their agency through its adoption, are seriously misguided. Covering should be challenged on principle by those who favour women's equality.

Definition

The covering of women is a practice that has traditionally been imposed upon women in the Middle East. It existed in the culture that predated the development of Judaism and influenced the patriarchal religions that developed in that area, including Christianity and Islam (Lerner, 1987). In some reaches of these religions covering has declined or become non-existent. In Judaism it survives in practices within fundamentalist communities where women shave their heads and wear wigs and hats. In Israel, however, some more extreme practices are developing, with several hundred ultra-orthodox women wearing burqas in order to be truly modest (Blomfield, 2010). In 2010, however, even fundamentalist Jewish men considered the trend had gone too far. In Christianity it survives in nun costume, though even nuns – the last representatives of extreme covering in the Christian religion – were released in the 1960s from the necessity to mortify their flesh with such costumes (Second Vatican Council, 1965). In some forms of Christianity, such as traditional Catholicism, Plymouth Brethren and the Amish, there are still rules about women covering their bodies and heads when they enter churches, or at all times in public, and a symbolic veil exists in popular culture in the form of the wedding veil. In Islam the wearing of head coverings has taken diverse forms according to region and culture. In fundamentalist Judaism and Islam, however, the practice is being enforced once more, propelled by patriarchal vengeance against the liberation of women, and the threat this poses to men's complete power in the family over women and children. Presently the forms of covering practised in the ancient Arab Middle East are being exported to other parts of the world through the power of oil money along with fundamentalist forms of Islam (Manji, 2003; Ali, 2006; 2007). The forms that are being disseminated range from the headscarf, through the jilbab, which covers all of the body in one or more overgarments, to face coverings in the form of the niqab which covers the face leaving a slot for the eyes, and the burqa in which all of the face is covered with a net grill over the eyes. The headscarf is regularly called the 'veil' in discussions of this topic, though the term veil might more appropriately apply to face coverings. I shall use the term headscarf or hijab here for covering of the head alone for the sake of clarity. I shall refer to garments that cover the face as face-veils or burqas.

Not a religious requirement

Muslim and feminist critics of the headscarf reject the argument that it represents piety, and constitutes a religious requirement of Islam (Lazreg, 2009). They point out that covering did not take place in many areas of the Muslim world until the recent emergence of political Islam from the Middle East. An argument from tradition is not appropriate in relation to the practice of covering. As most scholars point out, covering is being adopted in many societies where it is quite new as a practice, or where it had died out and is being reintroduced. Santi Rozario points out that the burqa is being introduced to Bangladesh where, until recently, few used the burqa, though over 87 per cent of Bangladeshis consider themselves to be Muslims (Rozario, 2006). There was now, she says, 'widespread use of the burqa', and she relates this to the spread of 'Islamist' movements (Rozario, 2006, p. 368). The argument that covering is a requirement of Islam is spread through the propaganda of these fundamentalist movements and is particularly persuasive for women converts who are not attracted to moderate branches of Islam but to the teachings of fundamentalist preachers who actively proselytise. Converts have a particular reason for covering, in the fact that they may not look sufficiently Muslim if they do not, and the whole point of their conversion is to represent Islam (Droogsma, 2007). One serious problem with the idea that covering represents piety is that it renders Muslim women who have rejected covering or never felt the need for it, into inauthentic Muslims.

Feminist criticisms of the headscarf

A fierce debate has been taking place within academic feminism and between feminist activists and NGOs internationally about whether the headscarf is inevitably harmful to women, or whether, despite its problematic past as a practice of women's subordination, it can be reclaimed and serve to promote women's empowerment, choice and agency. The opponents of the headscarf who are most passionate in their rejection, are usually those who have been brought up in Muslim societies and communities in which either their mothers and grandmothers wore the veil and tried to enforce it on their recalcitrant daughters, or their mothers never wore it and brought up their daughters to consider it quite unnecessary (Amara, 2006; Lazreg, 2009). Often they are members of the Iranian diaspora and have particular reasons to feel strongly on the issue as they have observed the cruelty of the hijab's enforcement in that country (Moghissi, 1999). I shall detail the feminist criticisms here, and should acknowledge my debt to Marnia Lazreg (2009), for her very helpful and detailed exposition of the feminist arguments in her book *Questioning the Veil*.

Making a difference

CEDAW identifies practices that arise from harmful social attitudes towards women as creating stereotypes of the sexes (Jeffreys, 2005). It is rather clear that covering constructs a difference between the sexes. The covering of women marks them so that they are readily identifiable as members of the subordinate sex class in public space. The readily identifiable difference is politically necessary under a system of male domination because it is necessary to know who occupies the dominant sex class status of the male and who occupies the subordinate status of the female. In an egalitarian system, whether a person was male or female might not be so important to the vast majority of social interaction. However, it is important under male domination where 'gender' establishes a person's place in a power hierarchy. The covering of women is an extreme form of the construction of visual gender difference. The feminist movement of the 1970s sought to break down gender stereotypes so that women and men would have more freedom to wear what they wished and engage in whatever activities they wished. This was an important part of the feminist message at that time and led to the inclusion of the remark about sex 'stereotypes' in the Convention on the Elimination of All Forms of Discrimination against Women in 1979.

Gender difference in appearance, though challenged at that time, was, of course, not eliminated. It is the bulwark of the two-sex, two-gender system of male domination and could not easily be dislodged. From the 1990s onwards, gender differences in appearance reappeared with a vengeance (Jeffreys, 2005). Shoes for women with extremely high heels were promoted by fashion designers and television programmes such as *Sex and the City*, so that by the present time in the West it is expected that women seeking to look smart or dressed up will wear shoes that are extremely difficult to walk in, and may even be unable to walk at all. Women's fashions showed more and more of women's sexual characteristics, such as bum cleavage and breast cleavage, and women were expected to show large areas of their bodies so that their sex was on public view. But neither the covering or uncovering of women is generally criticised from the point of view of constructing sex difference, since this is a principle point of all patriarchal cultures, and so normalised as to be invisible as harm. Marnia Lazreg, however, criticises the establishment of sex difference by hijab. The hijab, she says, is 'comforting' for men because it reassures them that the world of male domination and women's subordination is working smoothly: women are in their place, 'There seems to be nothing like a hijab to symbolize more tangibly and palpably the putatively natural inequality between men and women' (Lazreg, 2009, p. 95). In the West such 'identity lines' are drawn clearly through the wearing of skirts, revealing clothing, long hair and high heels.

Headscarf apologists frequently use the argument that Western culture also enforces clothing rules that are harmful to women and girls, as a reason why feminists should mute their criticism of the hijab, lest they appear hypocritical (Scott, 2007). Joan Wallach Scott, for instance, is sharply critical of those who support the 2004 banning of the headscarf in schools in France. One of her main arguments is that the banners are not as critical of French culture's subordination of women as they are of Islamic practices, 'It is as if patriarchy were a uniquely Islamic phenomenon!' (Scott 2007, p. 4). The hallmark of 'liberty and equality' for the banners was, 'The visibility of the bodies of women and men, their easy accessibility to one another, the free play of seduction' (Scott, 2007, p. 168). She rejects outright the arguments of French men and women who are pro-banning, that they are moved by political reasons such as the importance of the French version of secularism – *laïcité* – or by arguments as to women's equality (Winter, 2008). She is remarkably positive about the veil: 'the veil signals the acceptance of sexuality and even its celebration, but only under proper circumstances – that is, in private, within the family' (Scott, 2007, p. 171). She accuses French feminists who had previously been critical of the harmful practices of French culture of forgetting their critique and throwing themselves hypocritically into opposition to the veil. In fact French feminists have been some of the most profound analysts of the problem of 'sexual difference' and the oppression that women experience from having to represent feminine gender upon their persons (Guillaumin, 1996).

In the West harmful beauty practices are imposed by the fashion and beauty industries, and through the media and sex industries (Jeffreys, 2005). The imposition of gender is not problematised, and most often seen as natural, but this is a different problem from the imposition of gendered practices by religion. Being disloyal to god carries a greater weight of community disapproval and punishment than being disloyal, even to very strong social norms, is likely to. Girls and women may feel afraid of divine as well as family and community retribution if they do not cover a particular part of the body. Religion is much more powerful as a force of social control and unquestionable, in a way that social custom alone is not. Nonetheless, it is important to develop the critique of harmful beauty practices in the West alongside the critique of harmful religious practices.

The necessity for women to wear the veil if they venture outside the home demonstrates women's confinement to the private sphere. Women can only enter public space on sufferance, and while obeying particular imperatives. The problematic public/private split, which has been so important to feminist legal theorists, is instantiated by veil wearing. Thus Dena Attar, a London feminist, wrote in 1992 in a piece inspired by the work of Women Against Fundamentalism, that, 'Whatever the wearer's motives . . . the message of hijab is still that a woman's presence in the world outside home must be in some way justified. Whatever the circumstances which lead to this, we cannot mistake it for feminism or liberation' (Attar, 2010, p. 73). Hijab wearing reinforces men's dominance in the public sphere, and serves to maintain women's exclusion from enjoying their citizen rights to occupy public space and engage in all those necessary activities that take place there, political engagement, work, enjoyment of nature, exercise.

The physical and psychological harms of the headscarf

Harmful cultural practices are 'harmful to the health of women and girls', and Marnia Lazreg's arguments are particularly pertinent here. She is critical of discussion of the hijab, which does not take into account the material reality of wearing it, the effect on the bodies and minds of girls and women. She writes of the devastating psychological effect of the enforcement of the hijab on girl children that she has observed. She explains that they would be 'lively, joyful', but 'as soon as they reached an age when they were made to wear a hijab, they would lose the spark in their eyes and become more self-conscious and less spontaneous' (Lazreg, 2009, p. 18). She considers that the hijab makes them aware of the 'social limitations that such change entails for them as girls' (Lazreg, 2009, p. 18), and argues that having to wear a hijab makes a girl or woman feel that her body is flawed and makes her a flawed human being. It makes a woman feel 'that her body is something to be ashamed of' (Lazreg, 2009, p. 27). Wearing the hijab, she says, requires the denial of needs of the body such as exposure to the sun and the breeze, and concealment of the body is like the ball and chain on a convict, 'a form of punishment as well as an apology for having been born female' (Lazreg, 2009, p. 27). She is particularly critical of the covering of children, pointing out that the enforcement of the hijab on pre-pubescent girls is increasingly common, saying of mothers who carry out this harmful practice, that they convey to the girl child 'that her body is an object of shame', and they cultivate in a daughter 'the denial of her body' and inculcate 'in her psyche and emotions her natural inferiority', all at an age when the girl is vulnerable and 'expects her mother to defend and protect her from harm, psychological or physical' (Lazreg, 2009, p. 29). She concludes that, 'The veil constrains the body, in one way or another, in spite of efforts made to represent it otherwise' (Lazreg, 2009, p. 31). An unrecognised psychological effect, Lazreg argues, is the fact that 'hijab makes a woman feel removed from her environment' because she wears 'a piece of cloth that covers the ears several hours a day' and this 'blunts sensory perception' (Lazreg, 2009, p. 105). The physical discomfort is augmented by the fact that the hijab is hot, Lazreg points out, and if a long dress is also worn, then this 'makes walking difficult' (Lazreg, 2009, p. 104). Lazreg states firmly that 'A woman who wears it cannot claim equality. One cannot be on both sides of the veil question' (Lazreg, 2009, p. 95). The purpose of the hijab, she says, is 'the empowerment of a man over a woman in the intimacy of their sexual identity as borne by their bodies' (Lazreg, 2009, p. 128), because for men, 'being in command is what the veil is about' (Lazreg, 2009, p. 127).

Reasons women give for wearing the hijab

Women give a variety of reasons for their adoption of the hijab. They do not usually say that they feel under pressure to wear it, as this would undermine their sense of agency. They provide positive reasons, usually those common to the literature of the fundamentalist organisations that promote the practice. Hijab wearers and advocates who argue that the hijab is a religious requirement do so on the basis that it fulfils the modesty rule that exists for women in Islam as well as in Judaism (Tarlo, 2010). This notion of modesty can be a little contradictory. According to modesty exponents, women should be modest when outside the house, and not attract the gaze of men to whom they do not belong by marriage, but in the home modesty can be cast aside, and women must fulfil the ordinary sexual corvée that women in the West are culturally required to engage in. I define 'sexual corvée', in my book *Beauty and Misogyny*, as the unpaid labour that women are required to perform to make themselves sexually exciting to men, both inside and outside the home (Jeffreys, 2005). In the world of fundamentalist Islam the sexual corvée is for the home only. In Syria, for instance, there is a marketplace dedicated to providing women with toys and garments to stimulate their husbands sexually in the bedroom (Koutsoukis, 2010). In a photo of the marketplace, women in chadors, flowing black garments with headscarves, are pictured looking at saucy underwear. The shops provide 'battery-powered knickers that fall to the floor at a clap of the hands', 'singing underwear with strategically placed vibrating lights, brassieres spun from sugar', 'garments marked with red bull's eyes that glow in the dark'. The owner of a Jordanian lingerie shop is quoted explaining that her best customers are 'mostly mothers who come in and buy for their daughters before they get married. It's accepted that this is part of what makes a happy marriage, and keeps a husband from wanting to take another wife'. It is a part of the housework the new wives will have to perform.

In Bangladesh, where the hijab is being adopted as a new practice, under the influence of Arab versions of Islam, women may have strategic reasons such as 'to persuade their families to allow them to attend university', or to repel unwanted attention from men. Many women openly admit they adopt the burqa, 'to avoid being pestered by men and boys on the campus or the streets of the city where it is located' (Rozario, 2006, p. 376). Women wear the burqa so that they may be allowed to escape seclusion and come out in public, but as Santi Rozario comments, this means that the 'onus of women's security is on women again' (Rozario, 2006, p. 376). The effect is to remove responsibility from the state for women's safety. If they are assaulted while not covered it is considered their own fault. It is an irony that some women justify their adoption of the hijab as a way to achieve freedom from men's harassment in public spaces. The hijab is, after all, a form of constraint imposed upon women by men. In a study of the motivations of American women who adopted the hijab and associated loose clothing on conversion to Islam, the younger women all stressed the importance of covering in order to avoid men's assaultive behaviour (Droogsma, 2007). As the researcher explains, 'Since they cannot control the men's behavior, they feel the need to change their own behavior in the hope of "not inviting" this unwanted attention. Unfortunately, women commonly adopt self-blame for men's poor behavior in order to regain some control over their lives' (Droogsma, 2007, p. 305). One interviewee describes the positive effects of hijab wearing thus, 'Nobody's touched me, nobody's tried to rub against my breasts or touched me, or stood extra close to me in line, you know' (Droogsma, 2007, p. 307). Rachel Droogsma is insistent that her research shows the importance of women's agency, however, hijab wearing helps them to resist many of the constraints in their lives, 'since it provides them with a greater feeling of control over their bodies and, thus, their interactions with others' (Droogsma, 2007, p. 311). In fact, the hijab is a constraint, rather than a way to resist constraints, and this understanding of the term 'agency' is unusual, meaning, as it does here, only the adoption by women of limitations on their behaviour to avoid men's abuse, accommodation rather than resistance.

Unfortunately, covering does not protect women from harassment, as research from the Egyptian Centre for Women's Rights demonstrates (Hassan, 2008). As part of a campaign to get state legislation against street harassment of women, the Centre surveyed 2,020 people: Egyptian women, foreign women residing in Egypt and Egyptian men. The myth that it is women's immodesty that causes harassment was well represented in the responses, with 62.5 per cent of Egyptian women respondents, and 65.3 per cent of the men identifying a picture of a woman wearing Western dress and a skirt as most likely to suffer harassment. In fact a considerable percentage of the women who reported sexual harassment in the survey were covered to some degree: 31.9 per cent of women wore headscarves; 21 per cent wore both headscarves and loose covering clothing; 20 per cent wore a cloak and face veil; and 6 per cent wore a burqa. As the report concludes, 'These results disprove the belief that sexual harassment is linked to the way women dress', since 72.5 per cent of the victims wore some form of covering (Hassan, 2008, p. 8). The research found that modesty requirements hampered the victims, by preventing them from reporting to the police for fear of damage to their reputations. Only 2.4 per cent of women reported the harassment they suffered.

The reasons given by the men for their harassment of women are illuminating. The male responders in the survey may require women to be covered so as not to sexually excite them, but they treat sexual harassment of women as a regular sport and source of great positive advantages, both in terms of creating sexual satisfaction and making them feel more secure in their masculine status. The vast majority of male participants stated they harassed women approximately once a day, while others stated they did so more than once a day (Hassan, 2008, p. 11). The men said that 'harassing behavior works to satisfy their repressed sexual desires', or that harassing women made them feel 'more masculine, more confident, stronger in relation to women, powerful'. Hijab wearing upholds an important principle of male dominance, as the ECWR research shows: the idea that men are entitled to target women sexually without any responsibility, the 'male right of access', while women are entirely responsible for trying to divert the men's actions, and for whatever the men choose to do. The headscarf does not just give in to this notion, but helps to create and cement it with harmful effects on women's possibility of maintaining bodily integrity. The idea that men are sexually uncontrollable and that it is women's job to protect themselves from the 'male flood' (Dworkin, 1992), has long been recognised by feminist activists and theorists of male violence against women as a most harmful foundational myth of a rape culture. This is the myth that founds the wearing of the hijab.

Cultural relativism and covering up women

Despite the evidence that anti-hijab feminist critics present to show that covering is a harmful cultural practice against women, there are feminist scholars who defend the practice, cultural relativists in particular. The anthropologist Lila Abu-Lughod, for instance, writes about the burqa in a way that studiously avoids any form of judgement. Male domination is entirely absent from her account. She explains use of the burqa in Afghanistan as 'symbolizing women's modesty or respectability' and says that the burqa, 'marked the symbolic separation of men's and women's spheres, as part of the general association of women with family and home, not with public space where strangers mingled' (Abu-Lughod, 2002, p. 785). She observes that the burqa could be seen as a 'liberating invention because it enabled women to move out of segregated living spaces while still observing the basic moral requirements of separating and protecting women from unrelated men' (Abu-Lughod, 2002, p. 785). She says that she thinks of burqas as 'mobile homes', which is a positive appellation. They are associated she says, with, 'belonging to a particular community and participating in a moral way of life in which families are paramount in the organisation of communities and the home is associated with the sanctity of women' (Abu-Lughod, 2002, p. 785). The problem with this account is the absence of any men expressing their 'agency' by enforcing the practice or gaining from it. Covering up women and their exclusion from the public sphere is unlikely to have been invented by powerful women as practices that would benefit them. The problems that she describes women as having to negotiate need explaining, and perhaps even criticising, rather than being described as if men and male domination do not exist. Her account is determinedly free from a gendered or feminist analysis. Importantly, she warns, 'we . . . need to work against the reductive interpretation of veiling as the quintessential sign of women's unfreedom, even if we object to state imposition of this form, as in Iran or with the Taliban' (Abu-Lughod, 2002, p. 786). Who 'we' are is not explained.

The British academic Sophie Gilliat-Ray, who specialises in writing about Muslim issues, shows a cheerful insouciance in respect of the hijab and the seclusion of women in her handbook on understanding Muslims in Britain (Gilliat-Ray, 2010). The harmful custom of concealing women in the house is designed 'To protect the modesty of the womenfolk within the home' and 'curtains tend to be drawn as a barrier to the external gaze' (Gilliat-Ray, 2010, p. 136). Moreover women within the home have power, she considers, so that it might not matter if they are not allowed outside, 'It is within the unsegregated, private space of homes that the power . . . of women is often most evident' (Gilliat-Ray, 2010, p. 138). The covering of women is, she says, wrongly assumed by politicians and the media to be 'most problematic for Muslim women' and obsession with the issue 'reflects a minor issue compared with the other problems that women suffer' such as 'poor-quality, overcrowded accommodation, poverty or access to equitable health care' (Gilliat-Ray, 2010, p. 220). Questions of women's imprisonment and the destruction of their rights in the public sphere are here subordinated to general concerns that affect both men and women.

Ex-Iranian feminists have been most incisive in their criticism of the cultural relativists who promote or are sanguine about the hijab. Haideh Moghissi is dismissive of the idea that 'we should see the Islamic veil as a tool of female empowerment' (Moghissi, 1999, p. 41). Such ideas, she argues, are pushed by postcolonial theorists who require 'that we see Islamic dress, so mystified and misunderstood in the West, simply as clothing that may be worn to beautify the wearer, much in the same way as Western women are free to wear make-up' (Moghissi, 1999, p. 41). Shahrzad Mojab makes similar arguments (Mojab, 1998, p. 19). Postmodern or 'difference' feminists she says, call the critics of the hijab 'Eurocentric and imperialist' and profess to see hijab wearing as 'an authentic expression of a particular culture'. In fact they essentialise the culture of the other, creating a representative Muslim woman who must perforce wear the hijab or she is not authentic.

Choice and agency

The main argument that both liberal feminist theorists and the postcolonial and cultural relativist feminists select as to why feminists should temper their critique and learn to accept covering, is that women's 'choice' and 'agency' should be respected. Lila Abu-Lughod is positive about women exercising their 'agency' in wearing the hijab even in societies where they are trained from birth in the practice. She says that covering must 'not be confused with, or made to stand for, lack of agency' because women engage in it voluntarily as a sign of respect to men (Abu-Lughod, 2002, p. 786). Among the Bedouin, she explains, women engage in 'pulling the black head cloth over the face in front of older respected men' and this

> is considered a voluntary act by women who are deeply committed to being moral and have a sense of honor tied to family. One of the ways they show their standing is by covering their faces in certain contexts. They decide for whom they feel it is appropriate to veil.
>
> (Abu-Lughod, 2002, p. 786)

Women, in this account, are in charge. They do not have to show respect to men because men are the dominant class, but because they think it 'appropriate'.

Many feminist scholars have been critical of such representations of women's 'agency', which can seem little more than obedient and submissive behaviour. Naila Kabeer argues that for 'real choice' to exist for women there must be alternatives such as 'the ability to have chosen differently' (Kabeer, 2005, p. 13). The alternatives must indeed not only exist but 'be seen to *exist*' (Kabeer, 2005, p. 14). As to the emphasis in liberal feminist theory on the idea of 'agency', she argues that agency needs to be understood as an exercise of resistance, rather than an expression of traditional submission (Kabeer, 2005). In relation to 'agency' she says, 'Subordinate groups are likely to accept, and even collude with, their lot in society, if challenging this either does not appear possible or carries heavy personal and social costs'. If agency is to represent 'empowerment', she argues, this means 'not only actively exercising choice, but also doing this in ways that challenge power relations' (Kabeer, 2006, p. 14). She emphasises that there is a distinction between 'passive' forms of agency (action taken when there is little choice), and 'active' agency (purposeful behaviour) (Kabeer, 2006, p. 15). Kabeer's concept of 'transformative' agency is very different from that which Abu-Lughod identifies in women's expression of respect for men through covering their faces. It is a feminist approach.

Marnia Lazreg is scathing about the defence of the hijab that emanates from supposedly feminist scholars 'that seeks to correct the notion that the veil is a sign of "oppression" but in reality makes oppression more intellectually acceptable' (Lazreg, 2009, p. 6). Such an approach stresses the agency of those women who adopt the hijab:

> Its proponents engage in various degrees of sophisticated rhetorical hair-splitting in order to excavate the operative agency assumed to be lurking behind the veil, subverting its use, and turning it into a tool of empowerment. The implication is that the oppressed are not so oppressed after all; they have power.
>
> (Lazreg, 2009, p. 6)

Lazreg also calls into question the individualising approach of concentration on why an individual woman covers, without recognising that this affects other women and the girl child. When one woman adopts the hijab, the pressure is increased on other women and girls, and the institution of covering is strengthened rather than weakened (Lazreg, 2009, p. 11). Even if a woman 'chooses' to wear the hijab in the West where she is not forced to do so, her action 'validates its use for women in another country who may find it difficult to argue against it' and she is complicit with the force that may be exercised elsewhere.

Forcing women to cover

Feminist scholars and activists raised in a Muslim tradition are critical of the 'agency' approach, and they document the pressures that create the 'choice' to cover (Lazreg, 2009). Haideh Moghissi points out that in countries such as Iran, where the hijab was not worn by the majority of women prior to the imposition of compulsory covering under theocratic rule, the hijab should be seen as 'an integral part of the exercise of power by a misogynist theocratic state' and 'cannot be reduced to a cultural expression' (Moghissi, 1999, p. 19). But in Western multicultural states different forms of coercion prevail. Many girls are raised in families in which they are covered up by parental authority at young ages, even sometimes when toddlers. When girls have not been raised to cover then they may be forced to do so by men in their communities. These men include brothers and fathers, and other males in Muslim communities who may exercise physical or psychological force upon them.

Marie Macey describes behaviour of this kind in the UK city of Bradford where boys and young men hang around the schoolyard gates to head off girls who are not covered and put pressure upon them (Macey, 1999). Macey explains that, in Pakistani communities in the UK, Muslim men display great concern over 'appropriate' female dress and behaviour 'because these are taken to signify not only women's honour, but that of their families and of the wider community' (Macey, 1999, p. 52). The men may apply pressure on women to cover because they fear corruption from the West and threats to traditional values, and this pressure is part of a ubiquitous violence against women in these communities. 'Violence which crosses the public–private divide is organised and structured through Pakistani male networks (termed "the mobile phone mob" by Asian women)'. The tactics that these men use include 'threatening young women's parents in anonymous telephone calls', pressuring young women to stay at home, and 'organising searches for women who have fled home' and even 'issuing death threats to gays and lesbians;

and circulating leaflets exhorting Muslim men to rape Sikh women and murder homosexuals' (Macey, 1999, p. 49). The young men engage in these behaviours for the benefits that they acquire from them. In Bradford, Macey points out, they 'have constructed a form of Islamic identity which affords them peer-group status, community approval, *and* control over women' (Macey, 1999, p. 52).

Fadela Amara, a practising Muslim from a family in which the women did not cover, describes similar pressures that are causing girls in French cities to wear the hijab (Amara, 2006). She explains that she held a meeting for women and girls in 2002 to hear what women from the neighbourhoods were experiencing. The meeting had to be women only or the women would not have been able to attend. The girls related the forms of violence and constraint that they lived under.

> They talked about how they would dress in huge sweaters in order to cross the projects and then take them off when they reached school; the detours they would take to avoid the gangs of boys on their path; the difficulty of going out alone and the obligation to travel with groups of other young women for fear of attacks; their general confinement and the limitations on their going out; their limited access to sports and cultural activities; the tensions and aggression in their relations with boys; the impossibility of happy love relationships.
>
> (Amara, 2006, p. 111)

She is clear that the headscarf is a 'symbol of women's oppression' (Amara, 2006, p. 98). It is not 'simply a religious matter' she says, but a 'means of oppression, of alienation, of discrimination, an instrument of power over women used by men – men do not wear headscarves' (Amara, 2006, p. 100). In Leeds, UK, in 2010, an example of the coercion that women experience ended up before an industrial tribunal (Daily Mail Reporter, 2010). Ghazala Khan was sacked, two weeks into her employment, from an estate agency run by a traditional Muslim man, for refusing to wear a headscarf. Non-Muslim women workers were not required to cover, but a male employee found it intolerable that a woman from a Muslim background did not do so, and caused the agency owner to act. She was awarded £13,500 in compensation. This woman did exercise 'agency' in its more usual feminist understanding, as resistance rather than as capitulation.

Emma Tarlo, in her study of fashion and covering practices in the UK (2010), explains the pressures that can exist upon Muslim women to adopt a headscarf in London. In the Stamford Hill area of North East London, she says, a majority of Muslim women have worn jilbab or niqab in recent years, and this can create pressure upon Muslim women who do not cover. One 'religiously practicing [sic]' woman she talked to had recently moved from New Delhi where she did not wear the hijab and rejected it because she 'did not want to encourage the idea that women are the root cause of sin and must cover to protect men' (Tarlo, 2010, p. 51). But she came under pressure from her six-year-old son: 'He saw his mother dressed differently from the other Muslim mothers in the area and wanted her to conform to type' (Tarlo, 2010, p. 51). Marnia Lazreg, too, points out that sons play an important role: 'Muslim mothers are often under pressure from their sons to wear a veil' (Lazreg, 2009, p. 35). Also there was harassment of the Stamford Hill woman from men in the community, so that 'not to wear hijab in such a space was to make herself conspicuous and to attract unwanted attention and disrespectful comments from local Muslim men who perceived the absence of hijab as a sign of dubious sexual activity' (Tarlo, 2010, p. 51). Tarlo explains that the more Muslim women cover up, the more other women who have no desire to cover feel pressured to do so (Tarlo, 2010, p. 12). The reluctant women feel marginalised and are criticised or called 'name only Muslims' which impugns their piety. The women most likely to feel pressured are those who are actively religious but had not, previously, considered covering to be a religious obligation.

The political movement behind covering up women

Commentators who stress the agency of adopting the headscarf neglect to concern themselves with the forms of force, from family and community, which underlie women's 'choice' to cover. They omit another very significant detail: the fact that the hijab is promoted by an influential politico-religious movement of fundamentalist Islam, which pours forth propaganda via the mosque and the Internet. As some feminist activists have argued, the hijab operates for this movement as national flags once did for colonising states as they took over territory. In this case women's bodies are the territory, and the fundamentalist patriarchs can look at city streets, at lecture theatres and at schools to see how far they have penetrated with their ideology. An Iraqi participant in the AWID report on the challenge of increasingly powerful fundamentalisms to women's rights, described the phenomenon succinctly:

> To prove that you have politically dominated other groups, you either raise your flag on top of your building or even better the flag is the black cloth that women are wearing and they are walking all over the streets of that city . . . If every single woman of that neighbourhood is totally veiled, you have both social and political flags and you have proven that you have dominated.
>
> (AWID, 2009, p. 13)

The fundamentalist movement is masculinist and the propaganda comes from men. In such a context it is perverse to focus on the agency of women. Marnia Lazreg says that in her book she 'addresses' the hijab 'as an essential part of a trend that is largely *organized* and thus detrimental to women's advancement' (Lazreg, 2009, p. 3). She argues that as long as states either mandate or prohibit the headscarf, as long as political movements advocate for it, as long as 'organized networks with books, lectures, DVDs and course packets promote it far and wide, a woman can never be sure that she takes up a veil freely, in full awareness of its meanings and effects' (Lazreg, 2009, p. 130). Unfortunately, there has been considerable sympathy with the fundamentalist enforcement of the headscarf by persons who consider themselves liberal and left-leaning in the West, which can make it much harder for Muslim and ex-Muslim critics to speak out. The left-wing embrace of the headscarf as representing women's 'choice', can lead to some dilemmas for hijab apologists, however. Left liberals were represented at a 2004 conference organised in London by the Assembly for the Protection of Hijab (otherwise known as Pro-Hijab), which is a London-based international network and lobbying group that formed in response to the 2004 French ban on the wearing of headscarves by schoolgirls. As Emma Tarlo reports, the conference title was, 'Hijab: A woman's right to choose'. She explains that the conference was attended by a mix of hijab-wearing Muslim women and 'activists from Europe, Turkey and Tunisia, Muslim academics, legal specialists, human rights activists, left-wing politicians, a Catholic priest, a Sikh dignitary and a German feminist' (Tarlo, 2010, p. 44).

The good feelings of progressive, anti-racist camaraderie were rather spoiled by the fact that the guest of honour was a well-known Muslim cleric from Qatar, Sheikh Yusuf al-Qaradawi, who has explicitly negative views on homosexuality. There was a lesbian and gay picket outside the conference to protest, so that good liberals had to choose between solidarity with the hijab or with gay rights. Tarlo comments that the 'Audience determined to defend the wearing of the veil as a "human right"' (Tarlo, 2010, p. 44). Qaradawi also has other problematic views, telling a *Guardian* journalist that 'the notorious verse in the Qur'an which allows for the "beating" of wives by their husband' should be accepted, 'as a method of last resort – though only "lightly"' (Bunting, 2005). The support that exists on the Left for this fundamentalist Sheikh is puzzling. His invitation to London was issued by its Mayor, Ken Livingstone, known as Red Ken and seen as a hero in some sections of the Left. Livingstone described him as a 'progressive' (McKistry, 2005).

Tarlo describes another protest against the French ban in 2004 in London, where women's 'choice' was explicitly denied, rather than being waved about as a way to galvanise the support of liberal-minded persons. This was organised by the fundamentalist grouping Hizb ut-Tahrir (HT). This organisation is banned in several countries and has gained considerable notoriety in many others. In Western countries it focuses on recruitment on university campuses. Tarlo explains that HT assumes different names in order to retain access to university sites where it has been banned. Worldwide it is considered to have several million members. The event consisted of a day seminar on hijab, where there were banners carrying slogans such as 'Secularism dishonours women' and 'Hijab ban symbolizes war on Islam' (Tarlo, 2010, p. 111), and women chanted 'Do we want liberty? NO!' Freedom, democracy and personal choice were defined as '"Western concepts" which had no place in Islam' (Tarlo, 2010, p. 114). Organisers said that it was 'obligatory for women to wear jilbab and to cover hair, neck and bosom with hijab' (Tarlo, 2010, p. 115). They should also wear plain, thick material in dark or muted colours since they were meant to cover their beauty and conceal the female body. There was no room for arguments as to choice in relation to hijab because it was promoted as an 'obligation commanded by Allah' (Tarlo, 2010, p. 119). The political and religious propaganda in favour of this harmful cultural practice can be expressed with various degrees of aggression towards women, but the complicity of left-leaning progressives in supporting or tolerating it can provide yet another obstacle to women's ability to resist the coercion.

Escalation of the struggle

The forces of political Islam that promote the hijab have escalated their campaign in the last decade. Instead of simply demanding that girls and women wear the hijab and that this should be accepted in schools and workplaces, they have moved on, first to the jilbab, a form of covering that incorporates the hijab but also swathes the wearer head to toe in voluminous black robes with the face left uncovered, and then to the full face veil in the form of the niqab, which has a slit for the eyes, or the burqa, which has a veil over the eyes. Fundamentalist groups select stages for their confrontations with state authorities over covering up women by sending girl children or women so attired into schools, workplaces and courtrooms. In the UK the first confrontation took place when HT deployed a schoolgirl who sought to wear the jilbab in the classroom (Sandberg, 2009). In the UK, unlike France, girls are permitted to wear the hijab so long as this fits in with their school uniform in colour and design. Shabina Begum, 13 years old, went to school in Luton in September 2002 in the jilbab. She was accompanied by her brother and another man who told the assistant head teacher that she must be allowed to wear the jilbab because 'this was the only garment that met her religious requirements'. Shabina's brother talked of human rights and threatened legal proceedings if the school failed to grant those rights (Tarlo, 2010, p. 104). The assistant head teacher said he felt threatened by the attitude and approach of these emissaries of political Islam. Nonetheless, he told the girl to go home and change her clothes. Girls at the school were permitted to wear headscarves, trousers and longish skirts or shalwar kamiz (calf-length tunic and trousers), a uniform designed in 1993 after consultation with parents, students, staff and the imams of three mosques.

Shabina was kept at home for two years and denied an education by her male relatives while her case went to the High Court on the grounds that it was the school that had denied her an education, and denied her the right to express her religious beliefs. The school argued that the agreed uniform was Islamically acceptable, that the jilbab threatened health and safety, and that pupils needed protection from minority interpretations of Islam held by extremist groups active in the area that would put pressure on other pupils. The girl's case was not successful, but was then taken to the Court of Appeal where she was represented by Cherie Booth, wife of the then Prime Minister, Tony

Blair. It was successful at this stage on the grounds of the human right
to express religious belief. This victory was, according to Emma Tarlo's
account, welcomed by 'left journalists' and many human rights activists
as a victory for human rights, diversity and tolerance. The school took
the case to the House of Lords where the decision was reversed in March
2006 on the grounds that the shalwar kamiz uniform conformed
adequately to the requirements of Islam. Tarlo comments that this was
a case of 'a radical politico-religious agenda finding a vehicle for public
expression and a media only too hunger to lap it up' (Tarlo, 2010,
p. 110). She points out that HT advised Begum throughout. She also
provides another fascinating detail as further evidence of those who
considered themselves progressive giving support to this fundamentalist campaign. This is the fact that the *Guardian*'s front-page article
on the Court of Appeal victory was written by a member of HT, who
had recently joined the paper as a trainee journalist on a 'diversity programme'. The journalist later wrote a 'provocative' piece on the 2005
London underground bombings and was dismissed.

The involvement of HT was well recognised within the Muslim
community at the time. Ayesha Kariapper, in a report on covering in
the UK, written for the feminist NGO, Women Living Under Muslim
Laws, argues that this involvement 'helps draw links between a seemingly
individual case, which has polarized the UK national scene, and its
connections with political Islam, locally as well as abroad' (Kariapper,
2009, p. 61). The Muslim politician and Labour MP for Birmingham,
Khalid Mahmood, says, 'She . . . has been used as a political football
by HT. They have been working on this girl. They want an Islamic
revolution and they will try to disrupt anybody they can' (Kariapper,
2009, p. 61). Kariapper points out that HT 'aims to re-establish the
Islamic Caliphate as an independent state to unify the Muslim world'.
In August 2005 Tony Blair announced plans to ban HT but did not
follow through with this.

Begum's case is but one of several taken against schools in the UK
in the last five years. There has been an escalation in the level of covering
at the centre of the confrontations, which now involve not just the jilbab
but also the full-face veil. A teaching assistant was involved in one
confrontation in a junior school in Dewsbury in 2006. Aisha Azmi
attended a job interview wearing only a headscarf. She asked to wear a
niqab when she started work and this was agreed, but her confrontation
with the school authorities swiftly escalated beyond their ability to

continue compromising. She was asked to remove her face veil in the classroom because it made communication with the children difficult. The school argued that 'the children needed to be able to visually see the movement of Azmi's lips in order to learn the proper pronunciation of words' (Kariapper, 2009, p. 64). She said she would only remove the face veil if there were no male members of staff present; this was considered unacceptable by Kirklees Council, which suspended her. A tribunal upheld the school's decision. In Azmi's case again there appeared to be political Islamic forces backing her, as her father was the headmaster of the Islamic seminary attached to the Dewsbury mosque.

The decision in the Azmi case was welcomed by sections of the moderate Muslim community. Indeed, in 2007, one Muslim organisation offered to fund a school that was targeted by a 'covering' challenge. The Muslim Education Centre of Oxford (MECO) calls niqabs 'primitive, un-Islamic full face-masks' (Kariapper, 2009, p. 66). MECO is campaigning for the formal banning of the niqab from British schools and stated in a press release:

> The *niqab*, as all Muslims should know, is a cultural, class-based, pre-Islamic custom and is a un-Qur'anic innovation. Unfortunately, this non-Qur'anic garment is witnessing a contemporary resurgence due to the potency of Saudi petro-dollars, which is influencing fanatical *Wahhabi* theology and its Indo-Pakistani variants here and abroad . . . there is no scriptural authority at all for this chauvinistic perspective.
>
> (Kariapper, 2009, p. 66)

Ayesha Kariapper is firm about the way in which political Islam is orchestrating these covering cases, which purport to be about the rights of individual, self-directed women and girls. She says of the girls and women involved, 'there have always been Muslim male backers', and she draws attention to the fact that it is not women, such as mothers or sisters, who form the support teams for these challenges but only male relatives (Kariapper, 2009, p. 67).

As the covering of women as a political practice becomes more common, there are an increasing number of controversies and legal challenges around examples of its use. A new point of confrontation is the issue of the face veil in the courtroom. In Ontario, Canada, for instance, the issue has arisen of whether women should be permitted to give evidence in a courtroom, while wearing the face veil (Canadian Press, 2010). The Court of Appeal in Ontario is considering the case of a niqab-wearing woman who has to give evidence to support her report to police that her cousin and uncle repeatedly sexually abused her between six and ten years of age. The argument against the face veil is that it interferes with the justice process, both by preventing ordinary methods of telling whether someone is speaking the truth, through examining facial expression, and by making it harder for the female witness to make her case, through muffling her voice, for instance. The woman's right to wear the face veil, however, is defended by supposedly progressive organisations such as the Women's Legal Education and Action Fund and the Canadian Civil Liberties Association. The prohibition on her wearing the face veil, on the other hand, is supported by the Muslim Canadian Congress, which considers the veil a symbol of the oppression of women. In this way a 'moderate' Muslim organisation is ranged against an ostensibly 'feminist' group on the issue. Feminist support for the wearing of face veils can be blinkered in relation to the pressure on women to wear them. In legal theorist Natasha Bakht's discussion of the issue of face veils in courtrooms, she canvasses various reasons that women might wish to wear such veils, but does not mention force or reluctance. She castigates those who might find face veils inappropriate: 'Opposition to the *niqab* is usually a knee-jerk response to difference that is typically not grounded in any rational understanding of the actual circumstances at issue' (Bakht, 2009, p. 115).

In Perth, Western Australia, a similar challenge, the first of its kind in the country, was resolved in August, 2010 (Weber, 2010). A woman named Tasnim, who had been in Australia for seven years and wore the niqab at her citizenship ceremony, wished to wear the niqab that she had worn all her adult life when giving evidence as a witness. The case concerned the fraud trial of a head teacher of an Islamic school, who was charged with exaggerating the number of girl pupils in his school to get extra state funding. The defence lawyers argued that jury members needed to be able to see her face in order to properly assess her evidence. The Judge, Shauna Deane, ruled that Tasnim should give evidence without her face veil so that the jury could assess her demeanour. The judge said that her decision was not binding on any other courts. The intensely political nature of this confrontation is indicated by the claim from the defendant that he had received death threats and been physically attacked, suffering minor injuries, because he was seen as complicit in challenging Tasnim's right to wear the full face veil (ABC News, 2010). Those who defend the right of witnesses to wear face veils argue that the idea that judgement of 'demeanour' is reliable or useful in courts is contradicted by research, and no longer relevant (Bakht, 2009). In other jurisdictions such as New Zealand and the UK, judges have come to a variety of conclusions, with some seeking to get around the problem by getting women to give evidence without face veils, but behind screens, so that they are only visible to certain parties in the courtroom. There have been challenges to, and accommodations of, lawyers, jury members and witnesses who have appeared in court in face veils. So far there has been no case involving a judge in a face veil in the West, but women judges in Pakistan have worn them (Bakht, 2009).

In the UK in 2007 the Judicial Studies Board's Equal Treatment Advisory Committee gave its judgement on the issue of face veils in court (Mailonline, 2007). It ruled that wearing of the face veil in court should be decided on a case-by-case basis, but that Muslim women should be permitted to wear the garment providing it did not interfere with the administration of justice. Arguments as to the importance of allowing women to retain their face veils in courtrooms are based on the idea that the woman needs to wear a face veil for religious reasons, and that she would suffer serious distress and discomfort if required to remove it. But the practice of Islam does not require full face veils, and a woman's desire to wear one should perhaps be regarded in the same way as any other witness who wants to conceal their identity.

The further seclusion of women

The intrusion of political Islam in multicultural societies is creating an escalation in the seclusion of women. The requirement that women cover is now being extended to other practices that create sex segregation in public space, such as those that require women to have no physical contact with unrelated men. One point of confrontation centres on the handshake between women and men. In 2010 a woman translator engaged by the Australian embassy in Saudi Arabia refused to shake the hand of her employer, the male Australian ambassador (Zwartz, 2010). In this case the newly hired translator complained to the Australian Prime Minister and Foreign Minister that the ambassador tried to force her to shake hands, showed her disrespect, and needed cultural sensitivity training. But increased physical segregation is being mandated by fatwa websites for interaction with all non-related men in a range of contexts. Similar confrontations around handshaking are recorded on Islamonline as having taken place in the Netherlands (Islamonline, 2006). A female student who wished to train to be a teaching assistant refused to shake hands at the education centre, saying that Islam forbade physical contact with men above the age of twelve. Also an imam 'refused to shake hands with immigration Minister Rita Verdonk at a public event' (Islamonline, 2006). In January 2011, the Islamic fundamentalist group al-Shabab, which controls a district in Somalia, banned mixed sex handshakes (BBC, 2011). In the pronouncement, unrelated men and women were also banned from walking or talking together.

Islamonline, which is run from Qatar and Egypt and was founded by Sheik al-Qaradawi, the homophobic speaker mentioned above, whose presence as a speaker at an anti-hijab ban event provoked a picket, offers advice on this issue. It offers fatwas to petitioners who are mostly from the Arab world but include some from Germany and the UK. The fatwa section illustrates this trend towards increased segregation in response to a question about 'mixing between men and women' where 'many say that it is *haram* (unlawful) while others give a loose rein to themselves in this regard' (Islamonline, 2005a). The fatwa, by al-Qaradawi, kindly explains that, 'In principle, contacts between men and women are not totally rejected' and can be countenanced for good purposes such as education and charitable works. But there should be no 'transgressing the limits and forgetting about the nature of both sexes'. There are some explicit details about how men and women forced to be in each other's company should comport themselves. They should 'adhere to lowering the gaze. No lustful look should exist', and, 'General morality should be adhered to. In other words, a woman should be serious in speech and decent in way of walking, nipping any trial of Satan to spread immorality in the bud'. Most importantly, man/woman 'contacts . . . are not to be given loose rein'. Another petitioner asks, 'Many Muslim husbands order their wives not to speak to visitors or with any non-*mahram* man, while the husband addresses any woman. What is the ruling on this matter?' (Islamonline, 2005b). The fatwa in response states once again that Islam does not forbid women from talking to men or vice versa, but all Muslims, men and women, 'must observe *haya*' (shyness or modesty) in all their correspondence and conversations', but 'This shyness is a beautiful manner for both men and women, but more so for women, because it agrees with their feminine nature, which is why women do not initiate a conversation with strange men'. Women should, it is clear, only speak when they are spoken to. Men and women may greet each other, it continues, but not freely.

Banning the burqa?

One response to this escalation of confrontation in multicultural states has been to ban the burqa. The Belgian government banned face coverings in public spaces in April 2010 (BBC, 2010c). In July 2010 the French parliament voted for a ban on face veils in public by 335 to 1, with the centre left abstaining (Lichfield, 2010). The Spanish Senate voted in favour of a burqa ban in the same month (Minder, 2010). The British immigration minister ruled out a burqa ban for the UK (Stratton, 2010). Also, in 2010, Syria's Education Ministry announced a ban on face veils in all the country's public and private universities (Amos, 2010). The prohibition of face veils in public entails the administration of small fines to women who wear them as well as large fines for men who force their partners to cover. But the imposition of fines on men is unlikely to take place, since the women wearers are most unlikely to report their husbands. Such a course of action could cause them to be expelled from their marriages and communities, and may lead to violence against them. The moves by right-wing governments and opposition parties to seek burqa bans relates to the popularity of such bans with the public. Opinion polls suggest large majorities for banning the face veil, even in the UK where such a ban has been ruled out. The ban seems to be seen as a good way to bid for electoral support, particularly by right wing parties. The governments who are introducing measures to ban the face veil in 2010 are not doing so at the behest of feminist groups. They are right-wing governments, which are seeking to gain electoral advantage with a populist policy. From a feminist perspective, punishing women for wearing burqas is very problematic. They are the victims of misogynist fundamentalism, not those who organise and benefit from it.

Conclusion

This chapter has argued that the covering of women is incontrovertibly oppressive. It disenfranchises women of their right to enter public space on their own terms; it inculcates and represents harmful ideas about the necessity for women's modesty and women's responsibility for the control of men's biological urge to rape women; it interferes with women's physical and mental health; and it constitutes a form of political empire building on the part of fundamentalist movements, which endangers women's rights on many issues. The hijab is used as a wedge to get extreme Islamism into schools, into public places and onto many agendas. Alongside the demonstration of conquered territory, the covering of women serves fundamentalist Muslim organisations as a way of constantly escalating their challenges to more moderate Muslim or non-Muslim governments and institutions. Whereas once the headscarf was sufficient for the purpose of creating confrontation with governments in the West, the demand for covering is now being extended to include face veils. The fundamentalist patriarchs are in battle with Western patriarchs and moderate Muslims, using the bodies of women in their warfare. At issue is women's free access to the public world, streetscapes, public buildings, schools and courtrooms. The next chapter concerns another harmful cultural practice against women and girls that is justified by religion: polygamy. This practice, too, is in the news because of legal challenges, in this case by Mormon patriarchs in Canada, who seek to continue subordinating women through polygamy without fear of state interference.

7

A HAREM FOR EVERY MAN?

The rise of polygamy

Feminist legal theorists argue that the practice of polygamy contradicts a range of women's human rights, including the right to equality in marriage and the family, the right to health and economic rights (Cook, 2006). Nonetheless there are calls to legalise this harmful cultural practice in many different contexts presently, in the name of religion. While polygamy is legal in some majority Muslim states, it is generally prohibited elsewhere. One call for legalisation comes from a number of religious leaders in Muslim majority countries where polygamy is not presently legal, such as Uzbekistan and other succession states to the USSR (Pogrebov, 2006). Another is from minority groups within Muslim communities in countries such as Australia and the UK where polygamy is taking place unofficially, and some imams are calling for it to be officially recognised. There are Christian and Mormon forms of polygamy being increasingly practised too in the USA and Canada, and some fundamentalist Jewish patriarchs are promoting the practice of 'pilegesh' or concubinage. What is common to these different contexts is that religion is being used to justify the practice. The only exception to this is the case of publicly Christian Africa, where there is a revived acceptance of polygamy in some circles. In South Africa this is supported by the constitutional guarantee that pre-Christian polygamy should be protected. In that country, where the justification for the practice is from culture rather than religion, President Jacob Zuma is an open polygamist. Surprisingly, in the last decade, some legal and political theorists in Canada and the US have supported the calls of the patriarchs who are involved in the practice, for decriminalisation or legalisation. In this chapter I shall analyse the increasing frequency of the practice, its implications for women's human rights, and subject the arguments being used for legalisation to a critical feminist analysis. I shall argue that states should, rather than legalise the practice, move to further prohibit polygamy in the name of women's human rights.

Polygamy is a gendered practice, which originates in classical patriarchy and might more accurately be identified as polygyny, that is one man, several wives. Calls to legalise polygamy actually mean the legalisation of polygyny, a cultural practice that harms women and girls. There is no parallel practice available to women that might offer them equality. Nowhere is polyandry, that is, the taking of several husbands, practised in a similar fashion to polygyny. There are no examples, for instance, of women who marry young virgin boys who are chosen for them by their families, and then proceed to take extra 'husbands' as the first one ages and loses his attractiveness.

Marriage and women's human rights

Polygamy and other forms of marriage that harm women and girls should be understood as constituting servile marriage, which violates women's equality rights. Marriage and divorce are issues at the very heart of religious concerns. Marriage has traditionally created the power of an individual man, the paterfamilias, over a personal fiefdom of women, children and slaves. Male ruling elites have established the loyalty of those they govern, Carole Pateman argues, by extending to them the right to rule over women through the institution of marriage, as a compensation for their compliance (Pateman, 1988). Though there has been considerable progress towards a more egalitarian view of marriage in recent decades in the West, with women gaining the right to divorce, rights to shares of the family wealth and income, and the right to control their own bodies with the abrogating of the husband's right of sexual access, the institution originated in classical patriarchy where women's status was little different from that of slaves (Jeffreys, 2009). In most of the world, and for most of the world's women, laws on marriage, divorce and the custody of children are still grossly unequal, and in contradiction to women's equality.

Polygamy needs to be understood as more than a harmful cultural practice because it violates significant and well-recognised rights. Equality of women in marriage has been understood as the fundamental human right necessary to women. Article 23 (4) of the ICCPR, for instance, requires States Parties to 'take appropriate steps to ensure equality of rights and responsibilities of spouses as to marriage, during marriage and at its dissolution'. As feminist legal theorist Rebecca Cook points out, the term 'ensure' is usually interpreted as imposing a 'positive duty on States to achieve the stated goal' (Cook, 2006, Introduction, p. 4). Article 16 of CEDAW calls on States Parties to 'take all appropriate measures to eliminate discrimination against women in all matters relating to marriage and family relations' in order to ensure 'a basis of equality of men and women'. In a General Comment, the Human Rights Council, the body that oversees the ICCPR, states that 'Polygamy violates the dignity of women. It is an inadmissible discrimination against women' and 'should be definitely abolished wherever it continues to exist' (Cook, 2009, Introduction, p. 4). Cook explains that there is a growing consensus that polygamy is a practice of discrimination against women, but there is disagreement about the best 'transitional' measures to take to protect women and children who are already involved in the practice.

Multiculturalism and harmful marriage practices

Polygamy has become a problem for public policy in Western multicultural societies in the last decade and has attracted media and research attention. Polygamy is one of a range of harmful marriage practices, which, in their traditional and most brutally patriarchal form, are now embedded in Western societies (Warraich and Balkin, 2006). Male leaders of cultural minorities are starting to defend and promote these practices with a confidence derived from the tendency of governments of multicultural states to show respect for religious and cultural 'rights'. Recognition of these more harmful marriage practices by the state, from cultural or religious relativist impulses, results in the creation of a two-tier system of women's rights within these Western democracies. Women from the cultural majority have the rights enshrined in UN conventions, whereas women delivered to the rule of patriarchs in bargains made between male-dominated governments and community leaders, suffer severe disadvantage and do not have access to the same rights. Practices of 'servile' marriage, which I understand as marriages in which women have no choice as to marriage partner or are under pressure to acquiesce to the demands of family and are then subject to male authority, over contraception and abortion, over decision making, over modesty and honour rules, and over their bodies sexually, are increasingly evident in the West. They are created through arranged/forced marriages, through child marriage (under the age of eighteen) and through polygamy.

Though some feminist commentators have tended to defend the practice of 'arranged' marriage through recourse to cultural relativist arguments (Phillips and Dustin, 2004), there is an increasing volume of concern from feminist activists and theorists (Macey, 2009). Those seeking toleration of 'arranged' marriages seek to separate them from those that are clearly 'forced', but it is becoming clear that the distinction can be moot. It is hard to make distinctions when emotional pressure from families and communities, such as threats of ostracism, or coercion through threats of the emotional harms that parents will suffer, are understood as forms of force. There are strong pressures, often, upon the parents and not just the daughters. The parents who fail to force their daughters to enter marriages that they have arranged for them can suffer serious reprisals. In 2010 a UK couple who visited Pakistan in order to explain why their daughter would not go ahead with an arranged marriage were murdered on arrival in what was called an 'honour crime' (BBC News Birmingham, 2010).

Concern over 'forced' marriages has been created in countries such as the UK by evidence that these can lead to serious violence and death in the form of the euphemistically termed 'honour' killings (Welchman and Hossain, 2005). 'Honour' killings of young women who acquired boyfriends or sought to avoid 'arranged' marriages, led the UK government to set up a Forced Marriage Unit at the Home Office to assist the repatriation of young women trafficked overseas for marriage (Phillips and Dustin, 2004). The work of organisations such as Karma Nirvana and the books written by its founder Jasvinder Sanghera, who escaped a forced marriage, have shown the prevalence and serious harms of forced marriage and argued that it should be criminalised (Sanghera, 2007; Sanghera, 2009). Sanghera considers that the inadequate response to the problem of forced marriage in the UK is caused by concern about appearing to be racist. She reports that police officers tell her they often know that a girl is being forced but feel unable to act because of fears they will be accused of racism. Meanwhile, as she points out, the psychological harm that girls and women face from the practice is demonstrated by the fact that Asian women commit suicide at three times the average of women 'from other ethnicities' (Sanghera, 2009, p. 67), and by the disproportionate rates of self-mutilation among these women and girls (Bhardwaj, 2001).

The UK government, however, decided not to criminalise the perpetrators and brokers of forced marriage on cultural relativist grounds and the concern that this would drive the practice underground (Macey, 2009). Marie Macey explains that when the UK's Forced Marriage Unit conducted a consultation on whether this practice should be criminalised, there were few participants, and those in favour of criminalisation tended to be Children's and Young People's Services and those who had experienced forced marriage, whereas those against included all the Crown Prosecution and Probation Service respondents (Macey, 2009, p. 73). Those with the closest experience of the harms of the practice were most likely to call for it to be legally prohibited. Macey considers that it is the multiculturalist ideology of cultural relativism that has paralysed the policymakers. Polygamy is one form of servile marriage into which girls are being 'forced', or suffering the problem of having their sexual/emotional/reproductive/economic futures 'arranged' for them.

Polygamy in multicultural societies

Polygamy is able to be practised within countries such as the UK and Australia despite laws against it, such as bigamy laws, because these only apply to marriages that are recognised and civilly registered with the state. They do not apply to marriages performed under religious laws alone. Thus Muslim men, Mormons or Christian Patriarchs can acquire multiple wives in the ceremonies of their cults without attracting punishment. This is the way that polygamy is developing as a practice in the UK. Women Living Under Muslim Laws (WLUML) has published a most informative research report on the problem that shows how 'informal' marriages harm the rights of women and girls in the UK (Warraich and Balchin, 2006). When marriages are not civilly recognised, WLUML explains, they are called 'limping marriages', because the girls and women involved have no rights. They cannot obtain civil divorces, because they were never officially married in the first place, and have no rights to maintenance and inheritance. WULML has called for the registration of mosques and other places of worship as places in which marriage can be officially solemnised so that women cannot be victimised by unrecognised unions. The lack of registration of marriages is a boon to the practice of polygamy. The government recognises polygamous marriages that have taken place in other jurisdictions in which such marriages are legal, though it will not allow men to import more than one wife to the UK under immigration laws (Reid, 2009). The Home Office estimates that there are fewer than 1,000 recognised polygamous marriages in the UK. But the government acknowledges that it has no way to estimate the number of polygamous marriages that are performed under customary and religious law and not recognised. These are likely to be much more numerous. Men can get around the prohibitions in immigration law on importing more than one wife, by engaging in sham divorces in which wife number one is divorced but continues to live with her husband, who can then import another wife. This process can go on to encompass an official wife, and several 'ex' wives living under one roof. Also men can circumvent the law by importing extra wives on tourist or other visas, but not wife visas, and subsequently cohabiting with them (Reid, 2009).

The most usual practice, however, is likely to be that in which men simply marry the extra wives under customary or religious law. In some cases they will tell wife number one that they will officially register the marriage and then deliberately fail to do so, since this gives them more power in the relationship and makes the girl or woman completely dependent, especially where she accepts the dictates of fatwa sites that say a woman cannot divorce her husband without special permission, whereas he can divorce her by *talaq*, that is saying the words 'I divorce you' three times (Reid, 2009). This creates serious problems for the young women. Not only do they suffer the harms associated with both arranged/forced marriages and polygamy in general, but they cannot secure divorces (since they are not officially married), cannot remarry and suffer social and financial penalties. In some cases a man may acquire several 'wives' through customary and religious law and be officially married to none of them. It is likely that similar practices are implicated in the growth of the practice in Australia and in Muslim minorities in other multicultural states (National Times, 2008). Similar problems with polygamy exist among migrants to France from North Africa, such as those from Mali. The French government counts the first wife to enter as the only legal wife, and this 'creates obvious tensions within families and especially among women, forcing many of them to live in the shadows, subordinated to co-wives, who are in fact their juniors, or even evicted from their homes to protect the legal status of their husband and "first" wife' (Sargent and Larchanche-Kim, 2006, p. 21). As a result, secondary wives live with the fear of becoming homeless and without an income. Where several wives live together in state housing, this is likely to be extremely overcrowded and create problems with jealousy and violence.

Harmful effects of polygamy on women

The harms of polygamy differ as to context, but reports from all forms of the practice, across both multicultural states and states where polygamy is a traditional practice, demonstrate severe harms to women and children. Rebecca Cook argues that the harms of polygamy are: that it constitutes a form of patriarchy; that it harms the exclusive relationship that women can expect in marriage; that harms arise from competitive relationships with co-wives; that it harms mental health; that it harms sexual and reproductive health; that it harms women economically; that it harms women's citizenship; and that it harms the children of polygamous unions (Cook, 2006).

Mormon polygamy

The harmful effects of polygamy are plentifully evidenced in the stories of women who have escaped the practice in the Fundamentalist Church of Jesus Christ of the Latter Day Saints (FLDS) in the US and Canada (Moore-Emmett, 2004; Jessup and Palmer, 2007). These women describe a common array of harms to the equality of women and girls. Emily Duncan, in an article about Mormon polygamy in the US, which calls for legalisation, nonetheless states that these women have, 'no sexual autonomy; are exposed to sexual, physical, and verbal abuse; have limited access to education and other opportunities; are unable to gain or maintain financial independence; and all too often live in poverty' (Duncan, 2008, p. 326). Their marriage as young teenagers to strangers usually considerably older than themselves, who already have several wives, is evidence of polygamy as a form of patriarchy in practice. Harms to psychological health are reported such as the struggles over jealousy among the wives as they compete for recognition from their patriarch husband. Other harms to physical and mental health result from violence from husbands and other wives, and from incest, both father/daughter, and older brother/younger sister being rampant. There is evidence of considerable violence to wives and between wives, and to children. Women and children risk being 'reassigned', as they are the property of the church, if they displease the patriarchs. Male disciples who disobey can find that their wives and children are reassigned to another patriarch. Harms to sexual and reproductive health result from the fact that they are denied access to contraception and forced to bear very large numbers of children and are unable to deny sexual access. Harms to the children of polygamous unions are clear in the treatment of boys in fundamentalist Mormon communities. The majority of male children are likely to suffer the trauma of ejection and abandonment. These, called the 'lost boys', have to be forced out in order to enable polygamy to continue, otherwise there would not be enough girls to go around. These boys often end up on the streets or in low paid work if they are lucky, as they have little education or skills and no support network (Moore-Emmett, 2004).

The harm that Emily Duncan identifies as most serious is that of child marriage. The forced or 'assigned' marriages of girls from as young as fourteen years old in Mormon communities, constitute child rape on a mass scale. In an exemplary case against the FLDS leader Warren Jeffs, a fifteen-year-old girl was forced to become the wife of her thirty-two-year-old uncle. She escaped and was recaptured twice, and:

> On both occasions her father abused her; she lost consciousness during the second beating after her father had whipped her with a belt. Both the girl's father and uncle ultimately pled no contest to charges of child abuse, incest, and unlawful sexual conduct.
>
> (Duncan, 2008, p. 326)

In this case, as in most, no charges of bigamy (under which polygamy is prosecuted) were laid and the family was not investigated for other offences. The harms to reproductive rights are considerable in 'assigned marriages'. The girls and women have no right to withdraw consent to sexual use or to reproduction, and girls under the age of fifteen suffer high-risk pregnancies with a 60 per cent higher maternal death rate than older mothers. There is a high rate of birth defects in the children as a result of incest.

The economic harm to women is clear in the removal of girls from education, from skills training and from the workforce, so that they are unable to achieve economic independence, and the children of their 'marriage' are reduced to poverty. Polygamous husbands are frequently unable to provide financial support for all their wives and children and may, indeed, make no attempt to do so. In the case of polygamous husbands in Mormon groupings in the US, the numerous wives are often required to receive food stamps. The identity of the biological fathers is concealed from the children lest the authorities become aware of the welfare fraud that is taking place (Moore-Emmett, 2004). The children's ignorance that a man they lived with or nearby was in fact their father, or the necessity to lie about that fact, leads to some confusion, which may harm their mental health. Leaving the FLDS cults becomes very difficult when girls and women are not sufficiently educated, worldly or skilled to be able to survive financially. The practice is enforced not just through violence and penury, but religious arguments are used to terrify girls and women into compliance. This creation of fear of hellfire can be understood as a harm to mental health and well-being. Religious threats, such as women being taught that 'if they defy the prophet, they "forfeit (their) chance at the afterlife"', enforce obedience to the norms and values of the sect (Duncan, 2008, p. 326). Women survivors of the practice speak of being controlled by religious arguments both that polygamy is ordained and necessary for the afterlife, and that men's authority and women's obedience is ordained by scripture (Moore-Emmett, 2004; Jessup and Palmer, 2007). The secrecy surrounding fundamentalist Mormon cults limits the possibilities of research into the effects of the practice, so that knowledge about women's experiences has to come from the personal accounts of survivors. In other contexts, however, such as the Bedouin in Israel, who are mostly Muslims, there has been research on the experiences of women and children and the harms to their health, and on the attitudes of the men who maintain the practice.

Muslim polygamy

Research on Bedouin polygamy gives detailed information on issues such as harms to the mental health of women and children, harms to children's education, as well as the thinking of the polygamous patriarchs. It examines, for instance, the issue of harms to women's equality within marriage, including the inequality that exists between wives, as well as that between the wives and the husband. Whereas in many societies where polygamy is practised, the senior or first wife has status in relation to later wives, in the Bedouin Arab community this does not follow. In the Bedouin case, the senior wife has lower status because, while the first marriage is usually arranged, later marriages are likely to be the result of choice. The polygamous husbands very generally acquire new wives when their previous wives get older and are less attractive to them sexually. This situation can be compared to the practice in the West in which men who can afford to do so cast off their first wives and take up with young women, and may repeat the process several times. In polygamy the difference is that the previous wives are not cast off to make their way in the world independently, and potentially partner again. They are compelled to live with the jealousy and straightened circumstances that their husband's decision to take extra wives may bring. One comparison of the mental health of Bedouin Arab senior wives in polygamy and monogamous wives, found that the wives in polygamy reported significantly higher levels of 'somatization, depression, anxiety, hostility, and paranoid ideation' (Al-Krenawi and Slonim-Nevo, 2008, p. 144). They also reported lower self-esteem, less marital satisfaction and more problematic family functioning

In the ex-Soviet republic of Uzbekistan, where polygamy among Muslims is on the rise, though rejected by the majority of women, similar harms to women result from competition between wives. In a 2006 study, 50 per cent of the men said that a second marriage was 'perfectly permissible' or 'permissible under certain circumstances' (Pogrebov, 2006, p. 59). Women were much less supportive because, as the author points out, women are the ones who suffer the downsides of the practice, thus only 3 per cent were positive towards it, and 65 per cent of the respondents in the research classified as 'housewives' condemned the practice. These women pointed out that the first wives suffered emotionally from the husband's preference for his second wife. One woman demonstrated the practical disadvantages first wives suffered thus, 'Have you ever seen a man who takes his wife to a restaurant? Usually they take their lovers there' (Pogrebov, 2006, p. 59).

Another study of Bedouin Arabs, this time in Oman, gives good evidence of the patriarchal nature of polygamy, illustrating the power and advantage the practice affords to men (Profanter and Cate, 2009). It looks at 'The Male Perspective' and the men's views are illuminating. One man said he 'wanted a young woman because I needed love and romance' so he told his wife that he would take a second wife. He lives with the second wife and admits: 'I am not fair with my first wife' and the children from his first wife 'do hate me a little' (Profanter and Cate, 2009, p. 234). Another spoke of replacing a wife he had grown tired of: 'my wife was getting old to give me all that I need. So I remarried . . . the love goes to the second wife because she's still young' (Profanter and Cate, 2009, p. 235). The researchers comment that in another case too the man spoke of needing a new wife because he needed the sexual access, saying, 'I do not maintain physical contact with my first wife because she is old' although he was only two years older than she was (Profanter and Cate, 2009, p. 235). In such cases women are clearly denied the right to equality in marriage and family life.

Christian polygamy

Similar harms to women result from Christian polygamy. This form of polygamy is practised in cultural contexts where polygamy is the traditional marriage form, as well as in some fundamentalist Christian communities in the West. Christian men engage in polygamy in Africa, despite the fact that this is not supported by their religion. African churches, however, choose not to notice on the grounds that they need to keep some men in the congregation. Research on this form of polygamy presents useful information on the wives' attitudes and the motivations of the men involved. The wives, like women in polygamy in Bedouin culture, are opposed to the practice and they express a clear understanding of its harms to equality, harms to their mental health and economic harms. In research on the rapprochement between certain forms of Christianity in Benin and the practice of polygamy, Douglas Falen found that most of the women he spoke to opposed polygamy because it led to jealousy and competition over a man's resources (Falen, 2008). This, he points out, replicated the findings of other work on women's attitudes to polygamy in Africa. Other harms that they described included the fact that children of polygamous families did not 'get along', and that their schooling may be neglected because the father's resources could not cover all of his offspring.

The attitudes of Falen's male respondents in favour of polygamy clearly show that it is seen as serving male power and harms women's equality. One man stated clearly, in commenting upon recent legal changes in Benin that give official recognition only to monogamous marriages, that this was 'an importation of white people's legal principles in attempting to make women equal to men, which he claims is foreign to Africa' (Falen, 2008, p. 62). As Falen comments, 'In the face of contemporary women's more public and political roles in Africa, it is not unusual for men to resist legal reforms that undermine their authority over matters of marriage and women' (Falen, 2008). Most men, Falen notes, defend polygamy as a solution to their need for cheap labour in agriculture in the form of large families and numerous children. But some value polygamy as a means of 'controlling a wife' because a sole wife may 'become demanding and stubborn because she knows that her husband depends on her alone' (Falen, 2008, p. 63). These husbands said they benefited from the competition between multiple wives over their attention and access to resources. Another motivation for favouring polygamy was the 'enduring reason' that having many wives and children brings men prestige and inspires respect. Other men explained that they sought more wives 'when their wife is observing postpartum sexual taboos, or when she simply refuses to have sex' (Falen, 2008, p. 63). Most of Falen's male respondents explained that informal polygamous marriage was practised by men of all religions and was caused by men's search for multiple sexual partners. Christians who sought sex outside marriage tended to have 'outside wives' who were in some cases publicly recognised. Where the outside wives were kept secret the 'first meeting between a man's two families may take place at his funeral, at which time they may dispute the inheritance' (Falen, 2008, p. 63).

Though there is no published research on the growing cult of Christian polygamy in the US, websites of cult organisations provide useful evidence of the harms to women. This form of polygamy cannot easily be justified by tradition. The new cultic Christian polygamy represents a harmful cultural practice in the process of formation. The number of organisations that an Internet search reveals to be campaigning for Christian polygamy suggests that a substantial pro-polygamy movement exists. An Internet search on the term 'Christian Polygamy' brings up more than 791,000 hits. The website 'Christian Polygamy' identifies a 'movement' to promote the practice as beginning in 1994. At this date, Christian Polygamy Info tells us, a newspaper was started in the US that proclaimed that polygamy was bibilical and told the 'truth' that sections of both the Old and the New Testament allowed polygamy, and even that Moses had two wives (Christian Polygamy Info, n.d. a). The Christian polygamy movement, rather than being fuelled by the desire to maintain traditional harmful cultural practices, seems to be an angry reaction to the greater freedom of women to seek equality in their relationships and to seek divorces. In this respect it mirrors the motivations of male buyers in the mail-order bride market (Jeffreys, 2009). The pro-polygamy movement split in the late 1990s into two branches, one of which purports to be less harmful to women because it allows first wives to have some say in whether husbands may acquire a second one.

The acrimonious split resulted from bad publicity occasioned by the flight of women from Christian polygamy to wives' support groups where they detailed the harms they had experienced. The anti-polygamy organisation Tapestry Against Polygamy was founded in 1998 by women escaping Mormon polygamy, but it also attracted women escaping Christian polygamy. It opposed polygamy in general and welcomed the Christian wives who were escaping the practice (Tapestry Against Polygamy, n.d.). More recently, another anti-polygamy group has been established called Americans Against Abuses of Polygamy, which describes itself as 'a non-profit, conservative feminist, human rights organization, based in Texas' that will 'protect American women and children by educating the public on the realities of modern American polygamy' (Americans Against Abuses of Polygamy, n.d.). These organisations gave exposure to the harms to women within Christian polygamy and may have caused some of the patriarchs to distance themselves even more from those who were giving polygamy a bad name. The group that initiated the split decided that the errant Christian polygamists were being cruel to their wives by forcing them to accept that their husbands wanted to marry for a second time, thus breaking up marriages and driving disgruntled wives out. This group sought to maintain some respectability and feared losing credibility if the practice looked obviously cruel towards women. A negative picture might put off recruits and deter potential plural wives from becoming involved. To counter this threat it developed a doctrine of 'love not force', which stated that men should not force their wives to accept polygamy because if god was truly on their side, and meant for them to be polygamous, He would convince the wives and they would willingly accept the practice. Thus the authority of the husband was replaced by the authority of god. This 'love not force' doctrine is not accepted by some Christian polygamy organisations and the disagreement seems to be about the degree of brutal patriarchal power they adhere to. The 'love not force' branch of the movement describes itself as comprising 'committed Christ-centered, Spirit-led, Scripture-believing evangelical conservative

Christians, from all kinds of different denominational backgrounds'
(Christian Polygamy Info, n.d. a). This branch adheres to a more kindly
notion of male domination in which men will exercise a respectful power
over their wives rather than brute force. They define their version of
patriarchy as 'the "father-leadership" model, men following the
"footwashing, going-to-the-cross" example of Father God who gave in
selfless love' (Christian Polygamy Info, n.d. b).

The more brutal face of Christian polygamy, however, is rooted
clearly in men's rage at the ways in which women have achieved greater
equality. These less polite polygamists describe themselves as patriarchs
and they are not shy. These men need to be polygamous because they
have, according to some practitioners, more god-given testosterone
than others and therefore need more sexual outlets than just one wife.
Don Milton writes, on his website 'Christian polygamy', 'Shame on
you if you dare judge men who have been given by God an extra high
level of testosterone' (Milton, n.d. a). 'You cannot imagine what it is
like to go through life with the drive of an 18 or 20 year old and be
yoked with someone who has one seventh that drive,' Milton complains
(Milton, n.d. a). Milton is very angry that his first wife did not agree
to his taking a second one. He calls this 'persecution' and writes, 'it is
more painful than if you had been put in stocks in the public square.
You have been looked upon with hatred by your wife' (Milton,
n.d. b). He comments, 'It is sad that marriage has come to mean submission to women in today's world' (Milton, n.d. b). Citing biblical
references, Milton defines his version of patriarchal Christianity thus,
'Are you a man? Do you take your role as master of your wife seriously?
Do you rule over your wife as the Lord commands while not provoking
wrath?' (Milton, n.d. c). He advises that the way to achieve polygamy
without drawing unwelcome attention from the law is to divorce
wife number one (but still live with her) and then marry a second wife
religiously and civilly. The same practice could be employed on innumerable occasions and so a harem could be built up that was perfectly
legal. This is precisely the method employed by some patriarchs within
the Muslim community in the UK as we have seen.

There are many and varied forms of religious polygamy being
developed at present. Women who are involved in the Jewish tradition
of polygamy, which is experiencing a resurgence are called 'pilegesh',
roughly translated as 'concubines'. 'Pilegesh.org' provides personal ads

for men or heterosexual couples seeking extra wives, legal advice and Old Testament citations aplenty (Pilegesh.org, n.d.). 'Jewish Polygamy' offers similar resources (Jewish Polgyamy, n.d). There is a veritable explosion of religious polygamy websites dedicated to justifying the practice through religious texts, touting for extra wives, dealing with legal problems and offering personal experiences and advice.

Calls for polygamy to be legalised

In both the UK and Australia calls to legalise polygamy are being made by male self-styled representatives of the Muslim community (Malik, 2000). Joumanah El Matrah, manager of the Islamic Women's Welfare Council of Victoria and an opponent of polygamy, says that polygamy is likely to be increasing in Australia (National Times, 2008). This increase is empowering spokespersons such as Keysar Trad, who is the president of the Islamic Friendship Association of Australia, to call for legalisation. He explains what he sees as the advantages of polygamy for women (Trad, 2009). He says that the practice gives rights to women who, in Western society, would be men's mistresses, having to keep the relationship secret and having no protection when it ends. Islam, he explains, acknowledges polygamy as a 'fact of human nature' (presumably it is male human nature he has in mind) and sets up a regulatory framework. The value of polygamy is not recognised in Australia, he argues, because of prejudice against Muslim ideas on marriage and the family. Trad recognises that polygamy entails problems of jealousy for the wives, but considers this an advantage because it enables women to have 'a spiritually rewarding experience that allows women to grow while the husband toils to provide for more than one partner'. The self-abnegation involved may lead to 'euphoria' since, 'we become euphoric when we give to those in need, sponsor orphans and provide foster care, the ultimate in giving is for a woman to give a fraction of her husband's time and affection to another woman who is willing to share with her'. Islam, he explains, does not favour equal opportunities in this respect, since it does not permit polyandry. He offers as reasons, the need for men to be able to establish the paternity of their children and the fact that women may not be as interested in sex as their husbands are, leading to 'a perpetual state of conjugal frustration among men'. In polyandry this problem would be worsened and place an 'overwhelming burden' on the woman. Trad, and the small minority of other Muslim men in Australia who are calling for legalisation, are not being met with a positive response. Muslim women's organisations, government spokespeople and media editorials are hostile to the idea and argue that it is against women's equality (National Times, 2008). But this is not the case with the call to legalise Mormon polygamy in North America, where the response from civil liberties groups and legal theorists has been more positive.

Polygamy and women's human rights

The laws that states rely upon to prohibit polygamy are blunt instruments and gender neutral. They forbid bigamy or other kinds of cohabitation in ways that can criminalise the women involved in the practice without managing to target the harms that women suffer. They are old laws that are not based on human rights principles. It is for these reasons that some feminists in North America have begun to argue that the practice should be decriminalised or legalised, generally in relation to Mormon polygamy, so that plural marriages can be registered and all wives brought under the protection of the law. Beverley Baines, for instance, explains that the crime of polygamy in Canadian law, which dates back to the nineteenth century, derives from Christian moral values rather than concern for the welfare of women (Baines, 2007). This is clear from the fact that the law in Canada penalises both men and women for the practice of polygamy and is very general, potentially covering cohabitation as well as marriage. In suggesting that polygamy should be immediately decriminalised, a policy that she sees no chance of the Canadian government adopting, she says she is motivated by concern for three groups of women. These are women who are refused permission to migrate to Canada on the grounds that they are in polygamous marriages; women who are in polygamous marriages and would like to leave them but would not have access to support or property rights if they did so; and a third group of women who are opposed to legalising polygamy and would be in a better position to oppose legalisation on the grounds of gender equality once it was decriminalised. She argues that some forms of polygamy may not be harmful to women and even possibly beneficial, so decriminalising it would enable the specific abuses of women, which can result from this practice, to be targeted, such as coercion and harm to mental health, while not prohibiting the practice as a whole.

Critics of the present law on polygamy in Canada, though no prosecutions take place under it, argue that it is potentially unfair to women, making them liable to legal penalty for a practice over which they are likely to have no control. Demands to decriminalise, however, leave women in an extremely vulnerable position and remove the social opprobrium that should properly, considering the harmfulness of the practice, be attached to it. Decriminalisation would also leave the Canadian state with no legal penalty for a practice that is against women's equality in marriage and other human rights, and it would fail to fulfil its obligations under UN conventions. The federal justice minister of Canada (which has a conservative government) said in 2009 that polygamy had 'no place in Canada' after the British Columbia Attorney General sought advice on the status of the law on the issue. But this position is being tested presently, as the British Columbia Supreme Court is in the process of hearing a challenge to the state's polygamy laws on the grounds that they are unconstitutional because they violate the right to religious freedom (Stueck, 2010). Lawyers defending Canadian laws against the challenge are arguing from the basis of all the harms outlined in this chapter, and also point out that Mormon polygamy in Canada involves the trafficking of girls and women across state boundaries, usually from the US, for the purpose of sexual exploitation in plural marriage.

Considering that there are good reasons, on the grounds of women's human rights, to oppose decriminalisation of the practice, it is a matter of concern that there is now a call from civil liberties groups and even from a feminist legal theorist to go further than decriminalisation, i.e. for the legalisation of polygamy in the US. Legalisation would enable plural marriages to be registered and recognised by the state. The American Civil Liberties Union has adopted the policy that polygamy should be legalised on the grounds of freedom of religion. The policy, from 1991, states, 'The ACLU believes that criminal and civil laws prohibiting or penalizing the practice of plural marriage violate constitutional protections of freedom of expression and association, freedom of religion, and privacy for personal relationships among consenting adults' (ACLU, n.d.). The ACLU, in its policies on other issues relating to women's rights such as pornography, is libertarian and permissive, and can be seen as dedicated to upholding the freedoms of male citizens, so its approach to polygamy is not surprising. But support from feminists for legalisation is more of a puzzle. Emily Duncan, in the *Duke Journal of Gender, Law and Policy*, makes an argument that is very similar to that which some feminists make in relation to prostitution, saying that legalising it will make it easier to combat the recognised harms to women that the practice involves (Duncan, 2008).

Duncan explains how difficult it is to prosecute polygamists in the US, particularly in Utah and Texas where the biggest polygamist Mormon cults are situated. There is little enthusiasm for pursuing polygamists, particularly where there is considerable sympathy with the practitioners, as in Utah. It is very hard to gain evidence and find witnesses prepared to testify as the women involved are likely to show loyalty to the cult. There are other obstacles. The pursuit of polygamists causes, as she puts it, public relations disasters for the government as the media make much of pictures of children being removed. Also law enforcement and political officials are, she says, concerned about acting too aggressively against a practice some see as a 'protected religious activity' (Duncan, 2008, p. 324). Prosecuting polygamy is not a priority because it is not seen as serious and law enforcement officers are more likely to look at the crimes that, as Duncan expresses it, 'surround polygamy'. Duncan recognises and details the very serious harms to women and children that polygamy creates, but her response is to argue that it should be legalised and regulated to reduce the harms, as in the case of brothel prostitution, which has been legalised in some states in Australia, and in countries such as Germany, the Netherlands and New Zealand, using the same harm minimisation argument. As Duncan puts it:

> In the case of prostitution, many scholars believe the laws against the practice have only helped make life more difficult for prostitutes . . . Polygamy, like prostitution and alcohol consumption, is another area in which public policy could reflect practicality, not morality, and, in turn, allow for more effective regulation.
>
> (Duncan, 2008, p. 332)

Legalising polygamy, she argues, 'could positively affect polygamist women and children' (Duncan, 2008, p. 332).

In support of this argument she states that polygamy itself is not a problem, despite the copious research in many contexts that have shown women's desire to end the practice and the harms they have suffered within it. The problem is that a minority of polygamous families are 'dysfunctional', thus 'Condemning every practicing polygamist to prevent the abuses of some may be counterintuitive' (Duncan, 2008, p. 332). Another argument she makes is that polygamous practice is growing so it would not be practical to seek to end it, thus in Utah the polygamous community grew tenfold in the last fifty years and polygamists now constitute 2 per cent of the state's population. The growth is the result of a high birth rate and conversions. 'Polygamists', she says, are 'here to stay' (Duncan, 2008, p. 333). Legalisation could 'alleviate' some of the abuses through 'greater regulation' and would bring polygamous communities 'into the open' so that they can 'acclimate to society' when they no longer have to fear criminal charges. Laws and policies could be changed to support 'alternative family models'. The result of these changes would be that witnesses might be more willing to testify to abuses once other elements of their lifestyle were protected. The 'celestial' marriages of polygamists, those presently not registered by the state, could become official and appear on government records. Abuses could be more easily tackled under legalisation, by programmes such as Safety Net, set up by Utah's Attorney General, which brings together representatives of the cults and law enforcement officers to educate about and deter abuses. Underage marriages could be eliminated by requiring couples to 'appear before an independent civil authority' where someone outside the family could raise concerns or refuse to approve a marriage. When polygamy is out in the open, she says, 'society could learn to tolerate and eventually accept polygamists and their way of life' (Duncan, 2008, p. 335). Governments and law enforcement could study why polygamy leads to abuses in 'some, but not all, cases', and tailor regulations and laws to address the weaknesses that lead to abuse. In this way good polygamy would be protected and 'truly deviant practitioners' would be dealt with (Duncan, 2008, p. 337).

Duncan's arguments show a remarkable similarity to the arguments that legalisers use in relation to prostitution – another traditional practice of the exchange of women between men for sexual use – and share precisely the same flaws. One problem is defeatism, that is the assumption that nothing can be done since polygamy, or prostitution, like other harmful cultural practices, will always exist. In fact polygamy is already increasing and remedies need to focus on how to stop this harmful practice rather than on how to make it easier. Another similarity is the assumption in Duncan's arguments that, despite the considerable evidence of harms in relation to both practices, there is a good kind of polygamy/prostitution that can be separated off from the deviant and harmful form. Researchers of legalised prostitution in Victoria, Australia, the Netherlands and the state of Nevada in the US challenge these ideas (Farley, 2007; Sullivan, 2007; Jeffreys, 2009). They point out that all prostitution involves women being forced to disassociate emotionally from their bodies to survive the abuse and considerable harms to their physical and mental health; there is no benign version (Sullivan, 2007; Jeffreys, 2009). Similarly, in relation to polygamy, there is no reason to assume that underage marriage, violence, repudiation of extra boys, incest, poverty and the jealousy and competition with other wives and children that makes the lives of women in polygamy intolerable, would end if the practice became socially acceptable. Polygamy cannot be made compatible with women's equality in marriage and the family, and thus states are required to outlaw the practice and end the harmful attitudes that cause it, not go to considerable lengths to facilitate the patriarchs who are developing it.

Another assumption behind the legalisation argument is that criminalisation keeps the practice 'underground' and makes it hard to address the abuses. In relation to prostitution, at least, this argument is the most obviously flawed. Wherever brothel and/or escort prostitution has been legalised, a considerable illegal sector – several times the size of the legal sector – has developed alongside with precisely the same harms as before but now on a larger scale (Sullivan, 2007; Jeffreys, 2009). There is no reason why this should not turn out to be the case with polygamy too, as many patriarchs in the cults seek to protect their freedom to abuse in their own way. The idea that the harms of prostitution, most notably the violence involved in the everyday practices of the industry, which lead to bleeding and abraded vaginas, unwanted pregnancies and sexually transmitted diseases, beatings and rapes, would disappear in the light of legalisation was a misguided notion. Not only do they continue in the large illegal sectors, which are not monitored, once legalisation has taken place, but in the legal brothels themselves they persist (Jeffreys, 2010). Thus there is no reason to believe that the harms of polygamy will cease in the legalised version. Also, in relation to polygamy there is an extra form of coercion, which means women have less chance to exit: this is control through the terror of divine retribution. This would continue in a legalised environment and prevent girls and women from asking for help.

Fashionable polygamy

It is important to note that the practice of men taking on new and younger lovers while remaining married to their legal wives takes place in Western societies too, and can even achieve some degree of social and family acceptance if the men are rich and of high social status. The deaths of two extremely rich and influential Australian men in recent years has demonstrated a quite similar phenomenon. When Richard Pratt, a 'cardboard box king', had a Jewish funeral it was attended by his '11-year-old daughter, Paula, who lives in Sydney with her mother, Pratt's long-time mistress Shari-Lea Hitchcock' (Rule and Sharp, 2009). It was also attended by ex-Prime Minister, John Howard. Anne Summers, feminist author from Australia, delineates the difference between girlfriends and mistresses by explaining that mistresses are 'kept' and thus their keepers must be rich, 'in order to keep her in the style that makes it worth her while to surrender her independence' (Summers, 2009). Summers points out that the media magnate Kerry Packer bequeathed $10 million to his mistress in his will a couple of years earlier, but in that case the family would not allow her at his death bed or funeral. Pratt's mistress, on the other hand, was acknowledged by the family. As Summers points out, unlike girlfriends, mistresses 'must be on call whenever her master needs her, but there is little chance he will ever marry her' (Summers, 2009). One of Kerry Packer's ex-mistresses was kept on his payroll and employed to run a brothel for him when their four-year affair ended in the 1980s. She had the job of procuring for him, travelling the world to find prostitutes for him and his friends, according to his biographer, Paul Barry (ABC News, 2007), and later committed suicide. While 'mistresses' in the West may suffer from emotional and financial dependence, they differ from the wives in polygamy in having access to information and resources that give them a greater possibility of choosing to leave the men they are involved with, and become independent.

The feminist challenge to men's harmful practice of polygamy is complicated by the fact that polygamy has become fashionable in some circles in the US. The practice has been promoted through the US television series devoted to it in recent years, first *Big Love,* and then *Sister Wives*, broadcast in 2010, about a fundamentalist Mormon man with four wives. The term 'sister wives' comes from fundamentalist Mormonism and relates to the supposedly undying bonds that polygamy creates between plural wives. But the term is gaining a life of its own on the polygamy promotion website 'Sister Wives', which argues that polygamy is good for wives and does not mention the interest men might have in the practice. The 'Sister Wives' website is dedicated to 'practical poly advice and support', and contains numerous discussion threads between women on how to do polygamy effectively and how to survive its harms, particularly jealousy and poverty (Sister Wives, n.d.). The women involved range from some who are clearly caught up in the polygamy of the CPM, to some who profess no religion at all but aver that polygamy may, or does, serve their interests. It could be positive, the latter group argue, particularly in the provision of 'sister wives' who offer emotional and even sexual companionship to other women who all relate to the same man. The love that first wives may find with 'sister wives' is a recurring theme and in some cases this is clearly a sexual as well as emotional love, suggesting that polygamy is being used in such cases simply to create plural relationships. No support websites exist for plural 'husbands' who want to discuss their mental suffering in polyandrous relationships and this suggests that polygamy is thoroughly patriarchal even when supposedly practised as a form of sexual freedom. It is important in working out how to more effectively outlaw polygamy not to create problems for women involved in polyamory, a sexual libertarian practice of multi-partnering, which, though arguably against women's right to equality, may be more freely chosen by women who have alternatives, than the religious versions of the practice.

Conclusion

The practice of polygamy, in all its versions, turns the family into a private fiefdom for the exercise of men's power. It is manifestly against women's right to equality in marriage and the family and violates women's rights to health and their economic rights. It is not consistent with the obligations of states that are parties to conventions such as the ICCPR or CEDAW to decriminalise or legalise practices that violate women's right to equality, and arguments as to the right to religion should not allowed to trump this most important right. However, the legislation presently in place in states such as Canada to outlaw the practice is not adequate for the protection of women's rights. Bigamy laws were not intended to outlaw polygamy, which was not prevalent when they were introduced. They apply only to marriages registered by the state and cannot touch marriages formalised in customary and religious settings alone. Proponents of the legalisation of polygamy argue for the repeal of bigamy laws so that men may marry multiple wives legally and officially. This would give government sanction to this harmful practice and there is no reason to take this path, which would normalise the practice and enable it to develop unhindered. An approach is needed that gets to the heart of the ways in which polygamy is harmful to women, without inhibiting the rights of fashionable polyamorists to enter relationships of their choosing. Presently the energies of feminist legal theorists who recognise the harms of polygamy are concentrated on preventing decriminalisation or legalisation but there is a need for consideration of a solution that more effectively penalises the practice.

8

THE MASTER'S TOOLS

Islamic feminism and its critics

This chapter will examine the ideas and activism of a range of feminists who criticise the harmful effects of Islamic fundamentalism with inside knowledge, both those who have become atheists and those who remain Muslims. It will cast a critical eye at the surprising campaign against them by those feminists who take a strong cultural relativist position. These latter scholars see 'Islamic feminism', in which women's demands are framed through reference to religious texts, as the way forward. This approach has been seen by some as the only effective strategy in countries where there is religious rule, and any other forms of political action lead to serious reprisals. Feminists have not seen this as a suitable approach to Christianity. Mary Daly in the 1970s argued that it was pointless to seek to reinvent patriarchal religions (Daly, 1985b). Some feminists remained Christians but they did not seek to create a 'Christian feminism' and were often fiercely critical of the misogyny displayed there. In relation to Islam, however, similarly robust criticism is generally seen as unacceptable on the Left broadly and within the academy. Different rules are applied. I will suggest that those who treat Islam differently are practising a 'new orientalism' that exoticises Islam.

The feminist critics of Islam that I will examine here all grew up in Muslim contexts and none of them are 'Islamic feminists'. They are all incisively critical of Islam. The Canadian lesbian feminist Irshad Manji and Fadela Amara from France are practising Muslims, whereas Ayaan Hirsi Ali from Somalia, and Maryam Namazie from Iran are apostates, who have rejected religion. They are accused by cultural relativists such as the anthropologist Saba Mahmood as being guilty of serious faults such as imperialism, Westoxication, orientalism, racism and Islamophobia (Mahmood, 2009). They are seen as obeying the dictates of Western racists in destroying the reputation of Islam. This chapter will look at the arguments of those scholars of gender and Islam who make this critique, such as Saba Mahmood and Lila Abu-Lughod. It will also examine, by contrast, the work of scholars who are critical of the post-colonial and cultural relativist discourse. One of the latter, Haideh Moghissi, writes, 'It seems that we live in an era in Middle Eastern history in which Islamic fundamentalism cannot be challenged. Secular discourse to promote gender equality has been discredited as 'elitist', modernist or 'white' and 'North-oriented', and leftists and nationalists are told . . . that we must first affirm Islam, even its treatment of women, before we dare to speak of women's oppression in Islamic societies' (Moghissi, 1999, p. 134). I will argue that the work of the feminist critics of Islam is of great importance in confronting the harms that women face from religious fundamentalism. The work of their detractors, on the other hand, has a chilling effect on the climate in the feminist academy by making criticism of religion in general much more difficult. I will argue against the effectiveness of the 'Islamic feminist' approach with the aid of the work of significant secular and atheist feminist scholars.

Feminist criticism of Islam

Feminist criticism of Christianity has not elicited the angry response in the academy that criticism of Islam has occasioned. The implication behind accusations of Islamophobia and orientalism against critics of Islam is that they are being racist. It is this that makes criticism of Islam politically unacceptable in a way that criticism of Christianity has not been. This is surprising because the feminist critics of Islam have mostly been either practising Muslims or women raised as Muslims. They are not, for the most part, Westerners, but criticising a religion whose ideology and practical effects when wielded politically, they are well qualified to judge. As Ayaan Hirsi Ali explains at the beginning of her critique of Islam, *The Caged Virgin*, 'I hope to be able to make a con-tribution to ending the degrading treatment of Muslim women and girls by using my knowledge and experience of the Muslim faith' (Ali, 2006, p. 2). But still their views, and their right to air them, have not been well tolerated on the Left in the West, and in the academy. It is on the Left in particular that criticism of Islam is regarded as politically unacceptable, which is surprising considering that atheism, or at least secularism, has been so important to those who consider themselves socialists in relation to Christianity. But Islam, it seems, is different alto-gether; it concerns the 'other', the colonially oppressed, the underdog, and should therefore be respected.

I shall examine here the political work of practising Muslims first, going on to those who are publicly atheists and have rejected Islam. I shall consider the work of four women here but there are many more whose writings and activism deserve serious study. Irshad Manji and Fadela Amara are feminists who are incisively critical of the present day politics of Islam, as well as its sacred texts. Manji, a lesbian and feminist journalist remains, with considerable conflict, a practising Muslim (Manji, 2003). She describes herself as a 'Muslim refusenik', and says that if she lived in a Muslim society she would have abandoned Islam. 'Had I grown up in a Muslim country, I'd probably be an atheist in my heart. It's because I live in this corner of the world, where I can think, dispute, and delve further into any topic, that I've learned why I shouldn't give up on Islam just yet' (Manji, 2003, p. 215). But she is not sure that she will remain a Muslim, commenting at the end of her book, 'So, I'm down to my final fair shake for Islam. Whether I leave it behind will be up to me' (Manji, 2003, p. 223). The Canadian context gave her the tools to question the Islam in which she was brought up so that she questioned a great deal at her madresa, or Islamic school, and had to leave at thirteen. She rejected the segregation of girls in the school behind partitions, she hated the clothing she had to wear and she was appalled by the anti-Semitism she was taught. Of the concealing clothing forced upon her she writes, 'I entered its premises wearing a white polyester chador and departed several hours later with my hair flattened and my spirit deflated, as if the condom over my head had properly inoculated me from "unsafe" intellectual activity' (Manji, 2003, p. 12). She opposed the discrimination practised against girls, such as the requirement that girls begin obligatory prayer practice at nine, while boys did not have to do this until they were thirteen. She rejected the Islamic teaching against 'excessive laughter'.

In 1998 she started hosting *Queer Television* and received petitions against her presence on TV, as an out lesbian and perhaps one who engaged in 'excessive laughter'. She was attacked as a 'lying pig dyke' for her role (Manji, 2003, p. 141). Manji is strongly critical of what the Qur'an says about women and asks, in this context, 'What if the Koran isn't perfect? What if it's not a completely God-authored book? What if it's riddled with human biases?' (Manji, 2003, p. 47). Manji's statements about Islam are fearless and straightforward and apply to the religion itself, not just to fringe elements, 'For all our denunciations of Islam's fringe sickness, Muslims studiously avoided addressing the paralysing sickliness of the entire religion – the untouchability of mainstream Islam' (Manji, 2003, p. 51). She is particularly critical of the domination of Islam by its origins in the Middle East, the fact that the Qur'an has to be chanted in Arabic even by the majority of Muslims who do not speak the language, and that women have to wear costumes designed to keep out dust storms even in countries where these do not take place. A sign of the domination of desert Islam is the direction in which prayers must be offered, 'Why, then, *must* Muslims bow to Mecca five times a day? Isn't that a sign of being desert-whipped?' (Manji, 2003, p. 145).

Another strong critic of the influence of religious fundamentalism on women, who was born and raised in the West, is the French feminist Fadela Amara (Amara, 2006). Like Manji, she describes herself as a practising Muslim. Born in France of Algerian immigrant parents she became a socialist and feminist. Amara is clear about the importance of feminist opposition to fundamentalist Islam and states that 'the struggle for women's emancipation has become the epicentre of the combat against obscurantism and fundamentalism' (Amara, 2006, p. 162). She was a long-time and stalwart member of SOS Racisme and later set up a feminist organisation for Muslim women called 'Ni Putes, Ni Soumises', meaning neither whores nor submissives. Amara explains that when she was growing up in the projects in France she, like her mother and grandmother before her, did not wear the veil or feel under pressure to do so (Amara, 2006). There were no strict rules of segregating boys and girls. A big change took place with the development of Islamic fundamentalism in the 1990s, which had very negative impacts on the lives of girls and women.

In opposition to this change she set up 'Ni Putes, Ni Soumises', which organised a march to Paris. Fundamentalism was attractive to young Muslim males because of their vulnerability from the unemployment created by government policies. They acted to restrict the lives of their sisters and girls outside their families, and there was, as Amara puts it, 'growing male oppression' (Amara, 2006, p. 62). Girls complained that they were not allowed freedom of movement, had their wages confiscated and experienced physical violence. As the authority of fathers was undermined by unemployment, older brothers took on the roles of ruling in families. Later this dominion was extended to girls outside their families. They enforced curfews on girls, ensured that they were not allowed to go out alone, and forbade mixed-sex company outside the family. More and more girls found themselves confined to the home. The young men began surveillance of the young women who were not allowed to wear short skirts, tight-fitting jeans, low-cut blouses and short T-shirts. The boys used offensive remarks to control the girls in the street. Amara describes their behaviour as 'hypervirility' (Amara, 2003, p. 66). She says the only way for them to gain self-esteem and be 'recognized' inside and outside the projects was to act 'macho and violent', behaviour that was very harmful to those males who were less macho or homosexual, as well as to young women. Amara issues a sharp riposte to her cultural relativist critics. They accuse her, she says, 'of espousing neo-colonialism, of betraying my own community origins – showing their real intentions – and of mistreating Islam' (Amara, 2006, p. 157). Since she is opposing fundamentalism and is not rejecting Islam, they could, she says, be seen to be 'conflating Islam and Islamism (fundamentalism) in a vicious and shameful way' (Amara, 2006, p. 157).

Apostasy: ex-Muslim atheists

An increasing number of feminists who were raised Muslim are now going public about their rejection of religion and proclaiming their atheism. This is dangerous behaviour for them, considering the punishments for apostasy in Islamic law and the degree of opprobrium with which criticism of Islam can be met – let alone rejection of it. One of the best-known ex-Muslim atheists is Ayaan Hirsi Ali. Ali was raised in Somalia, Kenya and Saudi Arabia, moving around because of political instability in Somalia and her father's political activities. She suffered genital mutilation as a child and fled to the Netherlands at the age of twenty-two to escape an arranged marriage to a Somalian living in Canada, to whom she was being sent via Europe. Ali joined and worked for the Labour Party in the Netherlands. She became more and more concerned about the plight of Muslim women suffering domestic violence that she came across in her work as a translator, and the fact that she could not get the Party to take up this issue. She published a critique of the impact of fundamentalist politics and religion on women in 2006, *The Caged Virgin*, and a powerful autobiography, *Infidel*, in 2007. In a similar vein to Amara's descriptions of the plight of Muslim girls in France, Ali criticises the policies in the Netherlands that have led to the isolation of Muslim communities and toleration for the violence against women that takes place in them. There was, she felt, too much acceptance of a multicultural requirement to be tolerant of Islam and not appear to criticise it. She became an atheist.

Ali does not seek to protect Islam and limit her criticisms to fundamentalism or see the problem as the hijacking of Islam by a terrorist fringe. She states that 'Blair and Bush must stop saying that Islam is being held hostage by a terrorist minority. They are wrong. Islam is being held hostage by itself' (Ali, 2006, p. 41). Like Amara she is critical of the way in which Muslim communities are being segregated and isolated from the Western societies in which they exist. The ideals of multiculturalism are not enough, she says, 'We in the West need to make a concerted effort to counter Islamic education and all those other Islamic institutions that lead to self-segregation and thus contribute to the continuation of a hopeless tyranny over women and children' (Ali, 2006, p. 7). She considers that Muslim communities are being held back socially, politically and economically by the way women are treated within them.

Interestingly, though Fadela Amara and Ali hold different opinions on the intrinsic harmfulness of Islam, they have something in common. Both have taken up opportunities offered by right-wing governments in order to further their aspirations for Muslim women. Ali argues that Left parties have been so captured by cultural relativism as the correct anti-racist position, that they cannot be relied on to adopt programmes to support women from ethnic minorities on issues such as violence, forced marriage and honour crimes. Ali became exasperated with the failure of the Labour Party in the Netherlands to take the concerns of women seriously. She explains:

> I was getting sick of the evasive behaviour of the Labor Party, which has closed its eyes to the growing feelings of unease in society. Suppression of women does not seem to them an important theme, and they are not committed to admitting it occurs, addressing it, or correcting it.
>
> (Ali, 2006, p. 68)

She moved to the Liberal Party in 2002 because of 'the assurance by the party leader that I will be given the freedom to bring to the top of the political agenda the integration and emancipation of immigrant women' (Ali, 2006, p. 69). Fadela Amara made what could be seen to be a similar move. In 2007 she accepted nomination to the post of Minister for Urban Regeneration in the right-wing government of Sarkozy in France. Amara has clearly made a compromise in order to achieve her aims and has been criticised for it. Loic Wacquant, a male French sociologist now teaching at UC Berkeley, described her as a 'decorative puppet' who is in 'place to provide an "Arab face"' for Sarkozy (Baum, 2007). Wacquant asks how she could have 'joined the most rightward government of the past 50 years in France' and one which 'exploits class resentment and anti-immigration hostility'. But Amara says she is a 'leftist woman' who chose to join a right-wing government because 'there is a crisis' in the projects. She states that her political position has not altered and that may be correct, but it is interesting that, like others, she has found more promises of action on women's rights – even if they are not fulfilled – from the Right.

There is increasing confidence among Muslim atheists in the West to state their position publicly. The feminist Maryam Namazie set up the Council for Ex-Muslims in the UK in 2007 and a campaign against accommodation with Sharia law under the title, One Law For All. Namazie receives threats, usually on her mobile phone, such as the warning: 'You are going to be decapitated' (Rix, 2008). There are also Councils for Ex-Muslims in Germany and in Scandinavia. Coming out as an atheist for ex-Muslims is considerably more dangerous than it was for those who rejected Christianity at any time in the last century, because ex-Christians did not face death, only, in my case in the 1960s, the perturbation of the religious knowledge teacher at my school. Namazie was twelve when the Iranian revolution took place and suffered harassment in the street because her head was uncovered. Her school was closed for Islamicisation and the television news carried executions every day. She later went to work for the UNDP in Sudan only to find that Sudan became an Islamic republic six months after her arrival. At this point she became an atheist and started her campaigning against Islamic extremism, and particularly the introduction of sharia law in any form, because of the way in which it would inevitably, in her view, damage women's rights.

The assault upon the feminist critics of Islam

Despite their remarkable courage and political commitment, such Muslim and ex-Muslim feminist critics of religion have come under harsh attack from post-structuralist feminists. Saba Mahmood is particularly strident about the activists and theorists discussed above. She describes Irshad Manji's books as a 'shrill diatribe against Muslims' (Mahmood, 2009, p. 196). She attacks Manji for 'racism' and says 'Manji's identity as a Muslim lends particular force to her Orientalist and racist views', though it is hard to understand how a Muslim Asian woman's criticism of Islam can reasonably be ascribed to 'racism' (Mahmood, 2009, p. 199). She condemns these feminist critics for working with right-wing politicians and movements and supporting their campaign against Muslims, 'The arguments of these authors read like a blueprint for the neoconservative agenda for regime change in the Middle East' (Mahmood, 2009, p. 198). Of Fadela Amara and another writer, Chahdortt Djavann, she writes, 'These authors authenticate and legitimize the Islamophobia sweeping Europe today, lending a voice of credibility to some of the worst kinds of prejudices and stereotypes Europe has seen since the rise of anti-Semitism in the 1930s' (Mahmood, 2009, p. 197). She accuses Hirsi Ali thus: 'Excoriating Muslims for their unparalleled barbarity and misogyny, she scored points with the right wing' (Mahmood, 2009, p. 197). The cultural relativist opponents of the critics of Islam make a number of accusations against them, which we will consider here. In particular, they are accused of 'Islamophobia', an unfounded hatred and fear of Islam, and of orientalism, an exoticising and stigmatising of the Middle East.

Islamophobia

Feminist critics of the oppression of women in Muslim communities and states often receive the catcall that they are Islamophobic. In the last decade the idea that something called Islamophobia exists, is a form of racism, and needs to be vigorously opposed, has become a commonplace of Left-leaning commentators and scholars. It functions as a serious accusation because, like racism, it is difficult to disprove and may have the effect of silencing a critic through guilt and confusion. Haleh Afshar's work provides an example of how such accusations are used (Afshar, 2008). Afshar is a professor at the University of York in the UK. She is also a Baroness, sitting in the House of Lords, has an OBE, and is the chairperson of the Muslim Women's Network. Afshar, who does not cover, uses the accusation of Islamophobia in relation to feminist criticism of covering in particular. She says that 'the current climate of Islamophobia has burdened Muslim women who cover with additional problems in terms of their politics, their lived experiences and their life chances' (Afshar, 2008, p. 411). These women suffer because 'myths about the hijab have created a modern-day form of Orientalism that objectifies the women who cover and otherizes them as oppressed, perhaps exotic and possibly dangerous'. The Islamophobes who have 'such stereotypical views' she says, are 'Western feminists' who 'create stumbling blocks that bar the way to the feminist ideal of respect, unity and community of goals' (Afshar, 2008, p. 411). She says that the problem of Islamophobia may date back to the 1990s, 'with the shift in forms of prejudice from race-based prejudice to discrimination based on culture and religion', and increased after the terrorist attacks of September 11, 2001 (Afshar, 2008, p. 414). Islamophobia, in her view, is a 'discourse of hate' in which 'covered women are singled out as the living example of backwardness and fearful subordination'. Afshar quotes Jeremy Seabrook voicing what has now become the familiar Left standpoint: 'Officially, all right-thinking people have foresworn racism . . . Islamophobia is the half-open door through which it makes its triumphal re-entry into respectable society' (Afshar, 2008, p. 417).

The development of accusations of Islamophobia as substitutions for accusations of racism is an indication of the way in which many on the Left have elevated religion above race as a source of oppression. A number of thoughtful commentators have criticised this development. Marie Macey argues that recourse to the idea of Islamophobia to explain the economic disadvantage suffered by Muslims in the UK is misleading and diverts attention from the ways in which culture might affect economic status: 'It is arguable, however, that the relative disadvantage suffered by some minority ethnic groups is not the result of discrimination, but of cultural and/or religious beliefs and the lifestyle choices that follow from these' (Macey, 2009, p. 23). This perception is supported by the fact that the latest report on inequality in the UK shows that British citizens from the Asian subcontinent who are not Muslim, such as Hindus, Sikhs or Christians, do not suffer disadvantage in the same way (EHRC, 2010). The idea of Islamophobia implies that street violence and discrimination in jobs and services result from recognition that persons are Muslim. Benson and Stangroom argue that accusations of Islamophobia are being used to 'defuse and silence criticism of Islam' (Benson and Stangroom, 2009, p. 152). They attribute the rise in popularity of the concept to a 1997 Runnymede Trust report entitled 'Islamophobia: a Challenge for Us All'. The report defines Islamophobia as 'an outlook or worldview involving an unfounded dread and dislike of Muslims' with characteristics that include seeing Islam 'as inferior to the West – barbaric, irrational, primitive and sexist' (Benson and Stangroom, 2009, p. 152). As an example of the way the accusation is used to silence critics, Benson and Stangroom cite the election of Polly Toynbee, journalist and President of the British Humanist Association, as Islamophobe of the year in 2004 by the Islamic Human Rights Commission. As an atheist, Toynbee is a consistent and incisive critic of all the monotheistic religions. It is important that accusations of Islamophobia are not allowed to silence the feminist critique.

Orientalism

Feminist critics of Islam are also commonly accused of orientalism by their detractors. The epithet 'orientalist' owes its origins to the work of Edward Said, which has had a very considerable influence on feminist scholarship (Said, 1979). The cultural relativist anthropologist, Lila Abu-Lughod comments that Said's Orientalism 'has engendered feminist scholarship and debate' (Abu-Lughod, 2001, p. 101). In Said's understanding, the way in which the West views the Middle East is distorted by a colonial history in which European male pashas exoticised and sexualised the women of the harem, seeing them as passive and oppressed but sexually exciting. Said's work is employed to argue that critics of the way women are treated in Islam are patronising and colonialising by virtue of the fact that they question the practice of covering and other harmful cultural practices. Haleh Afshar, for instance, says that criticism of the voluntariness of the choice of women in the West who wear the veil is orientalist: 'the latter generalization mirrors nineteenth-century discussion about the exotic harem ladies of pleasure forever doing the belly dance and offering their bodies to a replete Pasha' (Afshar, 2008, p. 412). Names and references for the persons that she is criticising here are not given. She goes further to explain that, 'the new climate of Islamophobia has otherized Muslims in general and Muslim women in particular in a way that exemplifies aspects of what Edward Said termed Orientalism' (Afshar, 2008, p. 412). It has become increasingly difficult for feminist scholars to engage in critical writing about women's experience in the Middle East without their being accused of 'orientalism', an accusation that is taken seriously and has imputations of racism and generally quite unacceptable conduct.

Cultural relativism

The detractors of the feminist critics of Islam are cultural relativists, meaning that they object to any characterisation of Muslim women as being worse off, less possessing of agency, or more oppressed, than other women. Some are such hard-line cultural relativists that they are prepared to represent not just covering, but also the slavish repetition of practices of religious discipline by Muslim women, as no better or worse for women than any other forms of behaviour. These cultural relativists understand themselves to be progressive and broadly on the Left. Mahmood, for instance, teaches and writes in the area of post-structuralism and works with other post-structuralist scholars such as Wendy Brown and Judith Butler (Asad *et al.*, 2009), but she supports not only the religion of Islam, but Islamic practices that generations of feminist scholars both Muslim, ex-Muslim and others, have identified as those that are the clearest expressions of misogyny. Mahmood supports veil wearing, as 'an expression of and a means to a Muslim woman's submission to God's will' (Mahmood, 2009, p. 208). She is very annoyed at criticism by those she sees as secular liberals of 'the strict adherence to rituals of Islamic observance, the avoidance of the free mixing of the sexes and the adjudication of public and political issues through religious argumentation' (Mahmood, 2009, p. 209).

Saba Mahmood engages in a quite extreme form of cultural relativism in her defence of women in Egypt who are caught up in a new wave of religiosity in Islam (Mahmood, 2001). Mahmood seeks to gain respect for the exercise of 'agency' by her research subjects who teach each other about Islam in mosques and are extremely pious, praying the required amount of times per day, and engaging in veil wearing and various bodily practices that remind them to be modest and shy. She says that she goes beyond post-structuralism because that theoretical approach tends to understand the exercise of agency as being related to 'resistance'. She doesn't agree with that and says that agency should be understood as women seeking to tie themselves more firmly into dominant practice: 'we might think of agency not only as the capacity for progressive change but also, importantly, as the capacity to endure, suffer, and persist' (Mahmood, 2009, p. 217). Mahmood explains that feminists cannot accept that women want to submit because they are biased by liberalism and cannot compass 'stepping out of the simple opposition liberalism constructs between freedom and submission, instead exploring the forms of submission internal to a particular construction of freedom and the system of gender inequality in which such a construction resides' (Mahmood, 2009, p. 209). There is no coercion or constraint mentioned in her account of Egyptian women's practices of submission and subordination. There should be no hierarchy of values, she considers, 'I have argued that the liberatory goals of feminism should be rethought in light of the fact that the desire for freedom and liberation is a historically situated desire' (Mahmood, 2001, p. 223). The feminist critique is thus neatly dispatched, because it is merely the ephemeral product of a particular time in history. Another device for sidelining the feminist critique is guilt-tripping, that is accusing feminists who have the temerity to be critical of serious flaws, such as failure to respect 'difference'.

Guilt-tripping: feminist criticism of Islam is disrespectful of difference

The anthropologist Lila Abu-Lughod is an exemplary practitioner of the art of guilt-tripping feminists who are concerned about the human rights of women under Islamic regimes (Abu-Lughod, 2002). Abu-Lughod, for instance, says that 'we', by which she may mean feminists, 'need to develop . . . a serious appreciation of differences among women in the world . . .' (Abu-Lughod, 2002, p. 783). Her exposition of the importance of 'difference' is in an article that criticises what she considers to be the desire of Western feminists to 'save' the women of Afghanistan from the Taliban. She pooh-poohs the idea that the burqa is inherently harmful to women, defending it on the grounds of 'difference'. Western feminists, she considers, 'feel sorry for' and 'smugly superior' to 'women of cover' (Abu-Lughod, 2002, p. 787). It makes them 'feel good' to 'save' Afghan women from the Taliban. Afghan women might want to wear the burqa because they are 'different', so feminists must accept the 'possibility of difference'. They might want to continue wearing their burqas even after the Taliban have been defeated, so feminists need to ask themselves, 'Can we only free Afghan women to be like us or might we have to recognize that even after "liberation" from the Taliban, they might want different things than we would want for them?' (Abu-Lughod, 2002, p. 787).

Afghan women may just be 'different' from other women, she considers, and asks feminists to do 'the hard work involved in recognizing and respecting differences'. The implication here is that feminists who continue to campaign vigorously against the abuse of the human rights of Afghan women are somewhat lazy, just not wanting to do the hard yards. She advises feminists that 'We may want justice for women, but can we accept that there might be different ideas about justice and that different women might want, or choose, different futures from what we envision as best . . . We must consider that they might be called to personhood, so to speak, in a different language' (Abu-Lughod, 2002, p. 787). There is no question here that women might suffer a common oppression and have a common interest in ending it. In her view the 'different' approach of Afghan women is reflected in the fact that they 'looked to Iran as a country in which they saw women making significant gains within an Islam framework' (Abu-Lughod, 2002, p. 788). For the women of Aghanistan, Abu-Lughod considers, Islamic feminism is the way forward.

She is critical of the important and influential women's human rights group RAWA (Revolutionary Association for the Women of Afghanistan) for not taking up Islamic feminism. Feminists must be 'aware of differences, respectful of other paths toward social change that might give women better lives' and should call the very idea of 'liberation' into question. She asks whether 'liberation' is 'even a goal for which all women or people strive . . . Are emancipation, equality, and rights part of a universal language we must use?' (Abu-Lughod, 2002, p. 788). She identifies the 'we' in her article as 'As anthropologists, feminists, or concerned citizens' who should be 'wary of taking on the mantles of those 19th-century Christian missionary women who devoted their lives to saving their Muslim sisters' (Abu-Lughod, 2002, p. 789). The cry of Western feminists today, she says, is not to Jesus, but to 'human rights or the liberal West'. Abu-Lughod's hostility to the notion of 'women's rights' is clear in the way she speaks about NGOs dedicated to women's rights in Egypt and Palestine as a 'growth industry', a term that is not used positively (Abu-Lughod, 2010). Women Living Under Muslim Laws, an organisation of women from Muslim cultures, which is dedicated to improving women's existence in Muslim states, she describes as engaging in 'sensationalizing projects to save Muslim women from their cultures' (Abu-Lughod, 2010, p. 9). Abu-Lughod is critical of NGOs that highlight violence against women by men in their own communities such as domestic violence and honour killings, and asks why the NGOs do not campaign against the deaths of women in warfare, mainly that involving aggression by the US government, instead. For Abu-Lughod there is a good and justified feminism, which campaigns against the effects of 'occupation and siege' on the Palestinian family (Aub-Lughod, 2010, p. 12). Bad feminism engages in what she calls the 'culturalization' of violence, that is campaigning against stoning and violence meted out to women because they are women, by the men nearest to them. The correct object of assault should be violence women suffer in conjunction with their men, not from their men. It is male domination that Abu-Lughod considers it impolite to address, and feminists who do bring this into focus become the victims of her ire, as culturalisers, exoticisers and sensationalists.

Islamic feminism

The cultural relativists who traduce the feminist critics of Islam are not so acerbically hostile to Islamic feminism but are much more likely to favour this as the way forward. Islamic feminism is seen as culturally appropriate for Muslim women and has gained legitimacy as a form of feminism from its promotion within the Western academy. Islamic feminism is the practice in which Muslim women seek advances for women's rights through reinterpretations of Islamic scriptures. Opposition to polygamy, for instance, may be based upon the argument that Islamic texts show polygamy to be a practice suited only to a particular situation, such as one in which too many men have been killed in war, and only to be justifiable if the husband can treat all his wives equally, a condition that is impossible to fulfil. These are not 'feminist' arguments that are based upon the fact that polygamy is a practice of male power that is harmful to women. They are made in the literature of the well-known Malaysian Islamic women's organisation, Sisters in Islam (Sisters in Islam, 1991). In a pamphlet entitled 'Are Women and Men Equal Before Allah?' they argue that polygamy was invented to ameliorate the plight of orphans, though they do say they promote monogamy rather than polygamy. While feminist critics of Islam, like Irshad Manji, see the Qur'an as irremediably misogynist, Sisters of Islam reinterpret the apparently clearly sexist message. They say that women are not unequal in Islam because they have the good fortune of men being 'responsible' for them and being required to pay for their upkeep. As they explain, 'the Qur'an establishes that men . . . (have responsibility) over women

. . . it intends to establish a responsibility of men for the protection and maintenance of women in a restricted social context' (Sisters in Islam, 1991, p. 5). Men have responsibility to support women because 'Biologically, only women can bear the future generations of Muslims'. To this end, they say, 'The Qur'an created a harmonious balance in society by establishing a functional responsibility for males to facilitate this biological function of females'. The fact that men are required to support women financially does not, they explain, 'give men inherent superiority'. Men have a material advantage, Sisters in Islam says, thus they have a responsibility to spend 'for the support of women' (Sisters in Islam, 1991, p. 6). This is an expression of the separate spheres argument that is the common foundation in the work of apologists for fundamentalist religions. Difference, they say, does not mean inequality, but unfortunately it usually does. Systems of apartheid based on difference are constructed by those with the power to enforce them, such as whites in South Africa or men in male domination. It is women, not men, who are 'different' because men are the standard. Systems of apartheid do not emerge by some plan of nature, but are constructed by the powerful class in their interests.

'Islamic feminism' is often distinguished from the practice of 'Muslim feminists'. The latter descriptor indicates that the feminists in question are practising Muslims as well as being feminists rather than that their feminism will be framed by the scriptures. One criticism that is made of Islamic feminism is that it resembles not at all what might be considered to be its equivalent: 'Christian feminism' (Moghadam, 2002). Christian feminists, such as Mary Hunt (Hunt and New, 2010) and Rosemary Radford Ruether (1993) in the US, do not seek to derive their feminist arguments from the Bible, but rather criticise the Bible and the practice of Christian churches from a feminist perspective, something that would be plain dangerous and is not contemplated by Islamic feminists who may not cast any doubts upon the holy book. Islamic feminists are frank about the fact that their approach is tactical, they do not think any other way forward is possible. Thus Ziba Mir-Hosseini states, 'given the current realities of the Muslim world, in which the Islamists have the upper hand in defining the terms of reference of political and gender discourses, I would maintain that only those who are prepared to engage with Islam's sacred texts and its legal traditions can bring change from within' (Mir-Hosseini, 2006, p. 644). The rise of fundamentalist Islam has meant that Muslim women 'must' conduct the 'battle' for their rights 'in a religious language and framework' (Mir-Hosseini, 2006, p. 644).

The issue of Islamic feminism is most often discussed in relation to Iran, in which it has emerged most clearly as a force that seeks to influence government policy. It is understandable that feminists in Iran should seek to advance women's rights by using a strategy that can appear legitimate in that theocratic context, whereas 'Western feminism' would get no hearing or lead to punishment. However, Islamic feminism is appearing in worrying ways in the West. Thus a report of a consultation in the UK organised by the Muslim Women's Network, and chaired by Haleh Afshar, states on the first page that 'The women whose voices are recorded here spoke with passion and conviction about their desire to engage in decision-making processes both at the local and national levels and to fight for their *Islamic* [my italics] rights' (Muslim Women's Network, 2006). Christian feminists have never argued for their 'Christian rights' but for women's rights as human rights, as feminists of other faiths and none have tended to do.

Critics of Islamic feminism

Islamic feminists in the Iranian diaspora argue that their approach, applied within Iran, has achieved positive results that attest to its effectiveness. Mir-Hosseini, for instance, writes, 'only those who are prepared to engage with Islam's sacred texts and its legal tradition can bring change from within' (Mir-Hosseini, 2006, p. 644). Islamic feminist academics, or those cultural relativists who are their fellow travellers, argue that this movement can achieve real gains in theocracies. This may seem possible at the level of theory, but careful examination of the politics of women's rights in Iran does not support this enthusiasm. Critics of Islamic feminism argue that it has achieved very little (Mojab, 2001). Moreover, they argue that it is harmful to the secular feminism that is increasing in strength in Iran. Valentine Moghadam (2002), who identifies herself as a 'secular feminist' and a Marxist-feminist, considers that religious doctrine should not be the basis of laws, policies or institutions. Another significant critic is Shahrzad Mojab who says that 'postmodernists/relativists support Islam-based patriarchal gender relations' and brand 'The century-long secular feminist movements in Islamic countries' as 'Western', and 'Islamic patriarchal relations' as 'authentic cultural formations' (Mojab, 1998).

Barlow and Akbarzadeh examine in *Human Rights Quarterly* exactly what Islamic feminism achieved in Iran (Barlow and Akbarzadeh, 2008). They explain that there is presently a great deal of feminism going on in Iran and they use the terms 'religious-oriented' and 'secular-oriented' feminists because they consider that the terms 'Islamic feminists' and 'secular feminists' suggests too great a distinction between women who have areas of common ground. They explain that 'religious-orientated' feminism has 'proven to be a flourishing force since it does not challenge the Iranian regime' (Barlow and Akbarzadeh, 2008, p. 26). It was represented by a 'women's faction' in parliament that sought to reform the law. This achieved some improvements in the area of child custody, such that women could have custody of both male and female children to seven years. Also they achieved the raising of the minimum legal age for marriage to thirteen, though there are ways that this can be got around through gaining special permission to wed a young girl child. But, they argue, no substantive change was achieved. The Islamic feminists also tried to get CEDAW ratified, by arguing that it fitted into and represented women's Islamic rights. But the Guardian Council rejected this change that successfully went through parliament, on the grounds that it was 'unconstitutional and un-Islamic'.

Barlow and Akbarzadeh give an example of what they see as the betrayal by 'religious-orientated' feminists of their 'secular-orientated' sisters. A conference was held in April 2000 in Berlin to discuss the future of the reform movement and was attended by both groups of feminists. On return, however, the punishments for those who attended differed considerably according to their allegiance to Islam. The secular-orientated feminists got secret trials and two months in prison, whereas the religious-orientated women got public trials and were able to successfully appeal their prison sentences. The religious-orientated feminists did not protest the injustice, however, or seek to support their sisters. This created a schism. But Barlow and Akbarzadeh state secular-orientated feminism is getting its strength back. The only women to remain in the parliament are very conservative women and there are no women's factions left in politics. However, there is a move away from the strategies of Islamic feminism towards direct action politics of public protests and civil disobedience and some of those joining in are disillusioned ex-religiously-orientated feminists. A new alliance has developed, which augurs well.

The feminist response to cultural relativism about Islam

The problem of why post-structuralists and cultural relativists are prepared to support religion is addressed by Haideh Moghissi in her passionately argued and persuasive book *Feminism and Islamic Fundamentalism: The Limits of Postmodern Analysis* (1999). Moghissi experienced the impact of a fundamentalist government before leaving Iran for the US. Her book directly takes on what she sees as the harmful influence of postmodernism in the feminist academy, where it has led to a strange and dangerous alliance between two philosophies that should in theory be opposed: postmodernism and fundamentalism. Moghissi explains that she wrote the book because she had noticed a shift in the way that women's lives in Islamic societies were being written about in the academy 'from a sympathetic appreciation of the plight of women under fundamentalist rule to extravagant affirmations of Muslim women's "agency", gender-awarenesss, empowerment and security within a protected space', a trend that is well represented in the work of Mahmood and Abu-Lughod above (Moghissi, 1999, p. vii). This newly positive approach was the result of the influence of postmodernism with 'its well-advertised but fictitious radicalism' (Moghissi, 1999, p. 52) in the form of post-colonial theory. The result was a 'convergence . . . in the post-colonial, anti-Orientalist scholarship on Islam and gender' with a 'fundamentalist conservatism' (Moghissi, 1999, p. 47). The convergence resulted from 'postmodern relativism', which, she considers, dominates the English-speaking academy. This 'postmodern relativism' creates a 'style benchmarked by an uncritical pursuit of the culturally exotic and the untouched' so that no clear distinction is drawn between the position of fundamentalists and that of a large number of 'anti-representational post-colonial feminists'. This resulted in a 'tremendous cost' politically to women in the Islamic world. A particularly harmful aspect of these politics, she says, is 'nostalgic populism', which is the 'leading motif of the recent exuberant discussion of Muslim women's gender activism which represents "Muslim women" as empowered, militant and dignified citizens with a firmly integrated sense of self' (Moghissi, 1999, p. 49). The 'curious affinity' of postmodernism with the 'most reactionary ideas of Islamic fundamentalism' reflects the common ground these philosophies share in 'an unremitting hostility to the social, cultural and political processes of change and knowledge and rationality, originating in the West, known as modernity' (Moghissi, 1999, p. 52).

Moghissi strongly rejects Islamic feminism and asks now if 'a religion which is based on gender hierarchy' could be adopted as the framework for struggle for 'gender democracy and women's equality with men?' She asks 'if Islam and feminism are compatible, which one has to operate within the framework of the other?' (Moghissi, 1999, p. 126). She states unequivocally that 'no amount of twisting and bending can reconcile the Qur'anic injunctions and instructions about women's rights and obligations with the idea of gender equality' (Moghissi, 1999, p. 140), because 'The *Shari'a* unapologetically discriminates against women and religious minorities' (Moghissi, 1999, p. 141). Moghissi considers that the determination to find women's 'agency' in unsuitable places supports Islamism. She criticises 'Overheated excitement about Muslim women's agency' because this has the effect of 'promoting the viewpoints of the region's Muslim female elites' while discrediting and endangering the 'non-Muslim women who, under precarious, often frightening, conditions, are trying to reclaim women's voice and women's space in Islamic societies' (Moghissi, 1999, p. 146).

A new orientalism

The idea that Islamic feminism is most suitable for Muslim women is, I suggest, a patronising example of a 'new orientalism', which exoticises the Muslim woman. Those in the academy who castigate the detractors of Islamic feminism are guilty of this 'new orientalism'. This is the practice in which many in the Western academy, and perhaps the majority of those on the Left who consider themselves enlightened, exhibit an appeasement of Islamic fundamentalism that is profoundly negative for the rights of women. An example of 'new orientalism' is the fact that academic work that has an Islamic feminist perspective can be treated with quite different standards from those applied to other scholarly work. Thus scholarly journals that publish serious, peer-reviewed, theoretical and research-based articles, which would not be expected to publish pieces that proclaim that their theoretical framework comes from the Bible, do publish such pieces when precisely the same claim is made in relation to the Qur'an. Haleh Afshar from the UK, for instance, writes in the *Journal of Ethnic and Racial Studies* that 'With the death of the Prophet, Muslim women lost their most important champion' (Afshar,

2008, p. 422). This curious statement occurs in the middle of a considerable section on Islam, which includes comments on the behaviour of the Prophet's wives. It is, of course, not possible to reference such comments since the history and interpretation are both in doubt, as is the authorship of the sources. It is hard to imagine that such statements in relation to Jesus would be accepted in a peer-reviewed journal. The rules are different for Islam, and this may be because the Western academy, and the Left in the West, are involved in a form of 'orientalism' towards what they see as Muslim culture. Muslims may talk about god in the academy, whereas Christians have to employ rational and well referenced argument. The privileging of 'Islamic feminism' in academic discourse in the West should perhaps be understood as a form of reverse racism. It discriminates against all the brave apostates and secular feminists whether they labour undercover in Iran, or speak out in the diaspora.

Conclusion

Muslim and ex-Muslim feminists who criticise Islam have met with strong opposition from a surprising source: academics in the area of gender studies and the Middle East who might have been expected to be more positive towards other feminists on this issue. These detractors tend to be safely in US or UK universities and to be on the Left politically. They take cultural relativist positions in which whatever women do that does not show disrespect for Islam is identified as an expression of women's agency, from Islamic feminism to the slavish practice of Islamic rituals. Their work can be seen as 'orientalist', an accusation they usually make towards feminist critics of Islam because they make strong separations between East and West and exoticise the survival techniques of women in Islamic theocracies as positive if not progressive behaviours. Their denunciation of critics of Islam is a problem because it has made the feminist academy a place in which feminist atheism cannot easily be expressed. The fierce feminist critique of religion as patriarchal and misogynist, that animated feminism in the 1970s and 1980s has been severely undermined by a rehabilitation of religion in this cultural relativist work. Moreover the courageous ideas and activities of the feminist critics of Islam covered here, though some of them are known in humanist and rationalist circles, or even in the case of Ayaan Hirsi Ali in the malestream media, are likely to be little known to students of gender and women's studies who may even accept the tincture of racism that has been attached to their work. I argue for the work of these feminist atheists and critics to be taken into the mainstream of feminist scholarship and treated with the respect and support it deserves. The master's tools are unlikely to dismantle the master's house, whereas principled opposition to the whole construction may have more positive effects.

CONCLUSION

Liberating women from religious oppression

This book has argued that religion is on the rise and that, whatever the context – Christian patriarchy in the US; Islamic fundamentalism both in majority Muslim states and in multicultural states; Judaist fundamentalism in Israel and in other countries in the West – the subordination of women is the *sine qua non* of this development. This is because the rise of religion compensates men for the gender quake. This book has aimed to show that, though there are other socio-political reasons for the rise of religion, the significance of the power over women that it offers to men needs to be recognised. Religious institutions offer firm and steadfast bastions of male privilege, to which men can repair to escape the challenges created by changes in women's rights and equality in the last fifty years. Religious revivalism and extremism offer men compensation for the losses they have suffered as women have entered the public world, such as monopolies on lucrative forms of employment, domination of parliaments and public fora. In the home, some women are now so bold as to refuse unwanted sexual use and may wish to limit their childbearing. I argued in my book, *The Industrial Vagina* (2009), that the burgeoning sex industry offers a similar compensation to men for lost privileges. Prostitution and fundamentalist religion have in common men's desire for vengeance and compensation for their losses from women's increasing equality.

It is not just fundamentalist religion that constitutes a threat to women's equality. Women in most varieties of the monotheistic religions suffer discrimination in such important matters as the sharing of space and responsibilities in religious establishments, in ministry and in management. Religions based upon ancient texts created in times of the ancient slavery of women are not benign. Varieties of religion more usually understood as fundamentalist are engine rooms of misogyny, dedicated to casting women's status back to that which women experienced at the time in which the main religious texts were written; but those which are seen as moderate generally still employ those texts and do not seek to thoroughly disinfect them of their ancient prejudices.

This book has shown concern at the limitations and distortions that dominate discussion of the ways that religion harms women, particularly on the Left and in the feminist academy. I hope that the book will contribute to opening up academic and feminist discussion of such matters as Islamic feminism and the veil, as well as the subordination of women in Orthodox Jewish communities, because there is a grave need for more open discussion in the feminist academy. As I have shown, those feminists who criticise the ways in which religion harms women are unreasonably traduced in the academy, particularly by those who see themselves as progressive and on the Left. It is important that feminist scholars, as well as activists, are prepared to stand up against accusations that criticism of any variety of religion, including Islam, is inevitably racist and colonialist. Those feminists who are safer, by virtue of not facing punishment for apostasy, or working and writing in democratic states, need to support their sisters who are brave enough to stand up against threats and intimidation to detail the ways in which religion harms women.

I will not speak here about which strategies feminist activists should be adopting in Islamic republics or in other non-democratic contexts to deal with these threats that religion poses to women's human rights. A useful 2011 AWID report does consider this (AWID, 2011). This book has mostly been concerned with the impact of the rise of religion on women in Western democracies where the task of combating the ways in which religion oppresses women and girls is multi-pronged. This book has addressed a number of problems that need to be addressed: the ways in which governments are enlisting religions in the provision of services and policymaking with no concern for their misogynist agenda; the reluctance of governments to intervene in the private fiefdoms that religious patriarchs set up to maintain their power and privilege; incorporation of discriminatory religious law into legal systems; and the failure to challenge harmful cultural practices.

Secularism

The development of secularisation is important to ending the promotion and financial support of religion by governments. I say 'secularisation' because, even those states that many would understand as secular are often incompletely secularised and have made various compromises with religions. A movement towards greater secularisation is necessary because the use of arguments about the right to religion to justify subordinating women and girls can be most effectively countered in secular states. But the form that this secularisation should take has not been well discussed among feminist activists and scholars. Women Living Under Muslim Laws argues that there is a need for a feminist conceptualisation of secularism (WLUML, 2006). Secularism does not provide a sufficient answer, because secularists are not necessarily feminists and secular states can be hostile to the interests of women. Moreover secularism is usually understood as a separation between the public politics of the state and the private politics of religion i.e. it reproduces a public/private split that is very problematic for the interests of women. A secularism that serves the interests of women needs to smash the public/private divide in ways that extend human rights to all women equally. Also secular states may seek to create a level playing field on which all manifestations of 'religion' are seen as sacrosanct and beyond state interference, for instance. This does not serve women who are then trapped within patriarchal communities where their human rights are denied beyond and out of reach of state power.

There are many varieties of secularism in operation in states, some of which are more sympathetic to women's interests than others. Legal theorist Abdullahi Ahmed An-Nai'im points out, 'Secularism is in fact a multidimensional concept' that manifests in very different ways (An-Na'im, 2006, p. 14). He explains that secularism operates very differently in Mexico where 'there is such a strict separation of religion and politics that priests are not allowed to vote' and the Republic of Ireland where 'the Catholic Church wields so much political power that abortion is illegal on the grounds that it violates Church doctrine' (An-Na'im, 2006, p. 14). Despite the variety of the different forms that exist, I argue that secularism is the vital foundation of women's equality. The most important aspects of this secularism for women's rights are: an end to religious exceptionalism in equality laws; a prohibition on state financial support of religious organisations such as faith schools or faith welfare services; and no incorporation of aspects of religious law into the legal system. The state should not be involved in the funding of religions, either directly or through tax relief that enables religious organisations to become very profitable corporations. Religious organisations seeking to influence state policy should not be specially privileged through faith consultations. When religions are privileged in policy this disadvantages many constituencies within the state, including those that religions abhor, such as women, lesbians and gays, and those who have no religion or belong to minority religions that are not recognised. The official involvement of religion in affairs of state disadvantages women because, as this book has sought to show, religions are fundamentally patriarchal. Though they may be mellowed by the activities within them of determined feminists, and even allow women priests, they may at any time be subject to the determined influence of patriarchs who can point to what is said in the scriptures to roll back advances towards equality. Governments should not be persuaded that the 'right to religion' can negate the human rights of half of the world's people. Women's equality must be put in front of the rights of men to construct and promote their ideologies of male domination. The 'gentlemen's agreements' by which governments and male elites overlook harms to women in order to secure the loyalty and obedience of other groups of patriarchs, need to be challenged at every turn.

Transformative equality

Intervention is needed in the religious fiefdoms that patriarchs create to establish their control if transformative equality for women and girls is to be achieved. Feminist legal theorists have been clear on the necessity of breaking down the barrier between the public and private spheres if women's equality is to be achieved. Religious patriarchs uphold this barrier with fervour, because it enables them to create private fiefdoms in which they can hold back the progress of women's equality and justify this with reference to the wishes of their god. So long as the public/private split is respected, women's equality will be notional rather than actual. Feminist legal theorist, Rebecca Cook, is clear on the distinction between transformative equality and a formal equality that women are in reality prevented from accessing because of their subordination in the private realm (Cook, 2006). To support her case she quotes General Recommendation no. 25 of CEDAW, which notes that the convention aims to, 'eliminate all forms of discrimination against women with a view to achieving women's de jure and de facto equality with men in the enjoyment of their human rights and fundamental freedoms' (Cook, 2006, Introduction p. 2). This, she says, recognises the importance of transformative equality. It requires that states break open the bounds of privacy of the family within which girls and women are subordinated. This privacy is defended on the grounds of 'culture' in multicultural theory, but increasingly, as we have seen, on the grounds of religion, which is a weightier argument. Religion provides a good retreat for patriarchs, because cultures may change but the prescriptions of the holy books remain the same. When men's privileges are threatened, and the arguments as to rights and equality for women are difficult to challenge, they can default to religion. It is important for feminists to interrupt any 'gentlemen's agreements' through which governments make common cause with abusive men through privileging rights to the privacy of the family or the right to religion.

The right to exit

Theorists of multiculturalism, as we have seen, argue that respect by states for the privacy of cultures or religions is acceptable so long as a right to exit exists. This right to exit, feminist theorists maintain, must be a realistic one. If it is not realistic then it constitutes but a fig leaf of equality on the harsh reality of male domination. Presently girls and women within patriarchal fiefdoms are controlled by removal from education and the workplace so that they do not have economic independence, and by sequestration in faith schools, homes and communities so that they do not have access to ideas, supportive people and services that may help them leave. If girls and women are to be able to imagine opposition to forced/arranged marriages, for instance, they must know their rights and be able to imagine a different future. They must be prepared by education and training for economic independence. A realistic right to exit requires that governments committed to the rights of girls and women cease providing funding to faith schools. State schooling – which is universal and does not pander to particular interest groups – is likely to be most effective in giving girls information and access to alternatives. It gives children access to the world outside the fiefdoms in which they may be corralled, and makes greater social mixing possible. State education should not be acting as an agent of fundamentalist religions by imposing restrictions on girls that are demanded by self-appointed leaders such as Muslim councils, as to what they may see, how they may exercise and what they may wear.

Restrictions on the availability of homeschooling are needed too. Presently there are few regulations controlling homeschooling, save the necessity that the parents are seen as educationally competent to school their children. In Australia, homeschooling has been a way to overcome the problems of distance, but other motivations are now likely to be involved, such as the desire of parents to prevent their children from being contaminated by ideas outside the faith that has been chosen for them. To the extent that homeschooling is being used in the US and other countries to segregate children, cut off their options and indoctrinate them, it needs to be re-examined with the object of ensuring that children are not cut off from a right to exit thereby. But the right to exit is insufficient. It assumes that what takes place within the private fiefdoms of the home, family and community will in most instances be benign and worthy of respect. Something more proactive is needed. States need to intervene early in the lives of children and young people to protect them from getting into dangerous situations, particularly that of servile marriage.

Religious subordination disenfranchises women. As the legal theorist, Courtney Howland, argues, the state should be recognised as having an obligation to enable women to exercise their political rights by intervening in the private sphere: 'it is arguable that states may have a duty to pass laws prohibiting the practice of requiring wives to be obedient because it is inevitable that political rights, such as expression, association, and assembly are undermined by a rule of obedience' (Howland, 1999, p. 100). Religious arguments imprison women in harmful marriages and families. They constitute the bars of a cage made from the terror of hellfire rather than steel. Where the protection of the rights – and the lives – of girls and women are concerned, state intervention is necessary, and discussion should centre on the best ways to carry this out rather than focusing on masculinist notions of privacy and the right to religion.

One law for all

Respect by states for religious law means abrogation of the rights of girls and women. It is women who are adversely affected by such patriarchal accommodations, mainly through discriminatory rulings on marriage and divorce. Incorporation of any aspect of religious law into the legal system creates two classes of rights for women. Those who are persuaded that they should use religious law end up with second-class rights compared with other women who have recourse to laws fought for by feminists during two centuries, which provide more equal rights for women in marriage and the family. Beyond the outlawing of acceptance of religious law in state legal systems, it is necessary for governments to consider how to intervene to help women harmed by religious law in their communities. Political philosopher Clare Chambers argues against liberal understandings that state intervention in communities restricts freedom (Chambers, 2008). She considers that the state should intervene in the form of an 'equality tribunal' to which women from Muslim or Jewish communities could apply if, for instance, they were denied equal rights in marriage in a religious court. If found guilty of discrimination the court would have to pay compensation and this, she thinks, would cause attitudes to change towards equality. The state, she says, needs to 'be proactive in prohibiting those practices or forms of domination which are particularly harmful' (Chambers, 2008, p. 79).

Harmful cultural practices

In order to create a level playing field for women, however, special laws are needed, too, which target harmful practices against girls and women. Ungendered laws on bodily harm, on slavery and on marriage, do not adequately respond to the special harms that are visited upon girls and women, such as female genital mutilation and forced marriage. The former UN Special Rapporteur, Radhika Coomaraswamy, recommends that states should develop penal, civil and administrative sanctions in domestic legislation to punish violence in the family and provide redress to women victims, even if the violence is associated with a cultural practice (Coomaraswamy, 2002). The penal sanction, she says, should be strong and effective and not merely on paper. The mere existence of laws is not sufficient. Laws prohibiting female genital mutilation exist in the UK and in France, for instance, but they are not invoked (Dirie, 2008). Coomaraswamy argues that states should develop national plans of action to eradicate violence in the family, particularly violence relating to cultural practices, through health and education programmes at the grass-roots level. States should adopt, she says, all appropriate measures in the field of education to modify the social and cultural patterns of conduct that foster cultural practices in the family that are violent towards women. Jasvinder Sanghera, of the NGO working against forced marriage in the UK – Karma Nirvana – writes about the issue of how to educate children towards eliminating the ideology of honour that leads to so much suffering and violence against women and girls. She quotes UK director of the Crown Prosecution Service, Nazir Afzal, as saying that re-education has to target six-, eight-, or ten-year-olds, 'Anybody over the age of eighteen has already made up their mind, for them it's too late' (Sanghera, 2009, p. 290). Education will not be enough to enable all children to overcome the emotional attachments that families use to enforce their submission, to arranged marriages, for example, but it is a step along the way. Thus states need to fund NGOs, like Karma Nirvana, that conduct this education and provide support to those who need a way out. The concept of harmful cultural practices, however, has been unreasonably restricted in UN understandings. The practice of covering girl children and women is not usually explicitly included in this category. It fits very well, and concerns about religious sensitivity should not be permitted to override its inclusion.

The plan of action

The plan of action that Coomaraswamy calls for needs to cover all of the ways in which women's rights and equality are harmed by religion. This form of women's subordination needs to be understood and challenged as a whole, from the right of religions to dismiss female staff that become pregnant out of wedlock, to the justification of harmful marriage practices, through the right to religion. The range of forms of discrimination and violence against women that are justified by religion is extensive. As feminist activists and scholars work to delineate the ways in which girls and women are subordinated through religion, it will be easier to demand that governments prove their commitment to women's equality by limiting the harms that religions cause. A concern for women's freedom of religion from governments would provide a beginning towards this end. The necessary basis of women's freedom 'of' religion is the right to be free 'from' religion, and all the harms it creates for women's human rights and women's equality.

REFERENCES

ABC News (2007, 26 July) Ex-mistress ran Packer's brothel: Biography. *ABC News Australia.* www.abc.net.au/news/stories/2007/07/26/1989489.htm (accessed 4 April 2010).

ABC News (2010, 6 August) Assault on man at centre of burka-linked case. *ABC News Australia.* www.abc.net.au/news/stories/2010/08/06/2975560.htm (accessed 8 August 2010).

Abu-Lughod, Lila (2001) Orientalism and Middle East Feminist Studies. *Feminist Studies,* 27(1): 101–113.

Abu-Lughod, Lila (2002) Do Muslim Women Really Need Saving? Anthropological Reflections on Cultural Relativism and Its Others. *American Anthropologist* 104(3): 783–790.

Abu-Lughod, Lila (2010) The active social life of 'Muslim women's rights': a plea for ethnography, not polemic with cases from Egypt and Palestine. *Journal of Middle East Women's Studies* 6(1): 1–45.

ACLU (n.d.) American Civil Liberties Union of Utah. National ACLU Policy on Plural Marriage. www.acluutah.org/pluralmarriage.htm (accessed 11 November 2009).

Accord (2009) Employment in Faith Schools: Accord Equality Bill Report Stage Briefing. www.accordcoalition.org.uk/wp-content/uploads/2009/12/Equality-Bill-Employment-Briefing-Dec-09.pdf (accessed 12 January 2010).

AFP (2010) Vatican Changes Tune on Condom Use as Benedict XVI says prophylactic reduces risk of HIV. *The Australian,* 21 November.

Afshar, Haleh (2008) Can I see your hair? Choice, agency and attitudes: the dilemma of faith and feminism for Muslim women who cover. *Ethnic and Racial Studies,* 31(2): 411–427.

Ahmed, Leila (1992) *Women and Gender in Islam: Historical Roots of a Modern Debate.* New Haven, CT: Yale University Press.

Ali, Ayaan Hirsi (2006) *The Caged Virgin: A Muslim Woman's Cry for Reason.* London: Pocket Books.

Ali, Ayaan Hirsi (2007) *Infidel: My Life.* New York: Free Press.

Al-Krenawi, Alean and Slonim-Nevo, Vered (2008) The Pyschosocial Profile of Bedouin Arab Women Living in Polygamous and Monogamous Marriages. *Families in Society: The Journal of Contemporary Social Services.* 89(1): 139–149.

Al-Tikriti, Anas, Ridley, Yvonee, Hibatullah, Ihtisham, Patel, Ismail, and Salih, Roshan Muhammed (2008) What turns some Islamists to terror? *Guardian* Letters, 26 April. www.guardian.co.uk/uk/2008/apr/26/uksecurity (accessed 20 August 2010).

Amara, Fadela (2006) *Breaking the Silence: French Women's Voices from the Ghetto.* Berkeley, Los Angeles, London: University of California Press.

American Psychological Association (2007) *Report of the APA Task Force on the Sexualization of Girls.* Washington, DC: American Psychological Association.

Americans Against Abuses of Polygamy (n.d.) Polygamy is Abuse. http://polygamyisabuse.com/ (accessed 12 September 2010).

Amor, Abdelfattah M. (2002) *Study on Freedom of Religion or Belief and the Status of Women from the Viewpoint of Religion and Traditions.* Working Paper for Geneva-Based NGO Committee on Freedom of Religion or Belief and NGO Committee on the Status of Women. Unofficial Summary in English of E/CN.4/2002/73/Add.2, 5 April 2002. Geneva.

Amos, Deborah (2010) In Syria ban on veil raises few eyebrows. *National Public Radio,* 21 July. www.npr.org/templates/story/story.php?storyId=128671593&ps=cprs (accessed 12 October 2010).

An-Na'im, Abdullahi (2006) *Secularism from an Islamic Perspective. Dossier 28.* Women Living Under Muslim Laws. www.wluml.org/sites/wluml.org/files/import/english/pubs/pdf/dossier28/abdullahi-en.pdf (accessed 12 April 2010).

Arat, Yesim (2010) Religion, Politics and Gender Equality in Turkey: Implications of a democratic paradox. *Third World Quarterly.* 31(6): 869–884.

Asad, Talal, Brown, Wendy, Butler, Judith and Mahmood, Saba (2009) *Is Critique Secular? Blasphemy, Injury and Free Speech.* Berkeley, CA: University of California Press.

Askin, Kelly D. and Koenig, Dorean M. (eds) (2001) *Women and International Human Rights Law.* New York: Transnational Publishers.

Attar, Dena (2010, first published 1992) The Portable Cage. Women and Fundamentalism. In Cameron, Deborah and Scanlon, Joan (eds), *The Trouble and Strife Reader,* London: Bloomsbury, pp. 71–77.

AWID (2009) *New Insights on Religious Fundamentalisms. Research Highlights.* Toronto, Mexico City, Capetown: Association for Women's Rights in Development. www.awid.org/Media/Files/Challenging-Fundamentalisms-Research-Highlights (accessed 30 May 2011).

AWID (2010) Feminists On The Frontline: Case Studies of Resisting and Challenging Fundamentalisms. Toronto, Mexico City, Capetown: Association for Women's Rights in Development. www.awid.org/Library/Feminists-on-the-Frontline-Case-Studies-of-Resisting-and-Challenging-Fundamentalisms (accessed 30 May 2011).

Bachelard, Michael (2008) *Behind the Exclusive Brethren*. Victoria, Australia: Scribe Publications.

Baines, Beverley (2007) Polygamy's Challenge: Women, Religion and the Post-Liberal State. *Printemps*, 2(1): 23–28.

Bakht, Natasha (2009) Objection, Your Honour! Accommodating *Niqab*-Wearing Women in Courtrooms. In Grillo, Ralph, Ballard, Roger, Ferrari, Alessandro, Hoekema, Andre J., Maussen, Marcel, and Shah, Prakash (eds) (2009) *Legal Practice and Cultural Diversity*, London: Ashgate, pp. 115–134.

Balchin, Cassandra (2010) *Towards a Future without Fundamentalism. Analyzing Religious Fundamentalist Strategies and Feminist Responses*. Toronto, Mexico City, Capetown: Association for Women's Rights in Development.

Bamberger, Joan (1974) The Myth of Matriarchy: Why Men Rule in Primitive Society. In Rosaldo, Michelle and Lamphere, Louise, (eds), *Woman, Culture and Society*, Stanford CA: Stanford University Press. pp. 263–280.

Barlow, Rebecca and Akbarzadeh, Shahram (2008) Prospects for Feminism in the Islamic Republic of Iran. *Human Rights Quarterly*. 30(1): 21–40.

Baum, Geraldine (2007) Sarkozy deputy is no stranger to French slums. *Los Angeles Times*, 7 October. http://articles.latimes.com/2007/oct/12/world/fg-fadela12 (accessed 6 April 2010).

Bayes, Jane and Tohidi, Nayereh (2001) *Globalization, Gender and Religion: The Politics of Women's Rights in Catholic and Muslim Contexts*. New York: Palgrave.

BBC (2010a) Catholic Church sex abuse scandals around the world. *BBC News*, 23 April London: British Broadcasting Corporation. http://news.bbc.co.uk/2/hi/8576268.stm (accessed 20 May 2010).

BBC (2010b) US Church ordains lesbian bishop Mary Glasspool. *BBC News*, 15 May. London: British Broadcasting Corporation. http://news.bbc.co.uk/2/hi/americas/8684194.stm (accessed 20 May 2010).

BBC (2010c) Belgian lawmakers pass burka ban. *BBC News*, 30 April. London: British Broadcasting Corporation. http://news.bbc.co.uk/2/hi/europe/8652861.stm (accessed 12 October 2010).

BBC (2011) Somalia's al Shabab bans mixed sex handshakes in Jowhar. *BBC News*, 7 January. London: British Broadcasting Corporation. www.bbc.co.uk/news/world-africa-12138627 (accessed 19 January 2011).

BBC News Birmingham (2010) Birmingham Couple Murdered on Trip to Pakistan. *BBC News Birmingham*, 8 August. www.bbc.co.uk/news/uk-england-birmingham-10908372 (accessed 12 October 2010).

Beauvoir, Simone de (1972, first published 1949) *The Second Sex*. Harmondsworth: Penguin.

Beijing Declaration (1995) Fourth World Conference on Women. Beijing Declaration. United Nations. www.un.org/womenwatch/daw/beijing/platform/declar.htm (accessed 12 March 2010).

Bell, Diane and Klein, Renate (eds) (1996) *Radically Speaking. Feminism Reclaimed*. Melbourne: Spinifex Press.

Benedict, Ruth (1934) *Patterns of Culture*. Boston, MA: Houghton Mifflin Company

Benhabib, Seyla (2002) *The Claims of Culture. Equality and Diversity in the Global Era*. Princeton and Oxford: Princeton University Press.

Benson, Ophelia (2010,) Blasphemy, an unjustified privilege. *The Guardian*, 11 January. www.guardian.co.uk/commentisfree/belief/2010/jan/11/blasphemy-religion-atheism (accessed 12 March 2010).

Benson, Ophelia and Stangroom, Jeremy (2009) *Does God Hate Women?* London: Continuum.

Berger, Peter L. (1999) The Desecularization of the World: A Global Overview. In Berger, Peter L. (ed.), *The Desecularization of the World. Resurgent Religion in World Politics*, Washington, DC: Ethics and Policy Center and Wm B. Eerdmans Publishing Co., pp. 1–18.

Berkeley, Rob (2008) *Right to Divide? Faith Schools and Community Cohesion*. London: Runnymede Trust.

Berman, Paul (2010) *The Flight of the Intellectuals*. Melbourne: Scribe Publications.

Bhardwaj, Anita (2001) Growing Up Young, Asian and Female in Britain. A Report on Self-harm and Suicide. *Feminist Review*. 68, Summer: 52–67.

Bibby, Paul (2008,) Hillsong hits schools with beauty gospel. *Sydney Morning Herald*, 26 July. www.smh.com.au/news/national/hillsong-hits-schools-with-beauty-gospel/2008/07/25/1216492732905.html (accessed 3 September 2009).

Blakey, H., Pearce, J. and Chester, G. (2006) *Minorities within Minorities: Beneath the Surface of South Asian Participation*. York: Joseph Rowntree Foundation.

Bloch, Barbara (2009) I'm not religious but . . . A Secular Feminist Response to Interfaith Dialogue in Australia. In Dreher, Tanja and Ho, Christina (eds), *Beyond the Hijab Debate: New Conversations on Gender, Race and Religion*, Newcastle upon Tyne: Cambridge Scholars Publishing, pp.180–194.

Blomfield, Adrian (2010) Israeli rabbis clamp down on burka. *Daily Telegraph*, 30 July. www.telegraph.co.uk/news/worldnews/middleeast/israel/7919501/Israeli-rabbis-clamp-down-on-burka.htm (accessed 19 January 2011).

Bloom, Adi (2009) Compulsory sex education sparks fear that faith schools may impose agenda. *The Times Educational Supplement*, 1 May. www.tes.co.uk/article.aspx?storycode=6012631 (accessed 9 September 2009).

Book of Common Prayer (1559) http://justus.anglican.org/resources/bcp/1559/Churching_of_Women_1559.htm (accessed 30 May 2011).

Brissenden, Michael (2004) God and Politics mix at Hillsong. *7.30 Report*, 14 July. Australian Broadcasting Corporation. www.abc.net.au/7.30/content/2004/s1154131.htm (accessed 9 September 2009).

Brown, Andrew (2010) Fundamentalists against women. *The Guardian* 14 July. www.guardian.co.uk/commentisfree/andrewbrown/2010/jul/14/religion-reform-feminism-patriarchy (accessed 14 July 2010).

Bunting, Madeleine (2005) Friendly Fire. Madeleine Bunting meets Sheikh Yusuf al-Qaradawi in Qatar. *The Guardian*, 29 October. www.guardian.co.uk/world/2005/oct/29/religion.uk1 (accessed 12 October 2010).

Buss, Doris and Herman, Didi (2003) *Globalizing Family Values. The Christian Right in International Politics.* Minneapolis, MN: University of Minnesota Press.

Butler, Jennifer (2000) 300 Religious Right Participants Attend Beijing Prepcom. Ecumenical Women 2000 Plus, 1 June. www.globalpolicy.org/component/content/article/177/31727.html (accessed 20 March 2010).

Butler, Jennifer (2006) *Born Again: the Christian Right Globalized.* London: Pluto Press.

Butler, Judith (2000) Restaging the Universal: Hegemony and the Limits of Formalism. In Butler, Judith, Laclau, Ernesto and Zizek, Slavoj, *Contingency, hegemony, universality: contemporary dialogues on the left,* London: Verso, pp. 11–43.

Butler, Judith, Laclau, Ernesto and Zizek, Slavoj (2000*) Contingency, hegemony, universality: contemporary dialogues on the left.* London: Verso.

Cairo Declaration (1990) *Cairo Declaration on Human Rights in Islam.* Organisation of the Islamic Conference. www1.umn.edu/humanrts/instree/cairodeclaration.html (accessed 20 March 2010).

Canadian Press, The (2010) Niqab fight goes to top Ontario Court. *CBC News,* 8 June. Canadian Broadcasting Company. www.cbc.ca/canada/toronto/story/2010/06/08/niqab-testimony-ontario.html (accessed 19 January 2011).

Cantle, Ted, Kaur, Daljit, Athar, Mohammed, Dallison, Chris, Wiggans, Andy and Harris, Joshua (2006) *Challenging Local Communities to Change Oldham. Review of Community Cohesion in Oldham.* Final Report. Coventry: The Institute of Community Cohesion, Coventry University.

Carlson, Allan (1999) *The Natural Family is the Fundamental Social Unit: A Summons to Create Social Engineering.* World Congress of Families II. Opening Remarks. www.worldcongress.org/wcf2_spkrs/wcf_acc.htm (accessed 20 March 2010).

Carter, Paul (2007) Hillsong hosts Howard, Rudd in online telecast. *Courier Mail,* 9 August. www.news.com.au/couriermail/story/0,23739,22220165-5003402,00.html (accessed 11 September 2009).

Catholics for Choice. (2008) *Truth & Consequence. A Look Behind the Vatican's Ban on Contraception.* Washington, DC: Catholics for Choice.

CEDAW (1979) Convention on the Elimination of All Forms of Discrimination Against Women Reservations to CEDAW. www.un.org/womenwatch/daw/cedaw/reservations.htm (accessed 20 March 2010).

Chambers, Clare (2008) *Sex, Culture, and Justice: The Limits of Choice.* University Park, PA: The Pennsylvania State University Press.

Channel 4 (2007) *Dispatches: Undercover Mosque.* UK: Channel 4, 15 January.

Charlesworth, Hilary (1995) Human Rights as Men's Rights. In Peters, Julie and Wolper, Andrea (eds), *Women's Rights - Human Rights. International Feminist Perspectives,* New York: Routledge, pp. 103–113.

Cherry, Matt with Roy Brown (2009) *Speaking Freely About Religion: Religious Freedom, Defamation and Blasphemy.* London: International Humanist and Ethical Union.

Christian Polygamy Info (n.d. a) *Christian Polygamy Info: The History of the "Movement".* www.christianpolygamy.info/history/ (accessed 7 June 2011).

Christian Polygamy Info (n.d. b) *Love-Not-Force, the Movement's Standard.* www.christianpolygamy.info/ (accessed 5 October 2010).

CMBW (n.d.) *The Danvers Statement on Biblical Manhood and Womanhood.* Council on Biblical Manhood and Womanhood www.cbmw.org/Danvers (accessed 19 July 2010).

Communities and Local Government (2007, December) *Face-to-Face and Side-by-Side: A framework for inter faith dialogue and social action.* London: Home Office.

Communities and Local Government Committee (2010) *Preventing Violent Extremism. Sixth Report of Session 2009–10.* London: House of Commons, The Stationery Office Limited.

Cook, Rebecca J. (ed.) (1994) *Human Rights of Women. National and International Perspectives.* Philadelphia, PA: University of Pennsylvania Press.

Cook, Rebecca J. (2006) *Polygyny and Canada's Obligations under International Human Rights Law.* Ottawa: Department of Justice. www.justice.gc.ca/eng/dept-min/pub/poly/index.html (accessed 5 October 2010).

Coomaraswamy, Radhika (2002) *Cultural practices in the family that are violent towards women.* Report of the Special Rapporteur on violence against women. E/CN.4/2002/83. Retrieved February 28 2004 from www.unhchr.ch/Huridocda/Huridoca.nsf/TestFrame/42e7191fae543562c1256ba7004e963c?Opendocument.

Crouse, Janice Shaw (2010) *Feminists and the Family.* World Congress of Families. www.worldcongress.org/wcf3_spkrs/wcf3_crouse.htm (accessed 20 September 2010).

Daily Mail Reporter (2010) Muslim woman sacked from estate agency for refusing to wear a headscarf. *Daily Mail*, 3 October. www.dailymail.co.uk/news/article-1317342/Muslim-woman-sacked-REFUSING-wear-headscarf.html (accessed 12 October 2010).

Daly, Mary (1985a, first published 1968) *The Church and the Second Sex.* Boston, MA: Beacon Press.

Daly, Mary (1985b, first published 1973) *Beyond God the Father. Towards a Philosophy of Women's Liberation.* Boston, MA: Beacon Press.

Daly, Mary and Silver, Hilary (2008) Social exclusion and social capital: A comparison and critique. *Theory and Society.* 37: 537–566.

Dawkins, Richard (2006) *The God Delusion.* London: Black Swan.

Delphy, Christine and Leonard, Diana (1992) *Familiar Exploitation: A New Analysis of Marriage in Contemporary Western Societies.* London: Polity Press.

Department for International Development (2006) Press Release, 25 July. Ethnic minority groups share in 5 million pound fund to raise awareness of poverty in the developing world. http://webarchive.nationalarchives.gov.uk/+/www.dfid.gov.uk/news/files/pressreleases/ethnic-share.asp (accessed 20 April 2010).

Department of Justice (2008) Exceptions Review. *A Review of the Exceptions and Exemptions from the Equal Opportunity Act 1995 (Vic)*. Consultation Paper February 2008. Victoria, Australia: Department of Justice. www.justice.vic. gov.au/wps/wcm/connect/DOJ+Internet/resources/file/eb19014bdfe70b2/ ExceptionsReview_FinalConsultationPaper.pdf (accessed 11 September 2009).

Dines, Gail (2010) *Pornland: How Porn has Hijacked our Sexuality*. Melbourne: Spinifex.

Dirie, Waris (2008) *Desert Children*. London: Virago.

Dobash, R.E. and Dobash, R. (1979) *Violence Against Wives*. Somerset: Open Books.

Doward, Jamie (2011) David Cameron's attack on multiculturalism divides the coalition. London: *The Observer*, 6 February. www.guardian.co.uk/politics/ 2011/feb/05/david-cameron-attack-multiculturalism-coalition (accessed 8 February 2011).

Doyle, Leonard (2009) At last Blair is free to 'do God' and America loves it. *The Independent*, 6 February. www.independent.co.uk/news/world/americas/at-last-blair-is-free-to-do-god-ndash-and-america-loves-it-1547656.html (accessed 11 September 2009).

Droogsma, Rachel Anderson (2007) Redefining Hijab: American Muslim Women's Standpoints on Veiling. *Journal of Applied Communication Research*. 35(3): 294–319.

Duncan, Emily J. (2008) The Positive Effects of Legalizing Polygamy: "Love is a many splendored thing". *Duke Journal of Gender Law and Policy*. 15: 315–337.

Dworkin, Andrea (1974) *Woman Hating*. New York: E.P. Dutton.

Dworkin, Andrea (1982, first published 1978) *Right-Wing Women: The Politics of Domesticated Females*. London: The Women's Press.

Dworkin, Andrea (1992) Against the Male Flood: Censorship, Pornography and Equality. In Catherine Itzin (ed.), *Pornography: Women, Violence and Civil Liberties*, New York: Oxford University Press.

Dworkin, Andrea (1997) *Life and Death: Unapologetic Writings about the Continuing War Against Women*. New York: Free Press.

Dyke, Anya Hart (2009) *Mosques Made in Britain*. London: Quilliam Foundation.

Eagleton, Terry (2009) *Reason, Faith, and Revolution: Reflections on the God Debate*. New Haven and London: Yale University Press.

EHRC (2010, 11 October) *How Fair is Britain?* Equality and Human Rights Commission. www.equalityhumanrights.com/howfairisbritain (accessed 6 November 2010).

El Sadaawi, Nawal (2007, first published 1982) *The Hidden Face of Eve: Women in the Arab World*. London: Zed Books.

European Women's Lobby (2005) *Religion and Women's Human Rights Position paper of the European Women's Lobby* http://secure1.awid.org/eng/Issues-and-Analysis/Library/Religion-and-Women-s-Human-Rights-Position-paper-of-the-European-Women-s-Lobby (accessed 30 May 2011).

Fader, Ayala (2009) *Mitzvah Girls. Bringing up the Next Generation of Hasidic Jews in Brooklyn*. Princeton: Princeton University Press.

Falen, Douglas J. (2008) Polygyny and Christian Marriage in Africa: The Case of Benin. *African Studies Review*, 51(2): 51–75.

Family Law Council (2007) *Civil and Religious Divorce*. Australian Government: Attorney-General's Department. www.ag.gov.au/www/agd/agd.nsf/Page/FamilyLawCouncil_LettersofAdvice_CivilandReligiousDivorce-Part2 (accessed 12 October 2010).

Farley, Melissa (2007) *Prostitution and Trafficking in Nevada. Making the Connections*. San Francisco: Prostitution Research and Education.

Farnell, Richard, Furbey, Robert, Sham Al-Haqq Hills, Stephen, Macey, Marie and Smith, Greg (2003) *'Faith' in urban regeneration?* Bristol: The Policy Press.

Ferguson, Adele (2006) God's Business. *Business Review Weekly*. 29 June–5 July 2006.

Figes, Eva (1970) *Patriarchal Attitudes: Women in Sexist Society*. New York: Stein and Day.

Fourest, Caroline (2008) *Brother Tariq: the Doublespeak of Tariq Ramadan*. New York: Encounter Books.

Frazer, Elizabeth and Lacey, Nicola (1993) *The Politics of Community: A Feminist Critique of the Liberal Communitarian Debate*. Toronto: University of Toronto Press.

Friedman, Elisabeth Jay (2003) Gendering the Agenda: the Impact of the Transnational Women's Rights Movement at the UN Conferences of the 1990s. *Women's Studies International Forum*, 26(4): 313–331.

Fudge, Judy (1989) The Effect of Entrenching a Bill of Rights upon Political Discourse: Feminist Demands and Sexual Violence in Canada. *International Journal of the Sociology of Law*. 17(4): 445–63.

Fyfe, Melissa (2009) Government bows to religious right. *The Sunday Age*, 27 September. Melbourne, Australia.

Gallichan, Walter (1915) *Women Under Polygamy*. New York: Dodd, Mead and Company.

Giddens, Anthony (1997) *Sociology*. Cambridge: Polity Press.

Gill, Rosalind C. (2007) Critical Respect: The Difficulties and Dilemmas of Agency and 'Choice' for Feminism. A Reply to Duits and van Zoonen. *European Journal of Women's Studies*, 14(1): 69–80.

Gilliat-Ray, Sophie (2010) *Muslims in Britain: An Introduction*. Cambridge: Cambridge University Press.

Gimbutas, Marija (1991) *The Civilization of the Goddess: the World of Old Europe*. New York: Harper Collins.

Guillaumin, Colette (1996) The Practice of Power and Belief in Nature. In Leonard, Diana and Adkins, Lisa (eds), *Sex in Question: French materialist feminism*, London: Taylor and Francis, pp. 72–108.

Gweini (2008) *Faith in Wales. Counting for Communities*. Cardiff: Gweini: The Council of the Christian Voluntary Sector in Wales.

Halliday, Fred (1995) The Literal vs the Liberal. *Women Against Fundamentalism Journal*, 6(16): 18

Handrahan, L.M. (2001) Gendering Ethnicity in Kyrgyzstan: Forgotten Elements in Promoting Peace and Democracy. *Gender and Development*, 9(3): 70–78.

Hanif, Mohammed (2011) How Pakistan responded to Salmaan Taseer's assassination. *The Guardian*, 6 January. www.guardian.co.uk/world/2011/jan/06/pakistan-salman-taseer-assassination (accessed 8 January 2011).

Hanman, Natalie (2006) Unequal Opportunities. Do faith schools teach girls and boys in the same way? *The Guardian*, 9 May.

Harding, Sandra (1986) *The Science Question in Feminism*. Ithaca, NY: Cornell University Press.

Harris, Sam (2005) *The End of Faith: Religion, Terror and the Future of Reason*. New York: W.W. Norton.

Hasan, Khola (2009) The Medical and Social Costs of Consanguineous Marriages among British Mirpuris. *South Asia Research*, 29(3): 275–298.

Hassan, Rasha Mohammad (2008) *"Clouds in Egypt's Sky". Sexual Harassment: from Verbal Harassment to Rape*. Egyption Centre for Women's Rights. www.preventgbvafrica.org/system/files/SexualHarassmentResearchResults2008.pdf (accessed 14 October 2010).

Hedgehammer, Thomas (2011) The rise of the macro-nationalists. New York: *The New York Times*, 31 July. www.nytimes.com/2011/07/31/opinion/sunday/the-rise-of-the-macro-nationalists.html (accessed 21 August 2011).

Hickley, Matthew (2008) Islamic sharia courts in Britain are now 'legally binding'. London: *Daily Mail*, 15 September. www.dailymail.co.uk/news/article-1055764/Islamic-sharia-courts-Britain-legally-binding.html (accessed 12 November 2009).

Hills, John, Brewer, Mike, Jenkins, Stephen, Lister, Ruth, Machin, Stephen, Mills, Stephen, Mills, Colin, Modood, Tariq, Rees, Teresa and Riddell, Sheila (2010) An Anatomy of Economic Inequality in the UK. Report of the National Equality Panel. London: Government Equalities Office. www.equalities.gov.uk/pdf/NEP%20Report%20bookmarked.pdf (accessed 11 January 2011).

Hitchens, Christopher (2008) *God is not Great: How Religion Poisons Everything*. Sydney: Allen and Unwin.

Hoff, Joan (1996) The Pernicious Effect of Post-modernism on Women's History. In Bell, Diane and Klein, Renate (eds), *Radically Speaking: Feminism Reclaimed*, Melbourne: Spinifex Press, pp. 393–412.

Hollis, Patricia (1979) *Women in Public Places*. London: Allen and Unwin.

Home Office (2004, February) *Working Together: Co-operation between Government and Faith Communities*. London: Home Office Faith Communities Unit.

Home Office (2005, August) *"Working Together": Co-operation between Government and Faith Communities*. Progress Report. London: Home Office Faith Communities Unit.

Hossain, Sara (1994) Equality in the Home: Women's Rights and Personal Laws in South Asia. In Cook, Rebecca J. (ed.), *Human Rights of Women. National and International Perspectives*, Philadelphia, PA: University of Pennsylvania Press.

Howland, Courtney W. (1999) Safeguarding Women's Political Freedoms under the International Covenant on Civil and Political Rights in the Face of Religious Fundamentalism. In Hyland, Courtney W. (ed.), *Religious Fundamentalisms and the Human Rights of Women*, New York: Palgrave.

Hughes, Barbara (2008) A Wife's Responsibility to help her Husband. In DeMoss, Nancy Leigh (ed.), *Becoming God's True Woman*. Wheaton, IL: Crossway Books, pp. 116–131.

Hunt, Mary and Neu, Diann L. (eds) (2010) *New Feminist Christianity. Many Voices, Many Views*. Woodstock, Vermont; Skylight Paths Publishing.

Hussain, Jamila (2009) Finding the Women's Space: Muslim Women and the Mosque. In Dreher, Tanja and Ho, Christina (eds), *Beyond the Hijab Debates: New Conversations on Gender, Race and Religion*, Newcastle upon Tyne: Cambridge Scholars Publishing, pp. 152–166.

IGLHRC (2010, 17 November) *Governments remove sexual orientation from UN Resolution condemning extrajudicial, summary or arbitrary executions*. International Gay and Lesbian Human Rights Commission. www.iglhrc.org/cgi-bin/iowa/article/pressroom/pressrelease/1257.html (accessed 10 December 2010).

Imam, Ayesha M. (1997) *The Muslim Religious Right ('Fundamentalists') and Sexuality. Dossier 17*. Women Living Under Muslim Laws. www.wluml.org/node/277 (accessed 30 May 2011).

Ireland, Doug (2008) Forked Tongue. *New Humanist*. 123(3). http://newhumanist.org.uk/1776/forked-tongue# (accessed 20 March 2010).

Islamic Sharia Council (n.d. a) *How the ISC works*. www.islamic-sharia.org/index.php?option=com_content&task=view&id=12&Itemid=27 (accessed 22 May 2010).

Islamic Sharia Council (n.d. b) *Men Seeking Divorce*. Page 2. www.islamic-sharia.org/how-it-works/how-the-isc-works-2.html (accessed 22 May 2010).

Islamic Sharia Council (n.d. c) *Denying husbands marital rights*. www.islamic-sharia.org/marriage-fatwas-related-to-women/denying-husbands-marital-rights-2.html (accessed 22 May 2010).

Islamic Sharia Council (n.d. d) Being at different locations at the time of the Nikah? www.islamic-sharia.org/marriage-fiqh-of-marriage-life/being-at-different-locations-at-the-time-of-the-n-2.html (accessed 22 May 2010).

Islamic Sharia Council (n.d. e) *On the Testimony of Women*. www.islamic-sharia.org/general/on-the-testimony-of-women-2.html (accessed 22 May 2010).

Islamic Sharia Council (n.d. f) *Why is it necessary for women to wear an outer garment*. www.islamic-sharia.org/general/why-is-it-necessary-for-women-to-wear-an-outer-garment-2.html (accessed 22 May 2010).

Islamonline (2003, 26 July) *Source of the Punishment for Apostasy.* www.islamonline.net/servlet/Satellite?cid=1119503547222&pagename=IslamOnline-English-Ask_Scholar/FatwaE/FatwaEAskTheScholar (accessed 22 May 2010).

Islamonline (2005a) *Mixing between men and women.* www.islamonline.net/English/News/2006-03/28/article03.shtml (accessed 22 May 2010).

Islamonline (2005b) *Talking With the Opposite Sex.* www.islamonline.net/servlet/Satellite?cid=1119503544520&pagename=IslamOnline-English-Ask_Scholar%2FFatwaE%2FFatwaE (accessed 22 May 2010).

Islamonline (2006) *Netherlands Defends Muslim Student Handshake Refusal.* www.islamonline.net/English/News/2006-03/28/article03.shtml (accessed 22 May 2010).

Jaggar, Alison (1998) Globalizing Feminist Ethics. *Hypatia*, 123(2): 86–106.

Jeffreys, Sheila (1997) *The Idea of Prostitution.* Melbourne: Spinifex Press.

Jeffreys, Sheila (1999) Bisexual Politics: A superior form of feminism? *Women's Studies International Forum.* 22(3): pp. 273–86.

Jeffreys, Sheila (2005) *Beauty and Misogyny: Harmful Cultural Practices in the West.* London: Routledge.

Jeffreys, Sheila (2009) *The Industrial Vagina: the International Political Economy of the Global Sex Trade.* London: Routledge.

Jeffreys, Sheila (2010) 'Brothels without Walls': the escort sector as a problem for the legalization of prostitution. *Social Politics*, 17(2): 210–234.

Jeffreys, Sheila (2012, forthcoming) Who made Adam Smith's dinner? Feminist critiques of the international political economy. In Pettman, Ralph (ed.), *Handbook of international Political Economy.* Singapore: World Scientific Publishers.

Jessup, Carolyn and Palmer, Laura (2007) *Escape.* Camberwell, Victoria: Viking, Penguin Group.

Jewish Polygamy (n.d.) *Pilegesh.* http://jewishpolygamy.wordpress.com/category/pilegesh/ (accessed 22 November 2010).

Johnson, Jennifer A. (2010) To catch a curious clicker: a social network analysis of the online pornography industry. In Boyle, Karen (ed.), *Everyday Pornography*, London: Routledge.

Joyce, Kathryn (2009) *Quiverfull: Inside the Christian Patriarchy Movement.* Boston: Beacon Press.

Kabeer, Naila (2005) Gender Equality and Women's Empowerment: A Critical Analysis of the Third Millennium Development Goal. *Gender and Development.* 13(1): 13–24.

KAFA (n.d.) Lebanon – KAFA – *Legal Rights of Women – Muslim and Christian.* www.kafa.org.lb/MuslimCommunities.aspx (accessed 23 November 2010).

Kariapper, Ayesha Salma (2009) *Walking a Tightrope. Women and Veiling in the United Kingdom.* London: Women Living Under Muslim Laws.

Katz, Sue (1995) The Rise of Religious Fundamentalism in Britain: The Experience of Women against Fundamentalism. *Gender and Development*, 3(1): 42–44.

Keddie, Nikki (1998) The New Religious Politics: Where, When, and Why Do "Fundamentalisms" Appear. *Comparative Studies in Society and Society*, 40(4): 696–723.

Khuankaew, Ouyporn (2008) Keeping the Faith: Overcoming Religious Fundamentalisms. *Arrows for Change*, 14 (1& 2).

Kissling, Frances (1999) Roman Catholic Fundamentalism: What's Sex (and Power) got to do with it? In Howland, Courtney W. (ed.), *Religious Fundamentalisms and the Human Rights of Women*, New York: Palgrave.

Kitzinger, Celia and Perkins, Rachel (1993) *Changing Our Minds: Lesbian Feminism and Psychology*. New York: New York University Press.

Koutsoukis, Jason (2010) Lingerie entices shoppers on the road to Damascus. Melbourne: *The Age*, 22 May, p. 15.

Kukathas, Chandran (2003) *The Liberal Archipelago: A Theory of Diversity and Freedom*. Oxford: Oxford University Press.

Lazreg, Marnia (2009) *Questioning the Veil: Open Letters to Muslim Women*. Princeton, NJ: Princeton University Press.

Lehrman, Karen (1997) *The Lipstick Proviso*. New York: Anchor Books.

Lerner, Gerda (1987) *The Creation of Patriarchy*. New York: Oxford University Press.

Levin, Tanya (2007) *People in Glass Houses. An Insider's Story of a Life In and Out of Hillson*. Melbourne: Black Ink.

Levin, Tanya (2008) Why Mercy Ministries was godsent for Hillsong. *Sydney Morning Herald*, 18 March.

Lichfield, John (2010) Even in France, a full-scale burqa ban remains unlikely. *The Independent*, 17 July. www.independent.co.uk/news/world/europe/even-in-france-a-fullscale-burka-ban-remains-unlikely-2028672.html (accessed 12 November 2010).

Lichter, Ida (2010) Sharia Law Would Harm Aussie Muslim Women. *The Australian*, 23 March. www.theaustralian.com.au/news/opinion/sharia-law-would-harm-aussie-muslim-women/story-e6frg6zo-1225843990296 (accessed 13 April 2010).

Lister, Ruth (1997) *Citizenship: Feminist Perspectives*. Basingstoke and London: Macmillan.

Lynfield, Ben (2009) 'Sinful' city buses stoned by ultra-orthodox Jews. *The Independent*, 25 February. www.independent.co.uk/news/world/middle-east/sinful-city-buses-stoned-by-ultraorthodox-jews-1631370.html (accessed 12 November 2010).

MacEoin, Dennis (2009) *Sharia Law or 'One Law For All'?* London: Civitas, Institute for the Study of Civil Society.

Macey, Marie. (1999) Religion, male violence, and the control of women: Pakistani Muslim men in Bradford, UK. *Gender and Development* 7(1): 48–55.

Macey, Marie (2009) *Multiculturalism, Religion and Women: Doing Harm by Doing Good?* Basingstoke: Palgrave Macmillan.

Macey, Marie and Beckett, Claire (2001) Race, Gender & Sexuality: the Oppression of Multiculturalism. *Women's Studies International Forum*, 24(3): 309–319.

MacInnis, Laura (2009) U.N. body adopts resolution on religious defamation. Geneva: Reuters. www.reuters.com/article/idUSTRE52P60220090326 (accessed 10 April 2010).

Mackay, Neil (2007) Child abuse in mosques: lifting the veil of secrecy. *Herald Scotland*, 18 August. www.heraldscotland.com/child-abuse-in-mosques-lifting-the-veil-of-secrecy-1.827823 (accessed 12 November 2010).

MacKinnon, Catharine A. (1989) *Towards a Feminist Theory of the State*. Cambridge, MA: Harvard University Press.

MacKinnon, Catharine A. (2006) Postmodernism and Human Rights, in MacKinnon, Catharine A. *Are Women Human? And Other International Dialogues*. Cambridge, MA: The Belknap Press of Harvard University Press, pp. 44–63.

McKinstry, Leo (2005). Labour's Shameful Debt to Livingstone. London: *The Telegraph*, 15 September. www.telegraph.co.uk/comment/personal-view/3619738/Labours-shameful-debt-to-Livingstone.html (accessed 1 June 2011).

McMahon, Anthony (1999) *Taking Care of Men. Sexual Politics in the Public Mind*. Cambridge: Cambridge University Press.

McSmith, Andy (2006) God will be my judge on Iraq. *The Independent*, 4 March. www.independent.co.uk/news/uk/politics/blair-god-will-be-my-judge-on-iraq-468512.html (accessed 20 September 2009).

Maddox, Marion (2005) *God Under Howard: The Rise of the Religious Right in Australian Politics*. Sydney: Allen and Unwin.

Mahmood, Saba (2001) Feminist Theory, Embodiment, and the Docile Agent: Some Reflections on the Egyptian Islamic Revival. *Cultural Anthropology*. 16(2): 202–236.

Mahmood, Saba. (2009) Feminism, Democracy, and Empire: Islam and the War on Terror. In Herzog, Hanna and Braude, Ann (eds), *Gendering Religion and Politics: Untangling Modernities*, New York: Palgrave Macmillan pp. 193–216.

Mahoney, Monica and Taj, Shahien (2006) *Muslim Women Talk Wales*, Project Report, 24 April. Wales: Saheli Association.

Mailonline (2007) Muslim veils 'should be allowed in court'. *The Daily Mail*. www.dailymail.co.uk/news/article-450427/Muslim-veils-allowed-court.html# (accessed 10 December 2010).

Malik, Zubeida (2000) Polygamy law set for challenge. *BBC News*, 18 June. http://news.bbc.co.uk/2/hi/uk_news/791263.stm (accessed 12 November 2010).

Manji, Irshad (2003) *The Trouble with Islam. A Muslim's Call for Reform in Her Faith*. Sydney: Random House.

Margolin, Ruth (2009) School entrance locked for 'modesty reasons'. *Jewish World*, 11 October. www.ynetnews.com/articles/0,7340,L-3802166,00.html (accessed 13 April 2010).

Miller, James (2000) *The Passion of Foucault*. Cambridge, MA: Harvard University Press.

Millett, Kate (1972) *Sexual Politics*. London: Abacus, Sphere Books.

Milton, Don (n.d. a) *Future Wives*. www.christianpolygamy.com/ (accessed 12 September 2010).

Milton, Don (n.d. b) *Persecution*. www.christianpolygamy.com/ (accessed 12 September 2010).

Milton, Don (n.d. c) *The Seven Steps to not Sinning*. www.christianpolygamy.com/ (accessed 12 September 2010).

Minder, Raphael (2010) Spain's Senate votes to ban burqa. *New York Times*, 23 July. www.nytimes.com/2010/06/24/world/europe/24iht-spain.html (accessed 12 January 2011).

Mir-Hosseini, Ziba (2006) Muslim Women's Quest for Equality: Between Islamic Law and Feminism. *Critical Inquiry*, 32(4): 629–645.

Mirza, Munira, Senthilkumaran, Abi and Ja'far, Zein (2004) *Living Apart Together: British Muslims and the Paradox of Multiculturalism*. London: Policy Exchange.

Moghadam, Valentine (2002) Islamic Feminism and Its Discontents: Toward a Resolution of the Debate. *Signs*, 27(4): 1135–1171.

Moghissi, Haideh (1999) *Feminism and Islamic Fundamentalism: The Limits of Postmodern Analysis*. London: Zed Books.

Mohanty, Chandra Talpade (1991) Under Western Eyes: Feminist Scholarship and Colonial Discourses. In Mohanty, Chandra, Russo, Ann and Torres, Lourdes (eds), *Third World Women and the Politics of Feminism*, Bloomington, IN: Indiana University Press.

Mohanty, Chandra Talpade (2003) Under Western Eyes Revisited: Feminist Solidarity Through Anticapitalist Struggles. *Signs Journal of Women in Culture and Society*, 28(2): 499–535.

Mojab, Shahrzad (1998) 'Muslim' women and 'western' feminists: the debate on particularly and universals. *Monthly Review*, 50(7): 19–30.

Mojab, Shahrzad (2001) Theorizing the Politics of 'Islamic Feminism'. *Feminist Review*, 69: 124–146.

Moore-Emmett, Andrea (2004) *God's Brothel: The Extortion of Sex for Salvation in Contemporary Mormon and Christian Fundamentalist Polygamy and the Stories of 18 Women Who Escaped*. San Francisco: Pince-nez Press.

Morgan, Robin (1989) *The Demon Lover: on the Sexuality of Terrorism*. London: Methuen.

Mubarak, Fatheena (2006) *Women's Inter Faith initiatives in the UK: A survey*. London: Inter Faith Network.

Muslim Council of Britain (2007) *Towards Greater Understanding: Meeting the needs of Muslim pupils in state schools*. London: The Muslim Council of Britain.

Muslim Council of Britain (2010, 13 July) *Advice to Schools: Muslim Council of Britain Responds to News Reports (12 July 2010) on Advice to Schools*. www.mcb.org.uk/article_detail.php?article=announcement-897 (accessed 10 November 2010).

Muslim Women's Network (2006) *She Who Disputes – Muslim Women Shape the Debate*. Muslim Women's Network/Women's National Commission.

Narayan, Uma. (1997) *Dislocating Cultures. Identities, traditions, and third world feminism*. New York: Routledge.

National Times (2008) Gender Equality and Polygamy are not Compatible. Melbourne, Australia: *The Age*, 27 June.

Norris, Pippa and Inglehart, Ronald (2004) *Sacred and Secular: Religion and Politics Worldwide*. Cambridge: Cambridge University Press.

Nussbaum, Martha (2000) *Women and Human Development*. Cambridge: Cambridge University Press.

Nussbaum, Martha C. (2007) *The Clash Within: Democracy, Religious Violence, and India's Future*. Cambridge, MA: Harvard Bellknap Press.

O'Beirne, Maria (2004, March) Home Office Research Study 274. *Religion in England and Wales: findings from the 2001 Home Office Citizenship Survey*. London: Home Office Research, Development and Statistics Directorate.

Odone, Christina (2008) Learning to be British and Muslim. London: *The Times*, 29 June. www.timesonline.co.uk/tol/news/uk/education/article4231194.ece (accessed 12 September 2009).

O'Faolain, Julia and Martines, Lauro (eds) (1973) *Not in God's Image: Women in History*. London: Virago.

Okin, Susan Moller (1989) *Justice, Gender and the Family*. New York: Basic Books.

Okin, Susan Moller (1999) *Is Multiculturalism Bad For Women?* Princeton, NJ: Princeton University Press.

Okin, Susan Moller (2002) Mistresses of their Own Destiny: Gender, Groups Rights and Realistic Rights of Exit. *Ethics*, 112 (2): 205–230.

Okin, Susan Moller (2002) 'Mistresses of their Own Destiny': Group Rights, Gender, and Realistic Rights of Exit (2002) 112 Ethics 205–230

Oriel, Jennifer (2005) Sexual Pleasure as a Human Right: Harmful or Helpful to Women in the Context of HIV/AIDS? *Women's Studies International Forum*, 28(5): 392–404.

Parekh, Bikhu (2000) *The Future of Multi-Ethnic Britain: The Parekh Report*. London: The Runnymede Trust.

Pateman, Carole (1988) *The Sexual Contract*. Cambridge: Polity Press.

Pereira, Charmaine and Ibrahim, Jibrin (2010) On the Bodies of Women: the common ground between Islam and Christianity in Nigeria. *Third World Quarterly*, 31(6): 921–937.

Peters, Julie and Wolper, Andrea (eds) (1995) *Women's Rights – Human Rights. International Feminist Perspectives*. New York: Routledge.

Phillips, Anne (2007) *Multiculturalism without Culture*. Princeton, NJ: Princeton University Press.

Phillips, Anne (2009) *Religion: ally, threat or just religion?* In Phillips, Anne and Casanova, José, (eds) A debate on the public role of religion and its social and gender implications. Gender and development programme paper (5). United Nations Research Institute for Social Development, Geneva, Switzerland, pp. 39–58.

Phillips, Anne and Dustin, Moira (2004) UK Initiatives on Forced Marriage: Regulation, Dialogue and Exit. *Political Studies*, 52(3): 531–551.

Pieterse, Jan (1994) Fundamentalism discourses: enemy images. *Women Against Fundamentalism Journal*, 1(5): 2–6.

Pilegesh.org (n.d.) http://pilegesh.blogspot.com/ (accessed 22 November 2010).

Pitcher, Ben (2009) *The Politics of Multiculturalism: Race and Racism in Contemporary Britain*. Basingstoke: Palgrave Macmillan.

Plaskow, Judith (1990) *Standing Again at Sinai: Judaism from a Feminist Perspective*. New York: Harper and Row.

Pogrebov, Igor (2006) Prevalence and Assessment of Polygamy in Uzbekistan. *Russian Social Science Review*, 47(6): 57–64.

Pride, Mary (1985) *The Way Home: Beyond Feminism, Back to Reality*. Wheaton, IL: Crossway Books.

Profanter, Annemarie and Cate, Stephanie Ryan (2009) Deal Justly With Them . . . In Justice in Polygyny – The Male Perspective. *The Journal of Social Psychology*, 149(3): 223–241.

Putnam, Robert D. (2000) *Bowling Alone: The Collapse and Revival of American Community*. New York: Simon and Schuster.

Racial and Religious Tolerance Act (2001) Victoria, Australia. www.austlii.edu.au/au/legis/vic/consol_act/rarta2001265/s8.html (accessed 12 September 2009).

Razavi, Shahra and Jenichen, Anne (2010) The Unhappy Marriage of Religion and Politics: problems and pitfalls for gender equality. *Third World Quarterly* 31(6): 833–850.

Read, George (2010) Female Genital Mutilation cannot be defended as part of Islam. *The Guardian*, 15 October. www.guardian.co.uk/commentisfree/belief/2010/oct/15/female-genital-mutilation-yusuf-al-qaradawi (accessed 12 November 2010).

Reform About Reform. www.reform.org.uk/about/what-is-reform.php (accessed 19 July 2010).

Reid, Sue (2009) Polygamy UK: This special Mail investigation reveals how thousands of men are milking the benefits system to support several wives. *Mailonline*, 24 February. www.dailymail.co.uk/news/article-1154789/Polygamy-UK-This-special-Mail-investigation-reveals-thousands-men-milking-benefits-support-wives.html (accessed 5 November 2010).

Rex, John (1997) The concept of a multicultural society. In Guibernau, Montserrat and Rex, John (eds), *The Ethnicity Reader. Nationalism, Multi-culturalism and Migration*, Cambridge: Polity Press, pp. 205–219.

Rix, Juliet (2008) It's time to take a stand against Islam and Sharia. *The Times Online*, 12 March. http://women.timesonline.co.uk/tol/life_and_style/women/the_way_we_live/article3530256.ece (accessed 22 March 2010).

Romito, Patrizia (2008) *A Deafening Silence. Hidden violence against women and children*. Bristol: The Policy Press.

Rozario, Santi (2006) The new burqua in Bangladesh: Empowerment or violation of women's rights? *Women's Studies International Forum*, 29(4): 368–380.

Rubin, Gayle (1975) The traffic in women: Notes on the 'political economy' of sex. In Reiter, Rayna (ed.), *Toward an Anthropology of Women*, New York and London: Monthly Review Press, pp. 157–210.

Ruether, Rosemary Radford (1993) *Sexism and God-Talk*. Boston, MA: Beacon Press.

Rule, Andrew and Sharp, Ari (2009) They all came to farewell the cardboard king. *Sydney Morning Herald*, 1 May.

Runnymede Trust (2007, 11 May) *Local Decision-making and Participation Think-piece on Cohesion and Integration*. London: Runnymede Trust.

Saeed, Abdullah (2010) A plea for clear thinking about the burqa. ABC Religion and Ethics. *Australian Broadcasting Corporation*, 5 August. www.abc.net.au/religion/articles/2010/08/05/2974143.htm (accessed 10 December 2010).

Saharso, Sawitri (2003) Culture, tolerance and gender. A contribution from the Netherlands. *The European Journal of Women's Studies*, 10(1): 7–27.

Sahgal, Gita and Nira Yuval-Davis (1992) *Refusing Holy Orders. Women and Fundamentalism in Britain*. Virago: London.

Said, Edward (1979) *Orientalism*. New York: Vintage.

Sandberg, Russell (2009). The changing position of religious minorities in English law: the legacy of Begum, Russell. In In Grillo, Ralph, Ballard, Roger, Ferrari, Alessandro, Hoekema, Andre J., Maussen, Marcel, and Shah, Prakash (eds) (2009). *Legal Practice and Cultural Diversity*, London: Ashgate, pp. 267–282.

Sanghera, Jasvinder (2007) *Shame*. London: Hodder & Stoughton.

Sanghera, Jasvinder (2009) *Daughters of Shame*. London: Hodder & Stoughton.

Sargent, Carolyn F. and Larchanche-Kim, Stephanie (2006) Liminal Lives: Immigration Status, Gender, and the Construction of Identities Among Malian Migrants in Paris. *American Behavioral Scientist* 50: 9, 9–26.

Scott, Joan Wallach (2007) *The Politics of the Veil*. Princeton, NJ: Princeton University Press.

Second Vatican Council (1965) *Decree on Adaptation and Renewal of Religious Life*. Vatican. www.vatican.va/archive/hist_councils/ii_vatican_council/documents/vat-ii_decree_19651028_perfectae-caritatis_en.html (accessed 12 April 2010).

Seguino, Stephanie and Lovinksy, James (2009) *The Impact of Religiosity on Gender Attitudes and Outcomes*. United Nations Research Institute for Social Development. www.uvm.edu/~sseguino/pdf/Religiosity.pdf (accessed 20 September, 2009).

Sen, Amartya (2006) *Identity and Violence: The Illusion of Destiny*. London: Allen Lane.

Shaheed, Farida (2010) Contested Identities: gendered politics, gendered religion in Pakistan. *Third World Quarterly*, 31(6): 851–867.

Sippel, Serra (n.d.) *Unfulfilled. The Holy See backs off from its claim for full membership of the UN, settling for the rights already held by Palestine.* www.catholics forchoice.org/conscience/archives/c2004win_unfulfilled.asp (accessed 12 April 2010).

Sisters in Islam (1991) *Are Women and Men Equal Before Allah?* www.sisters inislam.org.my/BM/pubs-equality.htm (accessed 10 October, 2010).

Sister Wives (n.d.) Sister Wives website www.sisterwives.net (accessed 7 June 2011).

Sjoo, Monica and Mor, Barbara (1987) *The Great Cosmic Mother: Rediscovering the Religion of the Earth*. New York: HarperCollins

Steans, Jill and Ahmadi, Vafa (2005) Negotiating the Politics of Gender and Rights: Some Reflections on the Status of Women's Human Rights at 'Beijing Plus Ten'. *Global Society*, 19(3): 227–245.

Stone, Merlin (1977) *The Paradise Papers*. London: Virago.

Stonewall (2007) *The School Report. The experiences of young gay people in Britain's schools.* London: Stonewall. www.stonewall.org.uk/educationforall (accessed 20 September 2009).

Stratton, Allegra (2010) Copying French ban on burqa would be un-British, says Minister. *The Guardian*, 18 July. www.guardian.co.uk/uk/2010/jul/18/burqa-ban-unbritish-immigration-minister (accessed 10 December 2010).

Stueck, Wendy (2010) Polygamy leads to expulsion of boys, teen pregnancies and early sexualizing of girls, argues crown. Canada: *The Globe and Mail*, 23 November. www.theglobeandmail.com/news/national/british-columbia/polygamy-leads-to-expulsion-of-boys-teen-pregnancies-and-early-sexualizing-of-girls-argues-crown/article1811012/ (accessed 11 January 2011).

Sullivan, Mary (2007) *Making Sex Work: The Failed Experiment of Legalized Prostitution in Australia*. Melbourne: Spinifex.

Summers, Anne (2009) Mistress in a gilded cage. *Brisbane Times*, 3 May.

Sussman, Anna Louise (2010) Embattled Gender Analyst Leaves Post at Amnesty. WeNews. *Global Sisterhood Network*, 16 April. www.global-sisterhoodnetwork.org/content/view/2436/59/ (accessed 12 November 2010).

Tapestry Against Polygamy (n.d.) *About us.* www.polygamy.org/about.shtml (accessed 7 June 2011).

Tarlo, Emma (2010) *Visibly Muslim: Fashion, Politics, Faith*. Oxford, and New York: Berg.

Telegraph (2010) Man arrested over Malmo immigrant shootings. *The Telegraph*, 7 November. www.telegraph.co.uk/news/worldnews/europe/sweden/8115818/Man-arrested-over-Malmo-immigrant-shootings.html (accessed 12 November 2010).

Thompson, Denise (2001) *Radical Feminism Today*. London: Sage Publications.

Townsend, Mark (2010) English Defence League forges links with America's Tea Party. *The Guardian*, 10 October. www.guardian.co.uk/uk/2010/oct/10/english-defence-league-tea-party (accessed 12 November 2010).

Trad, Keysar (2009) Why should polygamy be a crime? *Sydney Morning Herald*, October 2.

UNFPA (n.d.) Millennium Development Goal 3: Promote gender equality and empower women. http://web.unfpa.org/icpd/mdgs-icpd.cfm#mdg3 (accessed 13 August 2010).

United Nations (1966) *International Covenant on Civil and Political Rights*. Geneva: Office of the United Nations High Commissioner for Human Rights. www2.ohchr.org/english/law/ccpr.htm (accessed 20 April 2010).

United Nations (1979) *Convention on the Elimination of All forms of Discrimination Against Women*. Geneva: Office of the United Nations High. Commissioner for Human Rights. www2.ohchr.org/english/law/cedaw.htm (accessed 20 April 2010).

UN threat to Islam (n.d.) *Beijing Plus Five: The United Nation's Advance on Islam*. Soundvision.com. SoundVision.com Islamic Information and Products. www.soundvision.com/Info/women/UNthreattoIslam.asp (accessed 26 February 2010).

UN Watch (2010) *Defamation of Religion Passes Human Rights Council*. http://blog.unwatch.org/index.php/category/defamation-of-religion/ (accessed 12 December 2010).

Victoria (2001) Racial and Religious Tolerance Act. State of Victoria: Victorian Consolidated Legislation. www.austlii.edu.au/au/legis/vic/consol_act/rarta 2001265/ (accessed 13 September 2009).

Walter, Natasha (1999) *The New Feminism*. London: Virago.

Warhurst, John (2006, 3 May) *Religion in 21st Century Australian National Politics*. Canberra: Australian Senate Occasional Lecture Series.

Warraich, Sohail Akbar, and Balchin, Cassandra (2006) *Recognizing the Un-Recognized: Inter-Country Cases and Muslim Marriages and Divorces in Britain*. A policy research by Women Living Under Muslim Laws. London: Women Living Under Muslim Laws.

Weber, David (2010) Judge order woman to remove face veil. Australian Broadcasting Corporation: *ABC News*, 19 August. www.abc.net.au/news/stories/2010/08/19/2987539.htm (accessed 11 January 2011).

Welchman, Lynn and Hossain, Sara (eds) (2005) *Honour: Crimes, Paradigms, and Violence against Women*. London: Zed Press.

Wikan, Unni (2008) *In Honor of Fadime: Murder and Shame*. Chicago, IL: University of Chicago Press.

Wilkinson, Richard and Pickett, Kate (2009) *The Spirit Level: Why More Equal Societies Almost Always Do Better*. London: Allen Lane.

Wilson, Kalpana (2007) Agency. In Blakeley, Georgina and Bryson, Valerie (eds), *The impact of feminism on political concepts and debates*. Manchester: Manchester University Press, pp. 126–145.

Winter, Bronwyn (2008) *The Hijab and the Republic: Uncovering the French Headscarf Debate.* Syracuse, NY: Syracuse University Press.

Winter, Bronwyn (2009) One Hijab does not fit all: Recontextualising the Case for Sexularism. In Dreher, Tanja and Ho, Christina (eds), *Beyond the Hijab Debates. New Conversations on Gender, Race and Religion*, Newcastle upon Tyne: Cambridge Scholars Publishing pp. 195–207.

Winter, Bronwyn, Thompson, Denise and Jeffreys, Sheila (2002) The UN Approach to Harmful Traditional Practices: Some Conceptual Problems. *International Feminist Journal of Politics* 4(1): 72–94.

Wintour, Patrick (2011) David Cameron tells Muslim Britain: stop tolerating extremists. London: *The Guardian*, 5 February. www.guardian.co.uk/politics/2011/feb/05/david-cameron-muslim-extremism (accessed 6 February 2011).

WLUML (1990) Women Against Fundamentalism. Newsletter 1, November, p. 2.

WLUML (2006) Introducing. Dossier 28. A Collection of Artiles. London: Women Living Under Muslim Laws.

WLUML (2010a, 17 February) United Kingdom: WLUML Statement in Support of Gita Sahgal. www.wluml.org/node/5986 (accessed 20 April 2010).

WLUML (2010b, 17 November) Pakistan: Ensure safety of Asia Bibi and her family and repeal Pakistan's blasphemy laws. www.wluml.org/node/6789 (accessed 10 December 2010).

Wolf, Naomi (1994) *Fire with Fire: The New Female Power and How it Will Change the 21st Century.* New York: Random House.

Women Against Fundamentalism (1990) Statement. Women Against Fundamentalism, Newsletter No. 1. p. 2.

World Congress of Families (2009) *Amsterdam Declaration.* www.worldcongress.org/wcf5/wcf5.home.htm (accessed 29 November 2010).

World Congress of Families (n.d.) *The Natural Family.* www.worldcongress.org/WCF/wcf_tnf.htm (accessed 29 November 2010).

Wright, Tony (2010) PM tells it as she sees it on the God issue. *The Age: The National Times*, 30 June. www.theage.com.au/opinion/pm-tells-it-as-she-sees-it-on-the-god-issue-20100629-zjad.html (accessed 11 January 2011).

Young, Iris Marion (1990) *Justice and the Politics of Difference.* Princeton, NJ: Princeton University Press.

Young, Iris Marion (2002) *Inclusion and Democracy.* Oxford: Oxford University Press.

Yuval-Davis, Nira (1997) *Gender and Nation.* Sage: London.

Yuval-Davis, Nira (1999) The Personal is Political: Jewish Fundamentalism and Women's Empowerment. In Howland, Courtney W. (ed.), *Religious Fundamentalism and the Human Rights of Women*, New York: Palgrave.

Zach (2010) Opposition Mounts to Gender Segregation in Public Places. *New Israel Blog*, 4 March www.newisraelblog.org/2010/03/opposition-mounts-to-gender-segregation-in-publicplaces/ (accessed 11 January 2011).

Zwartz, Barney (2008) Cult-rescue group 'concerned about' Mercy Ministries. *The Age*, 18 March. www.theage.com.au/news/national/exorcism-healers-totally-misguided/2008/03/18/1205602343838.html (accessed 12 September 2009).

Zwartz, Barney (2010) Saudi translator seeks apology for embassy incident. Melbourne: *The Age*, 2 August. www.theage.com.au/national/saudi-translator-seeks-apology-for-embassy-incident-20100801-111gu.html (accessed 10 December 2010).

INDEX